European Casebook on

Business Alliances

Edited by

Justin Greenwood

The Robert Gordon University, Aberdeen

Prentice Hall

London   New York   Toronto   Sydney   Tokyo   Singapore
Munich   Mexico City   Madrid

First published 1995 by
Prentice Hall International (UK) Limited
Campus 400, Maylands Avenue
Hemel Hempstead
Hertfordshire, HP2 7EZ
A division of
Simon & Schuster International Group

Typeset in 10½/12pt Palatino and Times
by Hands Fotoset, Leicester

Printed and bound in Great Britain by
T J Press (Padstow) Ltd

Library of Congress Cataloging-in-Publication Data

European casebook on business alliances / edited by Justin Greenwood.
     p. cm.—(European casebook series on management)
  "First published 1995 by Prentice Hall International (UK) Limited,
Hemel Hempstead, Hertfordshire"—T.p. verso.
  Includes bibliographical references and index.
  ISBN 0-13-338039-4
  1. Strategic alliances (Business)—European Union countries—
Case studies. I. Greenwood, Justin. II. Series: European
casebook series in management.
  HD69 . S8E87 1995
  658' . 044—dc20

95–6918
CIP

British Library Cataloguing in Publication Data

A catalogue record for this book is available from
the British Library

ISBN 0-13-338039-4

---

1 2 3 4 5   99 98 97 96 95

To Roger, my brother

Contents

Part 7 Size, Partnership and Associability

Exhibits

About the Authors

Alan Cawson is Professor of Politics and Associate Fellow of the Science Policy Research Unit at the University of Sussex. He is co-author of *Hostile Brothers: Competition and Closure in the European Electronics Industry* (1990) and *The Shape of Things to Consume: Delivering Information Technology into the Home* (1995). He is currently researching the innovation of advanced television technologies in Japan, Europe and the United States.

Maria Green Cowles is a post-doctoral fellow at The American University, Washington, DC where she is completing a book on *The Politics of Big Business in the European Union*. She has published articles on European multinational firms and their political activities in *International Economic Insights*.

Laura Cram is a lecturer in European Public Policy at the University of Strathclyde. She has contributed articles about social policy and information policy in ·the European Union.

Justin Greenwood is Reader in the School of Public Administration and Law at the Robert Gordon University, Aberdeen. He is a contributing co-editor of *Organised Interests and the European Community* (1992), and author of the forthcoming *Representing Interests in the European Union*. He has published articles on representing interests in the European Union in *West European Politics, Journal of Common Market Studies, European Journal of Political Research, Government and Policy, American Behavioural Scientist, Current Politics and Economics of Europe* and *Tourism Management*. He is currently leading an EU-funded study on the organization of biotechnology interests in the European Union; his colleagues on the team include a number of contributors to this volume.

Jürgen R. Grote completed his studies in political and social sciences at the University of Marburg in Germany. He has held teaching positions in German studies at the Universities of Genoa and Siena and in sociology at Instituto Superiore per le Industrie Artistiche (ISIA) in Florence. He then undertook doctoral research at the London School of Economics before moving back to Italy where he was engaged in various research projects at the European University Institute (EUI) in Florence. He has also been working as a consultant to various regional research institutes in Italy and is now coordinating a large international research project on problems of collective action at sub-central levels of governance at the Mannheim Centre for European Social Research (University of Mannheim). His research interests are in the fields of sub- and supranational collective action and in regional development policies, especially in the South of Europe.

Desmond Hickie is Head of the Human Resource Management Group at Liverpool John Moores University. His primary research interest is in technology and organizational change, notably in the aerospace industry.

Henry Jacek is Professor of Political Science at McMaster University in Hamilton, Ontario, where he is also past Chair of Department and Collaterel Faculty Member in the Faculty of Business. He is co-editor of *Regionalism, Business Interests and Public Policy* and has written numerous articles and chapters on business organization and public policy in Europe and North America.

Grant Jordan is Professor of Politics at the University of Aberdeen. His main research interests are in British central government and policy-making, interest group membership and group influence. Among his publications are *The Commercial Lobbyists* (1991), *Engineers and Professional Regulation* (1992) and *Government and Pressure Groups in Britain* (1987 with Jeremy Richardson).

Luca Lanzalaco is Associate Professor of Public Administration at the Bocconi University, Milan. He has written several articles about interest groups, industrial relations and political theory and has published a book about the Italian Confederation of Industry.

William A. Maloney is a lecturer in the Department of Government at the University of Strathclyde. His main research interests are in public policy and interest group politics. He is co-author (with Jeremy Richardson) of the forthcoming *Politics and Water Policy in Britain 1945–1994*.

Andrew McLaughlin is a professional economist and a senior fellow in European public policy at Glasgow Caledonian University.

Joaquim Molins is Professor of Political Science at the Autonomous University of Barcelona. His recent works include *Interest Groups in Spain* (1994).

Dan Morrison is a financial journalist living in Princeton, New Jersey. He formerly worked for Hill and Knowlton, Inc. in Brussels as a consultant to American and Japanese corporations.

Oliver Roethig is currently completing his doctoral thesis at the London School of Economics and Political Science. His research focuses on the involvement of the British, German and European trade union confederations in EU policy-making.

Karsten Ronit is a research fellow at the Centre for Public Organization and Management, Copenhagen. He has contributed to books and journals on interest groups in western and eastern Europe and within different industries. He is currently involved in a project on the organization of European bioindustry.

Bob Switky is an assistant professor at Canisius College in Buffalo, New York. He received his Ph D from the Claremont Graduate School in California. His present research includes European Union trade policy.

Peter Vipond was a principal lecturer in Financial Services at London Guildhall University when he produced the chapter for this book. He is now an Assistant Director at the British Bankers' Association with responsibilities in Banking Supervision and Market Risk. His main research interests are in international finance, especially with regard to regulatory frameworks. Recent publications include a chapter on the financial environment in Nugent *et al.*, *The European Business Environment* (1994) and an article on the regulation of trade in financial services in the *Journal of Financial Regulation and Compliance*.

Anna Wadsworth is an undergraduate completing the European Studies degree at the University of Aberdeen. She spent the third year of her study in Brussels and Germany.

Series Editorial

The idea of a series of European Casebooks on Management arose from discussions during the annual case writing competition organized by the European Foundation for Management Development (EFMD) in Brussels. The case writing competition itself was set up to encourage the production of more case studies in management with a specifically European content, to meet the growing demand in European business schools and training programmes of corporations. Begun in 1989, the competition has now established itself as a major focus of interest for case study writers.

However, knowing that many European cases were being produced outside the context of the competition, it was decided to extend the search for cases more widely. The project was taken up by Prentice Hall International in 1991, who undertook to publish the series, and appointed a Series Editor to manage the academic aspects of the collection of volumes.

From the inception of the project, the EAP European School of Management, a *grande école* of the Paris Chamber of Commerce and Industry, agreed to finance the costs of the Series Editor, and Prentice Hall funded secretarial assistance. As well as its financial support, EAP is well positioned to supply an appropriate academic infrastructure to the editorial management of the series. From its headquarters in Paris, it maintains establishments in Berlin, Madrid and Oxford, and its masters' level students train in three countries. EAP is one of the leaders in European multicultural management education and, of course, a major user of case studies with a European focus in its courses.

Early market research showed a strong and largely unsatisfied demand for case studies in European management, at a time when interest in the completion of the Single European Market was at its height. Calls for case study writers and for volume editors met a good response, and the major fields of management were quickly covered as well as several important specialized areas not originally considered.

There is an increasing number of titles available in this Series of European Casebooks on Management on a wide range of topics including Business Alliances, Business Ethics, Competing Through Services, Cooperative Strategies, Entrepreneurship and New Ventures, Environmental Issues, Finance, Human Resource Management, Managing Industrial and Business-to-Business Marketing, Industrial and Trade Policy, Informational Technology, International Business, Leadership, Management in Eastern Europe, Production and Operations Management, Research and Technology Management and Strategy. A full list of current titles is available from the publisher's UK address shown on page iv.

The case studies are intended to draw on the main developments and changes in their respective fields of management in recent years, focusing on managerial issues in corporations trading in or with the European Union. Although the principal concentration is on the non-governmental sector, the experience of governments and governmental agencies is included in some of the volumes to the extent that they affect the corporate sector. In the light of the title of the Series, cases dealing with European cross-border involvements have been given priority in inclusion, but material that relates to national experience or is conceptual or global in nature has been considered relevant if it satisfies the criteria for good cases.

A driving motive for developing the Series of European Casebooks on Management has been the wish to encourage the production of cases with a specifically European dimension. Not only have the regulatory background, institutional framework and behavioural traits of cases developed in the American business schools like Harvard always been barriers to their use in European management education, but the developing European Union has emphasized aspects of corporate development and strategy completely ignored in most American cases. With the build-up of cross-border business activity in Europe have come difficulties in cultural adjustment. The growing legislation of the European Commission in its '1992 programme' has imposed constraints and given freedoms, not known in an American context, in such fields as technology, patents, competition, take-overs and mergers, freedom of establishment and workers' rights. There was clearly a need for case studies which took account of the rapid changes occurring in the European Union and which analyzed corporations' responses to them. It is recognized in the kind of terminology which is now much more current in management thinking: 'European management', 'Euromanagers' and 'Pan-Europeanization' no longer raise eyebrows even if not everyone believes these are totally valid terms.

In selecting cases for their volumes, the Editors and the Series Editor asked the leading question again and again – what is a good case? It was not sufficient to take the accepted Harvard view. Cases are critically important to teaching at the Harvard Business School and have been since they were first produced in 1910. For example, in 1986 Benson Shapiro said that 'One must understand the fundamentals of course design, because each case must fit into the rubric of the course'. Shapiro also said the case writer should 'Ensure the case includes a balanced conflict'. In 1955, Robert Davies, also of Harvard, wrote that 'There are two kinds of cases . . . the *issue case* in which the writer poses a particular problem and the reader prepares a recommendation designed to overcome the problem, and an *appraisal case* in which the writer describes a management decision already made and the reader evaluates this decision'. Generally, cases now being written in Europe are less rigid and constrained. They reflect the multifunctional and multicultural aspects of modern European business. They are pedagogical, but less tied to functional disciplines than the Harvard cases described by Shapiro, and this again is probably because the boundaries of the functional disciplines themselves, like marketing and finance, are becoming less distinct. However, according to Paul Lawrence, in 1953, Many of the 'good' points of Harvard case study teaching are nonetheless incorporated into European case writing: the emphasis on complex, real-life situations, the degree of interest aroused, the use of 'springboard cases', and the need for good reporting.

The essentials of 'good' case writing in European management have been discussed extensively by the judges of the annual case writing competition organized by EFMD. They can be summarized as follows from the main points of a presentation by Robert Collins of IMD Lausanne at the annual conference workshop and prize-giving in Jouy-en-Josas, Paris, in September 1993.

Although writing case studies in management involves an element of opportunistic, investigative journalism, the pedagogical needs of students should be paramount. The case writer should be objective: there is no place for personal opinion or advocacy – the case writer or teacher is neither judge nor jury.

As far as the audience for cases is concerned, the case must be interesting. The setting or topic should be attractive and the case raise compelling issues. A decision-forcing case is more likely to turn students on than a descriptive or expository one – but the snag is that students do not generally like open-ended and vague cases. The case should be transferable – across faculty members, programmes and institutions.

In terms of product quality, the case should exceed audience expectations of both performance and conformance. The length of a case is important – it should give optimal time for reading and analysis, and the quality and quantity of data should be right. Assimilation is made easier when the case focuses on characters or issues, is structured, has internally consistent data, avoids jargon and is written in high-quality prose. It should be remembered that inexperienced students have a low tolerance of ambiguity and of data/ information.

Writing a good case involves creating a favourable climate among all the stakeholders in a company. They will not assist if there is not confidence, discretion and cooperation. In a company there are archetypal executives who must all be managed, for example, the 'champion' may steer the case writer through the company (but only when he or she is on hand); the 'guerilla' will appear to help, but snipe from out of sight; the 'security guard' will consider everything classified and not for discussion. The reality for a case-writer on site in a company is that not everyone will love you.

The teacher can maximize the benefits of a good case. Opportunities for customization and experimentation should always be sought – among different sets of participants, programmes and in-team teaching. A good teacher can exploit the richness of a case and the acuity of the participants.

Clearly, the case method is not the only pedagogical method of teaching management. Charles Croué of the École Supérieure de Commerce de Tours believes it is the most revolutionary, because unlike teacher-centred or self-tutoring methods, it is an active and interactive method.

The method encourages students to organize their work, to exchange different points of view in complex discussions, to find compromise by negotiating, and to improve their skills at oral presentation. They learn to compare different solutions and to synthesize information and decisions. They can observe the relationships between different disciplines of management – like marketing and strategy – and understand the difference between theory and practice. In the case-study method they do all this in a situation of reality, solving a real management problem. All of these skills prepare students well for manager status.

The case method has three main distinguishing characteristics which set it aside from other teaching methods. It is *cooperative* – students work in groups, they exchange information, and it improves their communicative abilities. It is *dynamic* – students are stimulated from passivity to effort. It is *democratic* – teachers and students have equal roles; there are no preset solutions, and ideas are freely exchanged.

Finally, the case method is well suited to the changing nature of management and business at the present time. The current environment is moving very quickly: case studies can 'catch' new events and issues as they happen (likewise, they may quickly date). They lend themselves well to performance measurement, as the managerial qualities of the students improve. The current wish for 'action-learning' is satisfied, and cases can be delivered using multiple media like videos and computers.

The present volume, by Justin Greenwood, of the Robert Gordon University, Aberdeen, covers an area as yet under-researched in the management literature: European business collective action for the purpose of exerting political influence. Whereas in most of the volumes of this Series, the corporation, its strategy and actions are the focus of the case, Justin Greenwood's compendium is concerned with the *collective* strategy of corporations intent on increasing their prosperity in the European Union.

The field of this collection of cases is the external environment of corporations in the European Union, and specifically concerns the corporations' action and interaction with political institutions of the European Union and their effect on public policy decisions. The point is made by the editor, and is clear in the cases themselves, that the activities of European business alliances is no side-show, they are highly important in the development of the integration process of the European Union itself. Simply numerically, the number of business interest groups in Brussels has grown rapidly to around three thousand today; but this interest representation is also very complex and intricate.

The cases in this volume are concerned with business sectors, or 'domains' where a sector is ill-defined; although others were included to investigate particular types of conceptual issue. Clearly, the European pharmaceutical industry, presented as a case study by the editor, is an example of such a major sector. A more conceptual issue concerns the strategic position which an industry holds in the European Union – and reference is made to industries with different levels of technology.

Justin Greenwood points out that business collective interests, as a study, fall between business studies and political science. The study of politics and markets is new in business courses, and therefore the contribution of this volume of cases is unique. The importance of the impact of collective business interests on European-level public policies and decision-making must be clear to everyone. The influence of the European Round Table of Industrialists at the 'macro' level, and the European Information Technology Round Table at a sectoral level are two of the best examples.

The editor's analysis and the cases themselves point to a dynamic, growing role for European-level business alliances and collective action in the future. It is difficult to imagine individual corporations as well as sector-wide groups of firms standing aside from vigorously pursuing collective strategies to influence European Union public policy formulation and implementation.

Justin Greenwood has opened a rich vein of research of instruction and prescription with this collection of cases, which sits very comfortably in the Series as a whole. In fact, readers of any of the other more corporate-focused volumes in the Series will benefit from a wider knowledge of the field explored by the cases in the *European Casebook on Business Alliances*.

Paul Stonham, Series Editor,
EAP European School of Management, Oxford

Foreword

The work of the European Union is increasingly impinging on domestic as well as international businesses, and those organizations in the private and public sectors which ignore the agenda of decision-makers in Brussels do so at their peril. This timely book contains a rich account of a large number of European business alliances formed or activated in the course of seeking to influence EC/EU decision-making, and provides new analyses of the practices and processes of lobbying in the 1990s.

A book of this kind would not have been published as recently as ten years ago – for lack of the necessary research and for lack of a buying public. Many of the successful techniques and pitfalls of lobbying in Brussels have not changed over time, as the case studies in this book show, but the Brussels world of pressure groups, professional advisers, lobbyists and consultants has expanded greatly, particularly since the signing of the Single European Act in 1986 and the EC's commitment to achieve a single European market by the end of 1992. Those developments have immeasurably strengthened the dynamics of European integration and have spawned an unparalleled burst of legislative activity (over eight hundred measures) at EC level – all of which has drawn corporations and their representatives, advisers and lobbyists into the maw of the European Union. European legislation is not likely to be the end of the story for business alliances, as attention shifts from decision-making in Brussels to implementing decisions made in national capitals, and then to the task of monitoring, evaluating and enforcing the new rules of the single market. Existing policy communities and networks have enlarged their field of action while new networks and configurations of interests have formed to take on single issues or long-term policy concerns which have recently arrived on the Brussels agenda. The myriad number of Euro-groups, changing names and structures by the month, increasingly including the interests of prospective EU member states in their deliberations, have been joined by multinational and national corporations, as well as by foreign governments, lobbying directly to seek the attention of the EU institutions. Exclusively national interest groups also dip into the Brussels pond as well as lobbying hard their own national governments and sympathetic members of the European Parliament. Because the EU is the world's largest trading bloc it is no surprise that lobbyists from all over the world are active in seeking to influence its decisions.

The activity of seeking to influence and of bringing pressure to bear on the EU is having to change as the Commission and MEPs in particular face a lobbying overload. Measures to restrict access to EU officials and MEPs are being contemplated as well as a code of practice and declarations of interest on the part of lobbyists. Single issue alliances of federations and/or individual firms are being formed to give extra competitive advantage to their stand-points by virtue of the breadth, depth and resources that are at their command. The transparency of the process of EU decision-making is also under greater scrutiny by elected representatives, interest groups and the mass media. The relative secrecy of the interactions between organized interests is part of the decision-making system which those who are concerned about the institutional 'democratic deficit' in the EU wish to open up. The Commission is often more directly accountable to particular organized interests than it is to the wider public interest through the Council of Ministers and the European Parliament. This aspect of EU decision-making is underscored by the Commission's dependence on information and expertise from outside about subjects for decision, given the relatively small size of its own staff. The information and expertise Brussels is looking for is often at the command of corporations and pressure groups with a direct interest in the decisions to be made at EU level. Hence the mutual dependence of key actors in the decision-making process, which is reinforced by the lack of scrutiny by others less directly involved or concerned.

The examples and case histories cited in this book also amplify the findings of previous studies that the business of influencing EU-level decisions is not for the faint-hearted or those short of funds. Decision-making in the EU is a multi-layered affair, subject to numerous legitimate, and some arbitrary opportunities for delay. This requires careful issue-management skills on the part of bureaucrats, diplomats and lobbyists alike, and often considerable expenditures, to keep track of and to keep up pressure on the decision-makers and the process of which they are a part. Such expenditures may however be fully justified in the eyes of commerical interests if they succeed in the writing of the rules of the market in such a way as to confer competitive advantages on a sector or a particular firm, or to remove the threat of competitive disadvantages which otherwise might have been approved by the EU institutions.

Although the expansion of the lobbying industry in and around Brussels has brought forward many new organizations representing a range of social groups, and wider public concerns, the fire-power advantage still lies overwhelmingly with business interests despite some institutional corrections designed to add balance to the overall representation of interests in the Union. The organization of markets in western Europe remains the core activity of the EU. As this activity deepens and its scope is extended, so businesses will increasingly need to seek representation and to build alliances in order to protect their interests. It can no longer be assumed that interest group activity at the level of the EU is necessarily supportive of the process of European integration, as some early integration theorists argued. This book provides many and varied insights into just how representation and influence can be secured across a wide variety of sectors and cross-sectoral coalitions of actors as well as by sectoral interests. As such it provides an invaluable and long overdue guide to the workings of EU institutions and to the techniques of pressure and persuasion brought to bear upon them.

Alan Butt Philip
Jean Monnet Reader in European Integration
and Director, Centre for International Business Research
Bath University
November 1994

Acknowledgements

I would like to thank Rachel Stewart for her dedicated technical support in the production of this collection. Without her help, the book would undoubtedly have been delayed by several months.

Justin Greenwood

Abbreviations

ABI	Association of British Insurers
ACEA	Association of European Automobile Constructors
ACP	African, Caribbean and Pacific Countries
ACTIP	Animal Cell Technology Industrial Platform
AEA	Association of European Airlines
AECM	European Independent Business Confederation
AECMA	Association of European Aerospace Companies
AEGRAFLEX	Association Européenne des Graveurs et des Flexographes
AFB	Association Française des Banques
AMCHAM	American Chamber of Commerce
AMFEP	Association of Microbial Food Enzyme Producers
ANOBCCEE	Association of National Organisations in the Bakery and Confectionery in the EEC
ANSI	American National Standards Institute
AT&T	American Telephone and Telegraph
BBA	British Bankers' Association
BBA	Belgian Bioindustries Association
BBC	British Broadcasting Corporation
BC-NET	Business Cooperation Network
BDB	Bundesverband Deutscher Banken
BEUC	Bureau Européen des Unions de Consommateurs
BIAC	Business and Industrial Advisory Committee
BIBM	International Federation of the Precast Concrete Industry
BIIC	British Insurers' International Committee
BIS	Bank for International Settlements
BRT	Business Round Table
BSB	British Satellite Broadcasting

BSkyB	British Sky Broadcasting
BT	British Telecom
CAACE	Comité des Associations d'Armateurs des Communautés Européennes
CASA	Construcciones Aeronauticas
CBEMA	Computer and Business Manufacturers' Association
CBI	Confederation of British Industry
CCIR	International Radio Consultative Committee (of the International Telecommunications Union)
CCMC	Committee of Common Market Automobile Constructors
CD	Compact Disk
CEA	Comité Européen des Assurances
CEC	Commission of the European Communities
CECD	Confédération Européen de Commerce
CEE	Comunita Economica Europea
CEFIC	European Chemical Industry Council
CEN	Committee for European Normalization
CENELEC	Comité Européen de Normalisation Electrotechnique European Committee for Electrotechnical Standardization
CENSA	Council of European and Japanese National Shipowners' Associations
CEMBUREAU	European Cement Association
CEO	Chief Executive Officer
CES	Committee of European Shipowners
CIAA	Confederation of the Food and Drink Industries of the EEC
CIFE	Council of European Industrial Federations
CIGR	International Commission on Agricultural Engineering
CIRFS	Comité International de la Rayone et des Fibres Synthétique
CLCA	Automobile Industry of the Countries of the European Communities
COMASSO	Association of Plant Breeders of the European Economic Community
CONFAPI	Confederazione Italiana delle Piccole Imprese
COSINE	Cooperation for Open Systems Interconnection Networking in Europe
CPS	Consumer Policy Service
CRAFT	Cooperative Research Action for Technology
CUBE	Concertation Unit for Biotechnology
DBS	Direct Broadcasting by Satellite
DG	Directorate-General
DGB	German Trade Union Federation

DOE	Department of the Environment
DTI	Department of Trade and Industry
DVB	Digital Video Broadcasting
EACEM	European Association of Consumer Electronics Manufacturers
EAIC	European Aerospace Industries Council
EAPO	European Association of Fish Producers Organisations
EBCG	European Biotechnology Coordinating Group
EBF	European Banking Federation
EBIS	European Biotechnology Information Service
ECACC	European Council of American Chambers of Commerce
ECF	European Caravan Federation
ECFED	European Community Federation of Youth Hostel Associations
ECIS	European Centre for Infrastructure Studies
ECJ	European Court of Justice
ECLA	Association Industrielle Européene d'Habillement
ECMA	European Computer Manufacturers' Association
ECPA	European Crop Protection Association
ECSA	European Community Shipowners' Associations
ECTEL	Association of the European Telecommunications and Professional Electronics Industry
ECTAA	Group of National Travel Agents' and Tour Operators' Associations within the EEC
ECU	Euopean Currency Unit
EDMA	European Diagnostic Manufacturers' Association
EEA	European Economic Area
EEC	European Economic Community
EECA	European Electrical Components Manufacturers' Association
EEIG	European Economic Interest Grouping
EFB	European Federation of Biotechnology
EFCSO	European Federation of Camping Site Organisations
EFCT	European Federation of Conference Towns
EFPIA	European Federation of Pharmaceutical Industry Associations
EFTA	European Free Trade Association
EFTGA	European Federation of Tourist Guides Associations
EHMA	European Hotel Managers' Association
EIW/RMDI	European Institute for Water, for Resources, Management and Development
ELRA	European Leisure and Recreation Association
ELTAC	European Largest Textile and Apparel Companies

EMSU	European Medium and Small Business Union
EMUG	European MAP Users' Group
ENSR	European Network for SME Research
EP	European Parliament
ERDF	European Regional Development Fund
ERT	European Round Table of Industrialists
ESC	Economic and Social Committee
ESNBA	European Secretariat of National Biotechnology Associations
ESPRIT	European Strategic Programme for Research and Development in Information Technology
ETAG	European Tourism Action Group
ETC	European Travel Commission
ETOA	European Tour Operators' Association
ETSI	European Telecommunications Standards Institute
ETTFA	European Tourism Trade Fair Association
ETUC	European Trade Union Confederation
ETUI	European Trade Union Institute
ETUCTCL	Europea Trade Union Congress for Textiles, Clothing and Leather
EU	European Union
EUCAR	European Council for Automotive Research and Development
EUREAU	Union of European Associations of Water Suppliers
EUROBIT	European Association of Manufacturers of Business Machines and Information Technology
EUROFIET	European Retail Trade Union Organization
EUROPARKS	European Federation of Leisure Parks
EUROPECHE	Association of National Organisations of Fishing Enterprises in the EEC
EUROPMI	European Committee for Small and Medium-Sized Independent Companies
EUROTOQUES	European Community of Cooks
EUTO	European Union of Tourist Officers
EWOS	European Workshop for Open Systems
EWPCA	European Water Pollution Control Association
EWWG	European Waste Water Group
FCC	Federal Communications Commission
FDI	Foreign Direct Investments
FEBC	Forum for European Bioindustry Coordination
FEDESA	European Federation of Animal Health
FEFANA	European Federation of Animal Feed Additive Manufacturers

FERCO	European Federation of Contract Catering Organisations
FEWITA	Federation of Wholesale and International Trade Associations
FIEEBTP	International Federation of European Contractors of Buildings and Public Works
GATT	General Agreement on Tariffs and Trade
GEBTA	Guild of European Business Travel Agents
GEDIS	Groupment Européene des Enterprise de Distribution Integrée
GIE	Groupment d'Intérêt Économique
GNP	Gross National Product
GSP	Generalized System of Preferences
HD-MAC	High Definition Multiplex Analogue Component
HDTV	High Definition Television
HOTREC	Confederation of the National Hotel and Restaurant Associations in the European Community
HQ	Headquarters
ICS	International Chamber of Shipping
IFPMA	International Federation of Pharmaceutical Industry Associations
IGPOL	Industrial Group on the Protection of the Ozone Layer
ILO	International Labour Organization
IMO	International Maritime Organization
IMU	International Metal Union
ING	Internationale Nederland Group
INTERLAIN	Comitédes Industries Lainières de la CEE
INTERTANKO	International Association of Independent Tanker Owners
ISA	International Standards Association
ISF	International Shipping Federation
IT	Information Technology
IVTIP	In Vitro Testing Industry Platform
JAMA	Japan Automobile Manufacturers' Association
JCIF	Japan Centre for International Finance
JETRO	Japan External Trade Organization
JMEA	Japan Machinery Exporters' Association
KNO	Kritische Niederlandse Ondernemers
LIBA	London Investment Banking Association
MAC	Multiplex Analogue Component
MAFF	Ministry of Agriculture, Fisheries and Food
MEP	Member of the European Parliament
MFA	Multifibre Arrangement
MINT	Managing the Integration of New Technology

MITI	Ministry of International Trade and Industry
MPAA	Motion Picture Association of America
MPEG	Motion Picture Experts Group
MUSE	Multiple sub-Nyquist Encoding
MVEG	Motor Vehicle Emmissions Group
MZES	Mannheimer Zentrum für Europäische Sozialforschung
NACE	Nomenclature Generale des Activitiés Economiques dans le Communaute Europeenne
NATO	North Atlantic Treaty Organization
NBC	National Broadcasting Corporation
NTSC	National Television Systems Committee
OBC	Banque Odier Bungener Courvoisier
OECD	Organization for Economic Cooperation and Development
ORGALIME	Liaison Organisation for the European Mechanical, Electrical and Electronic Engineering and Metalwork Industries
OSI	Open Systems Interconnection
OSITOP	Open Systems Interconnection Technical and Office Protocols
PAL	Phase Alteration by Line
RACE	Research and Development in Advanced Communications Technologies in Europe
RARE	Réseaux Associés pour la Recherche Européene
RTF	Radio Télédiffusion de France
R&D	Research and Development
RWA	Regional Water Authority
SAF	Svenska Arbetsgivareföreningen
SAGB	Senior Advisory Group Biotechnology
SBAC	Society of British Aerospace Contractors
SD	Selective Distribution
SECAM	Séquence à memoire
SES	Société Européene des Satellites
SME	Small and Medium-Sized Enterprises
SPAG	Standards Promotion and Application Group
SPRINT	Strategic Programme for Innovation and Technology Transfer
TDA	Timeshare Developers' Association
TUC	Trade Union Congress
UACEE	Union de l'Artisanat de la CEE
UAP	Union des Assurances Paris
UEAPME	European Association of Craft, Small and Medium-Sized Enterprises

UIEP	Union Internationale des Enterprises de Platrerie, Staff, Stuc et Activités Annexes
UIPCG	International Union of Confectioners, Pastrycooks and Ice-Cream Makers
UK	United Kingdom
UNICE	Union of Industrial and Employers' Confederations of Europe
UNCTAD	United Nations Conference on Trade and Development
USA	United States of America
USICG	United States Industry Coordinating Group on European Community Affairs
VCI	Verband der Chemischen Industrie
VCR	Video Cassette Recorder
VHS	Video Home System
VLSI	Very Large Scale Integration
WARC	World Administrative Radio Conference
WHO	World Health Organization
WSA	Water Services Association
WTO	World Tourism Organization
WTTC	World Travel and Tourism Council
YES	Young Entrepreneurs for Europe
YIP	Yeast Industry Platform

Introduction

Justin Greenwood

The passage of the Single European Act in 1985 opened up unprecedented possibilities for business to expand markets and benefit from economies of scale. Since the famous *Cassis de Dijon* case of 1979 in the European Court of Justice,[1] European law established that, unless injurious to health and the environment, a product good enough to be produced for, say, the Danish market, was good enough for the Portuguese market too. No artificial barriers to market trade could be constructed. The single market provided for the free movement of goods, capital, workers and services in the twelve member states of the European Community, and in 1993 a free trade area was subsequently extended to most of western Europe by agreement with the European Free Trade Area (EFTA) countries, excluding Switzerland.

Business and political leaders came to recognize that Europe's future lay in the ability to compete with the rest of the world, and particularly the USA, Japan and the newly developing economies of south-east Asia. This meant not an inward-looking 'fortress Europe', seeking to drive out products made beyond the walls of the club, but, rather an ambition to exchange products with the rest of the world under conditions of market competition. Europe's traders would need the discipline of world contest if their products were to continue to find buyers in the years to come. By 1992, Europe was almost finally open for business, and businesspeople and politicians were delighted to see their ambitions fulfilled. Although there are inevitable disputes over the economic benefits of the single market, the Cecchini report estimated that the project would be worth a gain of around 5 per cent of Europe's gross domestic product in a medium-term period (Cecchini, 1988). The costs of 'non-Europe' were therefore unthinkable if Europe was to continue to generate wealth to sustain its population.

The increasingly accepted idea that the future of European countries lay in their ability to remain competitive within a world economy has driven the pace of European integration. Together, a significant range of interests in

European countries have a collective interest in integration. While disputes remain about the extent of integration which is desirable, there remains a consensus within business and politics about the need for an effective free market, and the corresponding need to pool resources to ensure that it comes about. A timetable for the achievement of monetary integration, the 1992 Maastricht treaty with its 'pillar' structures for political union, deepening of the single market, and majority agreement for a social protocol, have dramatically increased the pace of integration, promising a train of further unification with its own momentum. Instead of simply having an economic community, we now have a European Union. In a whole range of areas of public life, competencies have been transferred from the national level to the European Community. Member states have increasingly ceded powers to the institutions of the European Union, such that the complexities of European decision-making are balanced between intergovernmental bargaining of the member states and the powers of the European Commission and Parliament, rather than being dominated by the final decision of the twelve national governments at the Council. In most economic areas, the European Parliament enjoys co-decision making powers with the Council. It is now hardly possible for one nation ruthlessly and recklessly to follow a path of single self-interest in economic fields, in that such self-interest has become bonded to the interests of the other members of the European Union: national self-interest has partly become a collective European interest. Indeed, almost forty years of working together has resulted in collective outputs being produced and recognized among the parties involved, whether nations, European institutions, businesses, or some other types of interest. There may now be no turning back.

Back in 1958, Ernst Haas foresaw a key role for business interests in driving the pace of European integration. Integration in one sector would become impossible, because real harmonization would require a range of other measures, thus involving 'spillover' from one sector to another (Haas, 1958). As business leaders came to see the value of European integration, so they would turn to their national governments and demand more, and form political bases in Brussels to make sure there would be no retreat. Businesses in other sectors would see the benefits on offer, and also demand European integration in a 'me too' type process. The end result predicted by Haas was full integration. Business interest groups were thus seen as a key factor in the entire process. Although the European Economic Community came about as a result of political initiatives imposed by political leaders on a reluctant business community, the roles were soon reversed and businesses demanded further integration from politicians. The examination of European business alliances is therefore no side-show, but a central factor in understanding the development of the European Union.

Haas' 'neo-functionalist' model of integration seemed highly plausible until the 'de Gaulle crisis' of the mid-1960s, which in effect established a national veto on European decision-making. By the 1970s, with the economies of western Europe in deep recession from the oil crises, Haas' analysis seemed extremely unlikely in that European integration appeared to be going nowhere. Haas himself virtually disowned the explanatory power of his ideas in 1976 (Haas, 1976). Yet by the late 1980s, scholars had dusted down Haas' works, because they seemed once again to have relevance in analysing what happened before, during and after the passage of the Single European Act. Firstly, as Maria Green Cowles explains in Case 16, business leaders from the largest firms in Europe played a key role in the emergence of the single market project. Secondly, what has happened since in a number of sectoral, or 'meso', areas, as many of the cases which follow make clear, can be attributed in no small measure to the actions of business interests. Key issues concerning the regulation and promotion of trade in medicines, for instance, one of Europe's key export areas, can be understood only by reference to the actions of business interests and the relationships which have evolved with public actors in the European Union (Case 2). The number of interest groups present in Brussels has grown from three hundred in 1970 (Butt Philip, 1985), to around three thousand today (Commission, 1992). The majority of these are business interests with the resources to fund a Brussels base. It is also estimated that there are around ten thousand 'lobbyists' working in Brussels today (Commission, 1992). This dramatic growth has brought its own problems, and the European Parliament in particular has been highly critical of the ethical standards of a minority of 'lobbyists'. In response, the Commission has encouraged the 'lobbying community' to develop its own self-regulatory code of conduct. This was duly launched in September 1994 by a number of public affairs consultancy firms, although whether it will gain widespread acceptance by both the 'lobbying community' on the one hand, and the European Parliament on the other, remains to be seen (McLaughlin and Greenwood, 1995).

Few businesses of any size can afford to be without representation in Brussels. For many sectors, their affairs are governed more by policies arising from the European Union than they are by those from their national governments. The stakes to be won and lost from the activities of the European Union institutions are high; as Maloney (Case 10) observes by citing Key (1956): 'where power rests, there influence is brought to bear'. The norms which govern European-level activities become powerfully entrenched. Furthermore, European decision-, and non-decision-making processes are extremely complex. European interest representation is therefore extremely intricate. It is quite possible for a business interest to lose years of painstaking work and millions of ECUs in a moment. McLaughlin (1992), for instance, provides an example of how a British government minister negotiated away a whole generation of technology development by a British car firm in bargaining over fisheries matters. Elsewhere, Pedlar (1994) has described how the timetable for European decision-making between the Parliament and the

Council necessitated the final decision on the Pregnant Woman's Directive being taken at the Council of Fisheries Ministers.

Not only is there a plethora of European-level decision-making institutions involved with different types of power at different stages in the decision-making process, but there are also complex political relationships between them and a considerable range of interests represented within them. Different sections of the Commission pursue different kinds of interests. As most of the sector cases make clear, this is one of the key issues which an interest will need to manage, and sometimes even exploit. In Case 12, McLaughlin quotes one Commission official describing the relationship between two of the directorates: 'Quite simply, it's war'. The support of national governments have to be enlisted, sometimes in competition with those of other governments. Bargaining between and within these institutions can produce extremely uncertain processes and outcomes. At the national level, the outcome of directives can be considerably influenced during their implementation because this type of policy instrument, the dominant form of European policy output, leaves the detailed arrangements for putting policy into practice to the member states themselves. The forms of interest representation are thus highly complex. However, the two broad issues which concern us are, firstly, the *logic of influence*, concerning the extent to which a business interest can influence policy outputs (means) and outcomes (ends); and secondly, the *logic of collective action*, that is, the factors which impact upon the ways in which business interests work together. Successful patterns of collective action are a necessary, though not sufficient, condition for successful influence. A model of some of the issues arising from these two factors appears in *Exhibit 1*, a kind of 'map' of European interest representation.

A simplification of Exhibit 1 would be to divide channels of representation into the 'national route', the 'territorial route' and the 'Brussels strategy'. These can take many forms, but, simplified almost to the point of distortion as 'ideal types', the national route might involve a national interest group seeking to influence European policy by enlisting the support of its national government, whereas the Brussels strategy might involve a Brussels-based European interest group going straight to the Commission. The 'territorial route' involves a local or transnational coalition. There are arguments and factors influencing the adoption of those routes, which have been reviewed in detail elsewhere (see, for instance, Greenwood *et al.*, 1992): many of these will become evident from reading the cases which follow.

It is important to remember that these routes are by no means mutually exclusive, and indeed, for many interests, the principal rule is likely to be to try to keep as many channels of influence open as possible, provided it helps. However, the growth in the number of Brussels-based Euro groups, where the Commission is based, will alert the reader to the increasing use of the more direct Brussels strategy in recent years. In part this is a reflection of the increasing competencies invested in the European Union. This process is

Exhibit 1 *Representing interests in the European Union*
(Source: *Greenwood and Jordan, 1993)*

Organizational form of corporate activity	Route	Voice	Target
Individual firm	Try to determine policy at national level	Self-representation	Commission and Directorates-General
Coalition (industry, territorial)			
National trade association	Influence Europe via national contacts		Council of Ministers
National federation			Working group
European specific coalition (e.g. direct firm membership, informal collective)	Brussels strategy	Commercial lobbyist	Parliament Economic and Social Committee
European federation of national federations ('super federation')			

evident in all of the cases which follow, including the case which examines a non-business interest, the European Trade Union Confederation. However, in non-business areas the process of transferring to the Brussels strategy is less marked, and in most of these the national level of organization remains the most significant. Of interest, however, is that business groups in newly emerging industrial areas, such as gene splicing technologies, have invested more resources in the European level of organization than in the national one, preferring to go straight to Brussels. This may be the pattern of the future.

Whilst the picture may seem highly chaotic, the underlying principles are not. The Commission, where policies start life, is extremely open to representation from outside interests. It is a very small bureaucracy (around 3,600 senior administrators), is overworked, and its increasing workload has not been matched by an increase in resources. Metcalfe (1992) considers that there is a 'management deficit' in the Commission, resulting in its being unable to manage its business alone. It has come to rely upon the resources which interests bring, such as information, expertise, cooperation and the ability to put policies into practice. It is not possible to understand the impact of European interest groups upon public policies without considering the types of resource which private interests, such as firms or business interest groups, and the Commission exchange. These resources are summarized below.

Business Interest Resources

1. Information and Expertise

Public policies are shaped around information. The small and overloaded Commission has become dependent upon specialist information brought by private interests. Sometimes, just one Commission official will be responsible for a whole subsector's affairs. Hull has described this official as 'a very lonely [person] with a blank piece of paper in front of him, wondering what to put on it' (1993, p. 83).

Firms and industrial associations may well have greater collective expertise than will the Commission official(s). Commission reports contain statistics given by industrial sources (see Case 5 on biotechnology). Sometimes, the Commission will ask an industry association to prepare a report on its behalf (see Case 2 on pharmaceuticals). Sometimes the Commission will contract a consultant to produce a report, who will in turn depend upon industrial sources for the information collected; indeed, sometimes, the consultant will be dependent for his or her livelihood upon a particular firm or sector (see Case 3 on consumer electronics), providing a key route of information input to the Commission.

2. Economic Muscle

Some companies will have greater resources at their disposal than certain member states. They are therefore bound to be significant political actors. Public policy-makers are dependent upon businesses to perform; key factors such as employment, balance of trade and wealth creation, and indeed the popularity of public institutions, including ruling parties, count on business activities. The European pharmaceutical industry, for instance, has a net positive balance of trade with the rest of the world of +12 per cent? compared with a net deficit for all sectors of −0.67 per cent (Case 2). The pharmaceutical industry represents a key player with which to compete with the rest of the world, and European public policy-makers cannot afford to ignore it. Crudely put: the more resources a business interest has, the more likely it is to be able to influence public policies.

3. Prestige Value

Status resources also influence access to public policies. The Commission, for instance, is particularly keen on high prestige, high technology domains which promise to deliver the goods tomorrow. In part, domains such as civil aviation (Case 4), consumer electronics (Case 3), information technology (Case 1), biotechnology (Case 5) and pharmaceuticals (Case 2) reflect to the Commission a desired self-image of a force for today likely to grow into something even bigger tomorrow. For these types of reason, particular attention is given in the cases to comparing industries using different levels of technology.

4. Power in Implementation

Groups such as farmers are powerful actors because they own significant land resources. It would be inconceivable for the Commission to develop a policy on, say, retaining hedgerows, without negotiating with farmers first, because farmers have the ability to make or break such a policy in that they would be the key actors responsible for implementation. If the farmers refused such a policy then the policy would undoubtedly fail.

5. Organization of the Interest into a Non-competitive Format

Interests organized into competitive groupings are unlikely to be successful because public policies will either be unable to arbitrate between the factions or will favour one type of interest at the expense of others. Any bureaucracy will find it extremely difficult to deal with competitive groupings, and indeed the Commission has devoted resources to assist with the organization of interests into single formats. Outside of business, the Commission even gives grants to groups to establish themselves as 'one-stop shops' such as is the case with consumer interests. Life is so much easier for officials if they have to talk to just one outlet which can put forward the views of all its members. There are things which interests can do to ensure that competitive formats do not emerge, and these factors are examined in some of the cases which follow. One of these is to ensure that the largest firms have the most say in the policy of the trade association while at the same time not squeezing out the interests of the smaller players.

In Case 3, Cawson draws attention to the fact that an interest need not be organized into a group under certain conditions. For instance, an interest can operate effectively through a single firm with the Euro group being a 'front' for a particular company, or little more than a 'letterhead' organization set up for the appearance of acting collectively. Thus in consumer electronics, where European firms are concentrated into three companies only – Philips, Thomson and Nokia – there is really no need for a Euro association.

6. Coherent Organization of the Interest and Decision-making Power Given to Representative Outlets

Many (though not all) 'super federations', or European federations of national federations (sometimes even European federations of European federations), are so cumbersome and so far abstracted from the constituent membership of firms that they are ineffective or have collapsed on coherence grounds (see, for instance, Case 12 on automobiles and Case 5 on biotechnology). Grant (1990; 1993), for instance, considers that many Euro groups are incoherent and unable to agree on anything worthwhile; their purpose, therefore is restricted to that of fraternal contact. McLaughlin, author of Case 12, once entitled a conference paper 'Underfed Euro feds' (1992), while he and another author in this collection (Jordan) once addressed the question: 'Why are Euro groups so numerous and so weak?' It is necessary, for instance, when reading position statements from the 'peak' (all business) association UNICE, to read between the lines for the compromises and disagreements which result in 'lowest common denominator' statements. However, there are examples of effective 'superfederations', and the conditions for effectiveness are carefully examined in Case 2, which looks at the highly successful European Federation of Pharmaceutical Industry Associations. Among the factors essential to the ability to work well is the capacity for speedy decision-making, which requires the delegation of powers to the secretariat to take action without the need for constant prior referral to the membership constituency beforehand. Also important in achieving coherent policy statements is the weighting of interests towards the most important interests, identified earlier.

A number of different group formats have emerged in recent years, in part in response to the difficulties experienced by superfederations. In the cases of cars (Case 12), biotechnology (Case 5) and tourism (Case 9) some direct firm membership formats are evident, while elsewhere, such as cement (Case 6) and retailing (Case 8) there are mixed formats involving both firms and associations. In general terms, the more direct the constituency representation, the more effective the Euro group is, although there are many varying conditions and exceptions to this dictum.

Unquestionably the most influential contribution to understanding the 'encompassingness' (i.e. actual membership *viz-à-viz* total potential membership) of groups was that made by Mancur Olson in 1965. Olson suggested that the most rational behaviour for an interest was not to spend money on the membership fee of an association but instead to 'free-ride' on its activities, gaining the benefits without contributing. 'Collective goods', such as achieving a favourable outcome to discussions with state authority on regulation, was an insufficient basis to ensure membership. To avoid this problem, groups would have to offer selective incentives to their members to join, such as low-cost insurance policies or other facilities on favourable terms. Yet as Jordan and McLaughlin have shown elsewhere (1991), it is possible that Olson over-intellectualized the membership decision, stressing too much rational, utility-maximizing sorts of behaviour and paying insufficient attention to other types of dynamics. All sorts of factors impact upon the membership decision, such as the status of belonging, the need for lonely company representatives in Brussels to mix socially, or the fear that not to belong would be to lose out on vital information or the ability to influence the positions of the trade association. At the European level it is almost impossible to use Olson's typology, not least because of the difficulty of ascertaining who precisely has influence with federated associations. Is it, for instance, the national association affiliated to the European association, or is it the member firm of the national association? Unclear lines of accountability such as these make collective action at the European level a complicated phenomenon. However, it is clear that effective collective action leads to effective patterns of interest representation. In turn, effective interest representation through one organization leads to it being the natural home for collective action in that business domain.

7. Ability to Help the Commission to Carry Out Policies

An interest can make itself extremely attractive to the Commission if it helps ease the Commission's overload problem by acting as an agency of policy implementation. One means of achieving this is through self-regulation. Hence, the European Federation of Pharmaceutical Industry Associations (EFPIA; Case 2) offered itself as the means through which standards of medical selling to medical practitioners could be regulated via the provision of a code of practice, established and implemented by EFPIA, as an alternative to the Commission formulating and negotiating a regulation or directive and overseeing its implementation. This form of regulation is extremely attractive to both governmental and industry sources in that, for the Commission's part, *inter alia* it does not use up resources, is flexible and involves a spirit of self-discipline. For industry, among other things it permits the opportunity to retain control over its own affairs. These arrangements can also benefit the consumer, although there are examples where this is not the case. The Commission can, in theory, exercise influence by insisting on more formal regulation if the scheme fails, although its dependency upon industry for resources, including cooperation and economic performance, can disable such a mechanism in practice. Although self-regulatory instruments are popular in a number of sectors throughout member states, their establishment is rare at the European level as a whole. This may be because of the inability of some associations to 'deliver the goods' and to keep its membership in line, abiding by such a code. However, the implementation of European directives at the national level often occurs through self-regulatory instruments (Sargent, 1987). Once again, the ability of a private interest to make itself indispensable to public authority by offering a solution to the problem of overload is a key resource: considerable influence can be exerted upon the impact of a policy during its implementation.

There are forms of assistance with Commission overload besides self-regulatory schemes. Hence Cawson (Case 3) provides details of the help given by Philips to the development of broadcasting technologies through research, production and secondment of personnel to Directorate-General (DG) XIII (telecommunications). This case provides a further example of the dependence by the Commission on private business. Without firms like Philips, Europe would be unable to compete in global markets in key technologies. Firms such as these, therefore, have a 'reserved seat' at the policy-making table in this domain.

8. Interest Group's Ability to Influence its Members

An interest group which entered into agreement with the Commission and which failed to make the agreement stick with its members would be of little use to the Commission. Conversely, one which can deliver authoritative opinion and carry its members is likely to be invaluable.

European Union Resources

European Union resources include the ability to regulate and the ability to promote, assist, encourage or, in theory, hinder an industry. This is achieved through resources including policy instruments (including deregulatory ones); harmonization and integration measures; mechanisms for implementation; enforcement activities (such as the prevention of anti-competitive behaviour); negotiations in global trade agreements (such as GATT); enabling action (such as the provision of infrastructure or trade development); and funding for processes such as industrial research and development, restructuring or regional policies.

When these resources are exchanged between actors, power dependency relationships arise. Each party becomes dependent on the resources of the other. The possession, or absence, of these 'bargaining chips', will determine whether the private interest enjoys 'insider' (Grant, 1978) status to policy-making and implementation. These become what Jordan *et al.* (1992) have called 'policy participants'. Those lacking sufficient bargaining chips are 'outsider groups' (Grant, 1978). Crudely put: the less public an interest makes its affairs, the more successful we can conclude it is because it is able to get its needs met on the 'insider track' of public policy-making. Conversely, groups who need to appeal for public support for their concerns do so because they are unable or unwilling to exert influence as an insider group. Increasing use of public appeal strategies may signify the erosion of insider status. Typically, business groups possess more of the types of resources required for 'insider status' than do non-business groups, although high status groups such as members of the judiciary can also be intensely 'resource rich'. Equally, the absence of the resources outlined above in the right combination might mean that an otherwise resource-rich interest does not enjoy the privileged access which one might expect. For instance, an economically powerful industrial domain which is poorly organized for political representation purposes at the European Union level may not achieve insider status (an example in the cases which follow is that of tourism). Similarly, the domain might not achieve its full potential for full insider status, and here Maloney *et al.* (1995) helpfully make the distinction among *core* (always centrally involved in policy-making and implementation), *specialist* (always centrally involved where technical issues are involved) and *peripheral* (only sometimes involved) insider status. Examples of each of these types of status can be found in the cases which follow.

These models indicate the types of ingrained forms of involvement by private interests in public policy-making. To understand this phenomenon, it is necessary to forget popular images of smooth talkers showing up one day offering dinner and persuasion and disappearing the next. Hired hands – lobbyists – are used, but only in particular contexts, such as 'an extra pair of ears' (Case 1), or by the most desperate where they have neglected to build the type of long-term relations with bureaucracies which would have afforded a channel of influence in the first place, or perhaps when all else has failed. If it is necessary to hire a lobbyist to fight a case, then the issue is probably already lost. Sectors are governed by permanent partnerships involving private and public (centred around permanent officials) interests, from which policies emerge and are implemented. If an interest is taken by surprise and has to react to a policy initiative coming from the Commission then it is too late to exert much influence. Such influence is exerted as the policy initiative takes shape, and continues during formulation and implementation. Indeed, where the 'public' stops and the 'private' begins may be indistinguishable. Thus, Colebatch (1991) thinks of state authority more as an arena within which activities occur, rather than 'public authority' and 'private interests'.

Perhaps the easiest way to think of policy-making and implementation in these ways is through the idea of a rather exclusive 'policy village' (Heclo and Wildavsky, 1974), with entry into the village governed by the ownership of resources. Typically, these villages involve a limited number of partici-pants, i.e. the relevant part of the bureaucracy (such as a section of a DG in the Commission), and the key representatives of private interests. Resource entry thresholds are so high that the occupants of this village are extremely settled, with highly developed and enmeshed interpersonal and interinsti-tutional relationships. Thereafter, analytic life becomes more complicated for us. A number of different terms have been developed and adopted by different authors, often varying in emphasis among the important factors involved but nevertheless all describing, more-or-less, the policy village idea. Richardson and Jordan (1979) used the helpful term 'policy community', contrasting this with the more open and looser type of 'issue network' (Heclo, 1978), where interests are thrown together over a particular issue (perhaps a proposal to build a road through a local community or a new industrial estate), often to disappear again when the issue subsides. Rhodes and Marsh (1990) employ the generic term 'policy network', including at the one extreme the closed and settled policy community and at the other the loose and unstable 'issue network'. However, confusingly, there are authors who have used these terms to mean different things (see, in particular, Wilks and Wright, 1987). What is more important to retain is the idea of closed and stable 'villages' from which policies are bargained over, settled, made and implemented, or loose 'issue networks' which are poor mechanisms for the resolution of policy disputes. The former are mechanisms of sectoral, or 'meso', governance, involving public and private interests.

The emphasis upon cases in this text means that the focus of our interest is upon sectors. Where these lack definition (such as tourism or bioindustry), they are better referred to as domains. There have been, and remain, attempts to understand state-wide policy outcomes by reference to the relationship between public and private interests, often comprising tripartite partnerships involving governments, business and labour interests. For instance, 'macro' economic policy directions, and wage and social policy agreements, have been negotiated between chief government ministers and 'peak' associations representing, respectively, all business and trade union interests. There may have been times in some countries where these 'corporatist' arrangements prevailed, most notably through periods of Keynesian economic policies, and, where such policies remain, policy-making is sometimes still characterised by such arrangements, such as in Austria (Traxler, 1994). However, as Streeck and Schmitter (1991) and Traxler and Schmitter (1994) have pointed out, the absence of 'state'-like properties at the European Union makes the development of corporatism extremely unlikely. Indeed, business interests operating at the European Union level have refused or been unable to engage in dialogue over employment issues (Case 18) to the extent that there has, until recently, been little for business and labour interests to engage in dialogue over. This may change following the provisions of the Maastrict treaty, and has done so in the case of the Works Council Directive. The lack of competencies in 'social' issues in the European Union has, however, historically been a key factor disabling the organization of 'peak' labour at the European level, and in many countries there is reluctance among labour interests to give up beneficial national level arrangements in favour of the European Union level (Case 19). Indeed, Schmitter has argued that the European level can be extremely disruptive to national level corporatist type arrangements. It is certainly the case that the refocus to the European level can be turbulent for settled public/private relations at the national level, or, as Ronit makes clear in the case of shipping, at the global level (Case 13). However, Switky (Case 11) provides an interesting example of where sectoral labour and business associations joined forces for common purposes in the European Union, and these sorts of alliance are clearly possible in circumstances involving certain types of conditions.

The sectoral emphasis in this text reflects an intellectual tradition. In 1964, Lowi claimed that, instead of understanding policies as the outcome of politics, the reverse was true, i.e. that 'policies make politics'; the idea that the type of policy under consideration influences the underlying politics (Lowi, 1964). For instance, quite different types of interests cluster around redistributive policies from distributive, and regulatory, types of policies. Thus, a policy favouring small firms within a particular industry at the expense of large ones is likely to result in competitive politics within the industry concerned, whereas if the policy is one which affects the entire industry more-or-less equally, there is likely to be a unified response. This is a quite different endeavour from attempts to understand policies as arising from grand, 'state-level' explanations of politics. Theories of this class, such as Marxism, (macro) corporatism, or (state level) pluralism (the idea of power being both widely, though differentially, distributed such that no one interest routinely dominates, and available to those able to organize) therefore has little place in this endeavour. Rather, the logic of 'policies makes politics' is to expect arrangements to differ between particular domains and policy types. Thus, understanding policy outputs and outcomes can only be derived from studying in each case under consideration the exchange of different types of resource between the players involved in the circumstances. The case study method is thus the methodological tool of this approach.

Two models dominate as analytic tools of sectoral governance: neo-pluralism and neo-corporatism. These both encapsulate the closed 'policy village' idea, and are therefore quite similar. Indeed, there is a long (and sometimes bitter) dispute as to whether there is a difference at all between them. Because some of the authors in this book are associated with these different traditions (some are associated with neither in particular), it is important that the reader is at least aware of the debate, because these concepts are used extensively in the cases which follow. Identifying the terms used can sometimes also help locate which tradition the author is associated with, although sometimes terms are used interchangeably. Because the terms neo-pluralism and neo-corporatism are used regularly in this book, it is clearly important for the reader to know what is meant by them. Unfortunately there is no agreement over their use, but my own interpretation goes as follows.

Relationships between private actors and those from the relevant specialized part of the state bureaucracy based on the exchange of sufficient power-dependent resources result in closed 'policy villages'. This is the idea of a neo-pluralist 'policy community', based on symbiotic, or close mutually dependent, relationships, from which policies are formulated. Neo-, meso-corporatism is the idea of a particularly close relationship between an economic interest and the relevant part of the governmental bureaucracy. The economic interest is organized by an outlet, such as a trade association, to produce authoritative opinion, entering into policy agreements with the relevant part of the state machinery which can be made to stick with the constituent members. The policy agreed to involves the private interest in implementing arrangements (such as self-regulation) through the organizing outlet, such that the private interest has 'crossed the boundary' and become part of the machinery of governance. In effect, private interests are performing public functions, such as the role played by many national associations of travel agents in providing self-regulatory codes which ensure that the public is protected if a tour operator goes out of business. It is the outlet's (e.g. trade association's) job to see that the interest it represents exercises discipline to keep to the agreement. Streeck and Schmitter (1985) call this process 'private interest government'. In effect, what I am suggesting is that neo-corporatism is a specialism of the more generalized (but nonetheless valuable) notion of the neo-pluralist 'policy community'. My own view is that the distinction is worth making because it is the possession of highly powerful economic 'bargaining chips', together with the ability of the outlet to organize the membership, which gives rise to such extreme symbiotic relationships. These are highly developed governance mechanisms. The distinction is not one of merely 'splitting hairs', but rather a difference in explanatory capacity. Neo-corporatism is an attempt to explain why highly developed 'policy communities' come about. To others, however, there is nothing in neo-corporatism which is not encapsulated by the original notion of the 'policy community'. Both views are represented in this book. Readers may note a preference among authors who consider the neo-corporatist distinction to be worth making to avoid use of the term 'lobbying', sometimes preferring the term 'interest intermediation' on the grounds that this may better denote the ingrained forms of involvement by private interests in public policy-making which can be found. However, use of the term 'lobbying' does not itself indicate any particular alignment and may have a wide currency in that it is a term which is widely understood. In respect of my own contributions to this collection, I have a preference for the term 'interest representation', which seems able to cover the spectrum of activities from ingrained interest intermediation to the world of the hired case presenters.

The idea of private involvement in public policy-making arising from the exchange of sufficiently powerful 'bargaining chips' helps to make sense of the seemingly chaotic world of European interest representation. Neo-pluralism and neo-corporatism are underpinned by the idea of a kind of balance in the exchange of resources between private and public authors. Where the resource exchange is extremely unbalanced in favour of the private interest, 'regulatory capture' may arise, where the public authority is in effect unable to exert influence over the private actor because the resources of the latter are too strong. All of these concepts are based upon resource exchange, which helps us understand public policy outputs and outcomes according to the possession and exchange of different resources. Yet there are some who would deny that it can be made sense of in this way, pointing to the presence of different 'winners' and 'losers' in different examples. Winners and losers, according to this perspective, can be both business and other types of interest, depending upon how 'campaigns' are conducted. Such authors would prefer instead to emphasize the tactics adopted by private interests in seeking to exert influence. What is required, according to this perspective, is a highly professional standard and a high level of organization in order to win one's case, capacities over which business interests have no monopoly, although it would be conceded that their resources may help them to operate thus. This would include developing permanent relations with officials in different institutions of the European Union, and in particular with the Commission and national civil servants and political leaders, and, increasingly, key politicians from the European Parliament. Indeed, all practitioners and scholars would accept the need for permanent relations (some of the concepts described earlier are built upon the idea that a permanent relationship will develop under certain conditions). Equally, all parties would accept that the following is at least extremely helpful advice to anyone representing a case in Europe:

1. Have a clear strategy.
2. Make yourself indispensable.
3. Develop long-term, permanent relations with authorities. Establish a track record as a provider of useful, accurate, well researched information. If you need to start forming a relationship when a problem arises them it is probably too late.
4. Find out who is drafting an item and get in early. If you have not been able to influence the Commission draft proposal then you have probably lost the case.
5. Prepare well for meetings. Beware of using hired hands to present cases where their knowledge of your issue will inevitably be limited. Leave a position paper behind.
6. Present with brevity and clarity.
7. Be aware of all sides of the argument. Keep it low key; do not 'over-lobby'. Appreciate the limits of what can be achieved.
8. Keep all viable channels of communication open.
9. Know the system, and get to know the points of 'entry' to the decision-making process.
10. Remain vigilant.

Such advice would be helpful to any interest in presenting a case at the European level. However, 'tactical' points are an insufficient basis for attempting to understand public policy outputs and outcomes. Instead, emphasis is given here to the exchange of resources between private and public actors which determines access to public policy-making and implementation.

Vipond, drawing upon the case of European banking and insurance (Case 7), explains how alliances can be understood in terms of the attempt by firms to make strategic business choices, involving anticipating and/or shaping market conditions. Each of the cases in this volume contribute to an issue relatively unexplored by the management literature, i.e. European business collective action for the purpose of exerting political influence. This is where this collection enters, and as such represents an intersection between business studies and political science. The study of politics and markets is an established tradition within public administration and political science, but the two subjects together are not much studied in business courses. Business prosperity depends upon the political environment within which it operates, and strategies of action, whether collective or single firm, are key issues to study. An interesting contrast is the chapter by Morrison, who provides examples of Japanese firms 'going it alone' in their representation (Case 15). There is evidence of this in almost all sectors, but, as Morrison points out, Japanese firms find themselves less often having to adopt 'satisficing', compromise types of behaviour within wide constituency Euro associations dedicated to representing the interests of European member firms. They are therefore freer to pursue more 'maximalist' strategies of achieving single-firm objectives. There are some instances where Japanese firms are permitted to be members of Euro associations, but in these instances membership is more used as a 'listening post' than a strategy of interest representation. In most instances, however, Japanese firms are simply excluded, forcing them to develop different patterns of interest representation.

Jacek, describing the case of American firms in Europe, also detects a tendency to act alone in the political arena (Case 14), based on the belief of the sufficiency of their market power. Yet, as Jacek also observes, they have also founded one of the most effective and admired of all collective action networks in Europe, the EC Committee of the American Chamber of Commerce in Brussels (AmCham ECC).

A final issue to consider in introducing the reader to the case studies which follow concerns the extent to which we can learn from case studies. The cases in this collection have deliberately been kept short. This at least ensures that the issues are not lost in a mountain of parochial description. Providing empirical case study evidence, if chosen strategically and conducted rigorously, is a way of contributing to conceptual understanding rather than aimless 'story-telling'. The cases in this collection have been chosen both to represent a broad range of business domains, from high to low technology to recently privatized public utilities, and to cover the types of issue involved and dimensions of business interest alliances and representation in the EU, such as 'peak' associations and their labour interlocutors, 'rich firm clubs', and representatives of small firms. Some of the cases have been selected so as to investigate particular types of conceptual issue. Eckstein (1979) has suggested that case study research should proceed by the selection of 'crucial cases', i.e. most or least likely scenarios for the type of issue under investigation to occur. For instance, investigating the idea that well defined business sectors will find it easiest to organise at the European level requires, at least, comparison of well (e.g. pharmaceuticals) and poorly (e.g. tourism) defined sectors. A number of the issues under investigation relate to the strategic position which an industry holds in the European Union. Thus, for instance, comparison is made between levels of technology-based industries. Similarly, a number of issues investigated relate to issues of firm size and territorial forms of organization, and here Grote (Case 17) has made an excellent contribution to the literature by developing a number of hypotheses. Key to the development of a broad set of Commission policies aimed at small firms is their management capacity, and their networking at both supranational and sub-central territorial levels. Deeply entrenched difficulties are apparent in these tiers of organization.

Selection of cases has been made to facilitate such types of examination, which emerge throughout the cases and in the conclusions. Indeed, I have elsewhere claimed that good case study evidence is essential for theoretical development. Without it, we risk being led up the garden path by ideas which are little more than speculation. This is not to suggest that an idea has to be measurable through positivistic techniques in order to exist, because ideas can be developed through the role of case studies in stimulating the theoretical imagination. However, it does mean that our starting point is case study methods as a means of learning more about the issues under investigation. It is to this endeavour that we now turn.

Note

1. The *Cassis de Dijon* case involved the manufacturer of a French liquor and the Federal Republic of Germany. Mindful of its drinks industry, Germany refused to allow the importation of this drink through the smokescreen of product purity and health. The European Court of Justice dismissed the German case, and in doing so established the principle of mutual recognition of products in Community law.

References

Butt Philip, A. (1985) 'Pressure groups in the European Community', Working Paper No. 2. University Association for Contemporary European Studies, London.

Cecchini, P. (with Catinat, M. and Jacquemin, A.) (1988) *The European Challenge 1992: The Benefits of a Single Market*. Aldershot: Wildwood House.

Colebatch, H. (1991) 'Getting our act together: a case study in regulation and explanation'. Paper presented to the XVth World Congress of the International Political Science Association, Buenos Aires, 21–25 July 1991.

Commission of the European Communities (CEC) (1992) *An Open and Structured Dialogue Between the Commission and Special Interest Groups*. SEC(92) 2272 final. Brussels: CEC.

Eckstein, H. (1979) 'Case study and theory in political Science', in Greenstein, F. and Polsby, N. W. (eds) *Strategies of Inquiry*. Reading, MA: Addison Wesley.

Grant, W. (1978) 'Insider groups, outsider groups and interest group strategies in Britain'. Working Paper No. 19. University of Warwick Department of Politics.

Grant, W. (1990) 'Organised interests and the European Community'. Paper presented at the 6th International Colloquium of the Feltrinelli Foundation, Corton, 29–31 May 1990.

Grant, W. (1993) 'Pressure groups and the European Community: an overview', in Mazey, S. and Richardson, J. *Lobbying in the European Community*, Oxford: Oxford University Press, pp. 27–46.

Greenwood, J. and Jordan, A. G. (1993) 'The UK: a changing kaleidoscope', in van Schendelen, M. P. C. M. (ed.) *National Public and Private EC Lobbying*. Aldershot: Dartmouth, pp. 65–90.

Greenwood, J., Grote, J. and Ronit, K. (1992) Introduction to Greenwood, J., Grote, J. and Ronit, K. (eds) *Organised Interests and the European Community*. London: Sage, pp. 1–41.

Haas, E. B. (1958) *The Uniting of Europe: Political, Economic and Social Forces 1950–57*. Stanford, CA: Stanford University Press.

Haas, E. (1976) *The Obsolescence of Regional Integration Theory*. Berkeley, CA: Institute of International Studies.

Heclo, H. (1978) 'Issue networks and the executive establishment', in King, A. (ed.) *The New American Political System*. Washington, DC: AEI.

Heclo, H. and Wildavsky, A. (1974) *The Private Government of Public Money*, London: Macmillan.

Hull, R. (1993) 'Lobbying the European Community; a view from within', in Mazey, S. and Richardson, J. J. (eds) *Lobbying in the European Community*. Oxford: Oxford University Press, pp. 82–92.

Jordan, A. G. and McLaughlin, A. M. (1991) 'The rationality of lobbying in Europe: why are Euro groups so numerous and so weak?' Paper presented to the conference on Euro Lobbying, Nuffield College, Oxford, 17 May 1991.

Jordan, A. G., Maloney, W. A. and McLaughlin, A. M. (1992) 'What is studied when pressure groups are studied?' British Interest Group Project, Working Paper Series no. 1, University of Aberdeen.

Lowi, T. J. (1964) 'American business, public policy, case studies and political theory', *World Politics*, vol. 16, pp. 677–715.

McLaughlin, A. M. (1992) 'Underfed Euro feds'. Paper presented to the Annual Conference of the Political Studies Association, Queens University Belfast, 21 April 1992.

McLaughlin, A. M. and Greenwood, J. (1995) 'The management of interest representation in the European Union', *Journal of Common Market Studies*, forthcoming.

Maloney, W. A., Jordan, A. G. and McLaughlin, A. M. (1995) 'Interest groups and public policy: the insider/outsider model revisited', *Journal of Public Policy*, vol. 14, pp. 17–38.

Metcalfe, L. (1992) 'After 1992: can the Commission manage Europe', *Australian Journal of Public Administration*, vol. 51, pp. 117–130.

Olson, M. (1965) *The Logic of Collective Action*. Cambridge MA: Harvard University Press.

Pedlar, R. (1994) 'ETUC and the pregnant woman', in Pedlar, R. H. and van Schendelen, M. P. C. M. (eds) *Lobbying the European Union: Companies, Trade Associations and Issue Groups*. Aldershot: Dartmouth.

Rhodes, R. A. W. and Marsh, D. (1990) 'New directions in the study of policy networks', *European Journal of Political Research*, vol. 21, pp. 181–205.

Richardson, J. J. and Jordan, A. G. (1979) *Governing Under Pressure*. London: Martin Robertson.

Sargent, J. A. (1987) 'The organisation of business interests for European Community representation', in Grant, W. (with Sargent, J.) *Business and Politics in Britain*, London: Macmillan, pp. 213–238.

Streeck, W. and Schmitter, P. C. (1985) *Private Interest Government*. London: Sage.

Streeck, W. and Schmitter, P. C. (1991) 'From national corporatism to transnational pluralism', *Politics and Society,*, vol. 19, pp. 133–165.

Traxler, F. (1994) From demand-side to supply-side corporatism? Austria's labor relations in a process of Change'. Paper presented to the XVIth World Congress of the International Political Science Association, Berlin, 20–24 August 1994.

Traxler, F. and Schmitter, P. C. (1994) Prospective thoughts on regional integration, interest politics and policy formation in the European Community/Union'. Paper presented to the XVIth World Congress of the International Political Science Association, Berlin, 20–24 August 1994.

Wilks, S. and Wright, M. (1987) 'Introduction' to Wilks, S. and Wright, M. (eds) *Comparative Government–Industry Relations: Western Europe, the Unites States and Japan*. Oxford: Clarendon Press, pp. 1–41.

PART 1

High Technology

Business Alliances in the Information Technology Sector

Laura Cram[1]

Introduction

The information technology (IT) industry is closely involved at all levels of the policy process in Europe. In an environment in which 'technology is now dominated by international collaboration and multinational companies' (Sharp and Pavitt, 1993, p. 129), major IT multinationals[2] are able to exert pressure on the EU policy process both as a result of their important position in the global economy and through the vestiges of their status as champion industries at the national level. IT firms are heavily involved in the policy process from the level of broad industrial policy debates, to the setting of standards and the allocation of resources within specific EU research and development programmes such as ESPRIT and RACE.[3] Indeed, 'Esprit is as much managed by industry as the Commission itself' (Peterson, 1991, p. 277; see also Peterson, 1992). Several officials in DG XIII (the directorate-general for telecommunications, information industries and innovation) have, for example, commented that they are in such close contact with industrial representatives from the IT sector that they could hardly consider this lobbying – there is an ongoing process of consultation between industry and the policy-makers.[4]

Since the mid-1980s there has been an explosion of collective activity between major IT companies (both European and non-European owned) at the European level. Clearly, the companies are managing to some extent to overcome some of the thorny problems of collective action identified by Olson (1971). Existing studies examine the nature of *technological* collaboration in the IT sector (Sharp and Shearman, 1987) and the incentives for collective action between *member states* in the area of IT (Sandholtz, 1992a, b). This case study presents an overview of the major collective fora in which *businesses* participate in the IT sector at the European level and examines some of the factors promoting or inhibiting alliances in the IT field for *political ends*.

Participation by the IT Industry in Collective Fora at the European Level

General Industry Associations

Formal Direct Membership

IT firms are not only influential within the IT sector, they include some of the most influential industrial actors in the EU policy process. The European Round Table of Industrialists (ERT), for example, is an association of about forty-five of Europe's largest corporations from both EU and non-EU countries. Formed in 1983, under the chairmanship of Peter Gyllenhammer of Volvo, this invitation-only group includes such major IT producers and users as Philips, Siemens, Olivetti, Daimler Benz, Volvo, Fiat and Bosch (Sandholtz, 1992b). Concentrating predominantly on broad strategic issues such as industrial competitiveness rather than on the nitty-gritty of individual policies (Grant, 1994), the ERT has become a powerful lobby. Indeed, it has been argued that the ERT played a significant role in launching the Single European Market programme and that, in particular, a major role was played by Wisse Decker (then ERT chair from Philips) (Sandholtz and Zysman, 1989; Green, 1993).

An analysis of the membership of the ERT gives some indication of the level at which many of the major IT companies participate in the EU policy process. Inevitably, ERT discussions are not centred on solely IT-related issues, and much more specialist organizations have evolved to deal with these. However, the direct access to the Commission president, to other Commissioners and to national governments, which membership of the ERT affords (Grant, 1994), provides a powerful incentive to participate. Likewise, an analysis of the ERT warns against an over-romantic view of the role of IT users in the policy process. Recent attempts by national governments and the European Commission to encourage a greater role for users provide a seductive prospect and may appear to indicate a greater democratization of the policy process – perhaps a shift away from the domination of multinational companies. It should, however, be remembered that the users of IT products are a very diverse group and many of the most powerful multinationals are heavy users of IT. As the membership of the ERT indicates, many of the users of IT products may be just as influential as the producers and equally enjoy privileged access to decision-makers.

Contacts at this level undoubtedly also help the producers to learn at the very highest level what the major users require from their products.

Federations of Federations

A myriad of federations of national industrial federations exist at the European level. These organizations exist at various degrees of specificity. The major IT firms are broadly represented within UNICE, the Union of Industrial and Employers' Confederations of Europe. Most members however, express frustration with the enforced blandness of UNICE positions (an inevitable consequence of the need to incorporate the views of all sides of industry) and rarely would a company depend on this as a sole channel of representation on any particular issue. In this respect, the IT industry is in line with most other industrial sectors, particularly those dominated by multinational companies (Collie, 1993). Firms prefer to retain recourse to a range of strategies in an attempt to maximize their impact on any given issue (see studies in Greenwood *et al.* 1992; Mazey and Richardson, 1993). Thus a preference for 'multiple strategies' (McLaughlin *et al.* 1993) prevails. In the IT field, a trend towards the establishment of ever more specialist groupings with carefully selected memberships is evident.

Informal Direct Membership[5]

A number of highly selective *informal* organizations of industrial élites have also begun to emerge at a working level. While the representatives from major multinationals, which participate in these groups, do not directly represent the policies of any of the companies concerned, these meetings have come to represent an important point of contact for senior industrialists. One such group, for example, comprises a select group of representatives from a number of important multinationals in Europe and the USA (as yet there has been no member admitted from Japan although there have been discussions on this subject). The group is a purely private organization with no representative from the EU institutions. The organization has no formal structure, no budget and a temporary chair rotates on a six-monthly basis between the various member companies. The usual format is that members are invited in turn by the various member companies, who will host a lunch. The host is entitled to introduce a topic for debate and members are asked for a spontaneous reaction to the issue on the agenda. The second half of the meeting is devoted to the discussion of 'current rumours'. In this way members keep themselves informed of up-to-the-minute developments in European industry.

While the organization is in no way a lobbying organisation, membership of the group is considered to be very important by its members.

Meanwhile, a similar organization has emerged alongside which includes some representatives from major Japanese multinationals. However, this group is very informal and highly dependent on the personalities involved. The exchange of information in these less structured groups is of prime concern to their members. While the groups themselves are not involved in the lobbying process, those armed with the information derived from participation in such fora are better able to target the relevant policy-makers and to identify suitable partners for future alliance.

Sectoral Organizations

Federations of Federations

At a more sectorally specific level, many of the major IT companies are represented at the European level through the Liaison Organisation for the European Mechanical, Electrical and Electronic Engineering and Metal-work Industries (ORGALIME, established in 1954). This organization, while encompassing many of the interests of IT companies, is once again, however, often considered rather too broad to deal with specific issues related to the IT industry. The more specialist sectoral federation which claims to gather together almost 100 per cent of European manufacturers in the field of business machines, information technology and telecommunications terminal equipment is EUROBIT (the European Association of Manufacturers of Business Machines and Information Technology, established in 1974). The equivalent organization in the telecommunications sector is ECTEL (the Association of the European Telecommunications and Professional Electronics Industry, established in 1985).[6] Meanwhile, associations of electrical components manufacturers are represented via the EECA (European Electrical Components Manufacturers' Association, established in 1973) and national consumer electronic associations have a European platform via the European Association of Consumer Electronics Manufacturers (EACEM, established in 1983).[7]

Overlapping membership of organizations is a persistent feature of business organization in the IT sector, but as Schneider (1992, p. 65) observed with regard to the organization of industrial interests in the telecommunications sector, 'the relationship between these associations is essentially non-competitive'. Indeed, in the IT sector, close consultation between the organizations will frequently lead to mutually supportive policy positions. These often overworked and understaffed organizations[8] are sometimes happy to avoid covering the same ground. Indeed, as a representative from ORGALIME said, 'ORGALIME is very pleased when a strong sectoral body exists, such as ECTEL or EUROBIT, and tends to let them get on with it'. As well as cooperating with their European counterparts, these organizations are often in close contact with their equivalent international organizations, particularly in Japan and the USA.

There are a number of incentives which encourage participation in the EUROBIT framework. Firstly, as the European Commission generally prefers to communicate with sectoral organizations rather than with individual firms (Grant, 1994), membership of EUROBIT is important to all firms in the IT sector. EUROBIT does not have a Brussels office, although it has a permanent secretariat in the offices of VDMA in Germany. Schneider (1992, p. 59) has argued that these modest administrative facilities may indicate a 'letterhead status' or that of a 'listening post'. The organization is, however, in constant communication with the European Union institutions and is not short of contacts in Brussels. The current president of EUROBIT, Dr Bruno Lamborghini, is from the Italian multinational Olivetti which has its own offices in Brussels. The secretary-general, Günther Möller, meanwhile, is from the German VDMA, which also has its own liaison office in Brussels. Likewise, many of the major member IT firms such as Olivetti, IBM, Bull, Philips and Siemens-Nixdorf have their own premises in Brussels. EUROBIT also, meanwhile, uses the VDMA offices in Brussels as a Brussels base where EUROBIT members can meet.

Many of those firms interviewed claimed that EUROBIT suffers from the usual problem of a broad-based organization: the encompassing of conflicting views results in a watering down of policy positions. The large IT firms frequently choose to act alone or to form small *ad hoc* groupings (see below) when an issue is of particular concern to them. This perhaps lends weight to the image of EUROBIT as a rather ineffectual 'letterhead' organization. There is, however, a further important feature of the EUROBIT organization. EUROBIT incorporates firms in the IT field regardless of their country of origin. Thus non-European-owned IT firms may participate via their national federations in the work of EUROBIT. This is of particular significance to US-owned and, to an even greater extent, to Japanese-owned firms. All the more so as the prevalence of 'invitation only fora' which regularly exclude these (particularly the Japanese-owned) firms from participation continues.[9] Following the acquisition of the controlling shares in ICL by Fujitsu in 1990, for example, and the effective debarring of ICL from the European IT roundtable, EUROBIT became an important platform for ICL and the firm allocated considerable resources to EUROBIT participation. Hence, whether the logic of influence or the logic of membership prevails in providing the incentive for collective action largely depends on the alternative channels of influence which are open to the firm in question. Not all firms in the IT sector enjoy equal direct access to the ears of the policymakers. It is also, of course, important for indigenous European-owned firms to remain in close contact with their international counterparts.

Direct Membership Associations

Direct membership associations play an increasingly important role in a number of industrial sectors, for example, in the areas of biotechnology (Greenwood and Ronit, 1992) and in the automobile industry (McLaughlin *et al*. 1993). Grant (1994) has argued that certain sectoral conditions favour the formation of these organizations. In particular, the industry should have a strong international orientation, the decisions of the EU should have an important impact on the sector and the industry should be dominated by a fairly small number of major firms. These features clearly exist in the area of IT. In the information technology sector, major European IT firms have long enjoyed the ear of the EU policy-makers via their direct participation in the European IT Roundtable. Established in 1979–80 on the initiative of Etienne Davignon, then European Commissioner for Industry, the European IT Roundtable brought together the twelve leading IT companies in the EU[10] (Sharp and Shearman, 1987) and played a critical role in the establishment of the EU ESPRIT programme.

The IT roundtable has since undergone a number of changes in membership, generally reflecting the pattern of take-over and merger in the IT sector[11] as well as the changing nature of new technologies. It continues, however, to provide an important forum for the discussion of IT-related matters. This group, rather like the ERT, provides a forum that tends to be more useful for discussing strategic policy issues (in this case related to the IT sector) than details of specific policies. The broad nature of representation within the IT roundtable, while reflecting the complex diversity of the IT sector (i.e. ranging from equipment manufacturers and service providers to the innovators in technology), encompasses too many conflicting interests to generate clear policy outcomes. In particular, there is often direct conflict between the interests of the IT companies – for example, Olivetti, Bull, SNI – and the interests of the telecom equipment manufacturers – such as Alcatel, Philips and the 'main' branch of Siemens. There is a tendency to water down policy positions in an attempt to generate consensus between the various actors. Once again, however, membership of this group provides an important point of contact and source of information. As one representative from a major IT multinational said of his firm's participation in the IT roundtable, 'we listen more than we talk'.

Participation in Standards Institutions

The IT industry is involved voluntarily at all stages in the standard-setting process, either through the participation of firms in national standards bodies or through the direct participation of firms in European standard bodies. Particularly since the launch of the Single European Market programme, the pace of standardization in the EU has been stepped up and the direct involvement of IT firms in the standard-setting process has increased. The formal European bodies concerned with standards in the IT field have traditionally been CEN and CENELEC.[12] Both institutions were formed as an umbrella for the regional cooperation of west European national standards institutions. However, in March 1988 the European Telecommunications Standards Institute,[13] which allows for the *direct* participation of manufacturers, users, public service providers, research bodies and national administrations on equal terms, was created (Besen, 1990). The institute has so far proved to be rather effective and, despite generating some highly controversial debates (most recently, for example, over intellectual property rights), it is generally considered to be the most important of the standards institutes. There is little doubt that the formal direct participation of IT firms and IT users in standard-setting is likely to continue. Within the CEN/CENELEC framework, for example, EWOS[14] was established in December 1987. EWOS was created by a number of the most representative European federations of IT producer and user organizations[15] (EWOS, 1993) to aid progress on the drafting of standards in the area of open systems interconnection (OSI). Meanwhile, in 1992, the executive structure of CEN was reorganized and the organization now makes provision for greater participation of economic interests (not merely through the national standards organizations) in the standardization process (CEN, 1993).

Formal channels of direct access are clearly opening up for IT firms in the standard-setting process. However, the IT firms have always played a major role even at an informal level. On the one hand, they have formed a number of organizations concerned with the promotion of standards.[16] On the other hand, major IT multinationals may attempt to influence the output of the various standards bodies by utilizing their multiple access points at the national level. Thus, firms often use their participation in national standard bodies – for example, DIN in Germany and BSI in the UK – as a means of influencing European level standards. All of the standards bodies stress that they are simply a structure to facilitate the work of their members. The organizations themselves have only small staffs, and standards are made in committees comprising representatives from member organizations who are, ultimately of course, members of the affected firms. Examining the structure of the European Association of Consumer Electronics Manufacturers

(EACEM), Cawson (1992) argued that Philips and Thomson have been able
to play a dominant role in the organization as a result of their heavy presence
in the various national member associations. In similar fashion, it is not
uncommon for one major multinational company or an alliance of
companies, represented in several of the national standards bodies, to weight
standards committees in their favour by sending multiple representatives.

Participation in the standards process is important for IT firms: in a
rapidly changing technological environment, the output of the organization
cannot be left to chance. On the one hand, there is the possibility that the
firm may be able to push its own proprietary standard to the forefront. On
the other hand, it is important that a standard is not passed which is contrary
to the interests of the particular firm. As McLaughlin and Jordan (1993,
p. 30) argue, 'a free-rider cannot expect to steer the vehicle'. However, the
voluntary nature of most industrial standards further complicates the
scenario. As one interviewee from a standards body stated:

> there is a complex game played by industry – they send people to standards
> meetings but then don't implement the standards. Or they get involved
> only at the point where something interests them in particular. Generally,
> consensus is achieved early but on the basis of an underlying non-intention
> to implement.

Clearly, the incentives to participate in the standards process are not
solely connected to the output of the organizations. Rather, the standards
bodies also provide an important collective forum for the IT firms.
Participation in the various technical committees can provide an important
early warning system for the IT firms, both on the priorities for standarization
which the European Commission is identifying and, just as importantly, on
the priorities of their competitors.

Participation in Collective Fora Connected to the EU Institutions
The close involvement of IT firms with their counterparts and with the EU
institutions has emerged not only as a result of the establishment of lobbying
alliances but also as a result of their participation in a myriad of collective
fora attached to the EU institutions. The range of collective fora is too
complex to cover here, but involvement of the IT industry occurs at every
level of the formal policy process in the EU institutions. Many of the critical
contacts which IT firms have established with each other have been formed
as a result of their participation in a whole range of EU research
programmes.[17] Each directorate within the Commission has a range of

advisory committees, and the IT industry is heavily represented in all the relevant committees. The most recent example of IT industrial participation at the highest levels of EU policy formulation has been its participation in the so-called Bangemann Group – the high level group charged with the task of formulating the series of recommendations to the European Council on 'Europe and the Global Information Society' (High-Level Group on the Information Society, 26 May 1994), which prepared the ground for the Commission's action plan, *Europe's Way to the Information Society: An Action Plan* (20 July 1994) (CEU, 1994). The action plan particularly stresses the need to maximize the involvement of the private sector in the realization of the global information society.

Specialist *Ad Hoc* Groupings

Increasingly, IT companies indicate a preference for action through *ad hoc* specialist groups. Sometimes this type of grouping arises simply because no existing organization quite encompasses the particular alliance of interests. Thus in the early 1990s, when the debate over the EU software directive split the IT industry, the major US and European IT companies (basically the owners of large portfolios of intellectual property) formed SAGE which set up in opposition to the organization of Japanese companies and the smaller IT firms.

Specialist *ad hoc* groupings serve a number of purposes. On the one hand, an alliance lends weight to the lone voice of a single company. On the other hand, small groupings are more likely to be able to reach a *workable*, yet *meaningful* consensus. As most of these groups are intended to wither on the vine when the issue in question has subsided or been resolved, they can also provide a cost-effective means of addressing an issue as they do not incur the administrative costs associated with more permanent fora. Not least, the problem of the free-rider is largely avoided as each member is forced to pull its weight within the group; the ultimate sanction of course being that dissatisfied partners will not seek out a persistent free-rider for future alliance.

However, the scenario is not quite this simple and it appears that, to a certain extent at least, firms remain keen to maximize the degree of certainty within these initially *ad hoc* arrangements. Thus, for example, in August 1993, Bull, Olivetti and Siemens signed a memorandum of agreement which formalizes their hitherto *ad hoc* cooperation in a number of areas (*Financial Times*, 16 September 1994). While the agreement (commonly known as the BOS alliance) clearly has a technical purpose (namely the collaboration of the three firms on a European-wide computer network) it also has important political goals – not least, the need to convince the Commission of the worth of their scheme.

Rationality of Collective Action in the IT Sector:
Horses for Courses

'There is a horses for courses approach in Euro-lobbying and companies must keep open a number of options when entering the policy process' (McLaughlin, 1994, p. 12). This general statement about Euro-lobbying applies specifically within the IT sector. Firms are constantly weighing up the costs and benefits of the various possible routes of influence and of the potential alliances which may be built. To pursue the racecourse analogy a little further: the question for the firms is not only which horse to back, but which role to play in the consortium of racehorse owners!

IT firms have a number of routes of influence available to them beyond those collective European fora presented here. For example, no company is foolhardy enough to forget the importance of the national route of influence, and most pursue simultaneous strategies of lobbying at the member state level as well as at the European level. Meanwhile, at the European level, a number of major IT firms have opened their own offices in Brussels. The offices are beginning to prove their worth by facilitating contacts not only with the EU institutions but also with potential partners in strategic alliances. The Philips headquarters in Eindhoven is, for example, within commuting distance of Brussels. Yet the director of the Philips' EC liaison office stresses the importance of a base in Brussels and the need to be where things are happening. Not least, the semi-social aspects of business life in Brussels are a critical means of keeping up to date with important events. Another option open to IT firms is the employment of political lobbyists or consultants. Few of the major IT companies, however, employ lobbyists. On the one hand, lobbyists are rarely well received in the Commission. On the other hand, few lobbyists enjoy the privileged access to EU institutions enjoyed by these powerful industrial actors themselves. On the use of consultants, however, there is less consensus. Many firms use consultants for information purposes if not for lobbying. However, as one representative from a major multi-national said, 'we are sometimes in a better position to sell information to consultants and lobbyists than to buy it'. There may be some evidence that Japanese IT firms are more inclined to make use of consultants (McLaughlin, 1994). However, again this is not uniform: the head of the Hitachi office in Brussels, for example, almost never employs consultants as he claims that they rarely have enough understanding of the Japanese IT industry to provide a useful service.

There are no cut-and-dried explanations of how or why a specific alliance or route of influence is chosen. As has been argued elsewhere, firms operating in the European policy process reflect more closely Simon's (1976) characterization of the firm as acting with a 'bounded' rationality than Olson's (1971) image of the 'purely' rational firm (McLaughlin and Jordan, 1993). In an uncertain world, firms do not have perfect information on which to take rational decisions. The IT sector, in particular, characterized by a highly diverse and changing group of participants, constant technological innovation and changing public policy approaches, is fraught with uncertainties. Thus, the alliance strategies which firms operate can be viewed as a process of trial and error. As the process is iterated, however, the firms are beginning to learn the types of alliance that are most effective and which best suit their particular needs.

There are certain conditions which firms identify as inclining them towards one alliance strategy rather than another. The factor which most firms identify as paramount is the nature of the issue. Hence, on an issue which relates to industry in general, they are likely to choose the channel through which they exert most influence at the general industry level (thus for ERT members, the ERT may be the obvious choice). However, on an issue which is likely to have a specific impact on an individual firm, few firms would hesitate to take unitary action. This has particular advantages in terms of speed of action – often critical in this fast-moving environment. However, if allies can be found swiftly, a joint position from a number of affected firms may well have more impact than a single voice which may be accused of 'special pleading'. The need for rapid responses from this type of specialist grouping may to some extent explain the increasing formalization of *ad hoc* specialist groups (for example, the BOS alliance). Close, repeated contact allows for greater certainty as to the likely positions to be adopted by potential partners and for a speedy reaction to the issue at hand. A rough sliding scale of preferred channels of action, according to the degree to which an issue affects an individual firm, can be identified as follows: individual action, specialist *ad hoc* alliance, the European IT Roundtable, EUROBIT and, at the most general level, the ERT. Most firms will, however, pursue a number of these options simultaneously while also lobbying at the national level.

The level at which the issue in question is administered and the attitude of public policy-makers to the issue may also have an impact on the decision of a firm to act alone or to seek some form of alliance. For example, if an IT multinational is trying to encourage the EU to launch a cross-border initiative, it will stress its presence in a number of countries and its close alliances with important industrial partners in yet other member states. On the other hand, if the same company is seeking support for a project under the structural funds (administered solely through national channels) it will seek to stress its national roots and its critical position in the national economy. Likewise, while the support of other major multinationals often lends important support to an individual company's position, if the priority of the public policy-makers is to increase the role of small and medium-size enterprises or of IT users, multinationals may choose to forge an alliance with representatives from these groups rather than to stress their close links with the other dominant actors in the field.

It must be remembered that not all European fora are equally open to all participants in the IT field. Hence, the alliances chosen and the collective fora on which companies are represented may differ significantly (see above regarding ICL's attitude to EUROBIT membership). Many Japanese-owned IT companies, in particular, have been excluded from the various collective fora in the IT field. Likewise, many Japanese firms are well aware that their voices carry little weight in EU policy circles. For many of these firms, strategic *ad hoc* alliances with European-owned firms allow them some voice in the policy debate.[18] Although US IT firms have been incorporated to a much greater extent than Japanese companies into the European collective fora, a number of US firms also stress that they will often seek out alliances with European firms to enhance their position in the European policy debate. On the other hand, US firms have also made use of their access to the US channels of influence when necessary. For example, during the recent controversy over intellectual property rights generated in ETSI, a number of US companies, including IBM, Motorola and Digital, chose to lobby through a US organization – the Computer and Business Manufacturers' Association (CBEMA). Lobbying on this issue in the US resulted, ultimately, in a formal complaint from the US government to the European Commission. Thus, on occasion, a rather precarious position on the sidelines can have its advantages.

The clear trend in the IT sector is for IT firms to be increasingly involved directly in the policy process – at the broadest strategic level of EU industrial debate, when dealing with specific IT industry concerns, in the standard-setting process and when dealing with the specific details of particular policies. There is less and less willingness to be represented through third parties, whether these be industry associations or professional lobbyists. The complex nature of strategic alliances in the IT sector reflects the rather promiscuous nature of an industry in which a constant balance is being sought between collaboration and competition. The evident trend towards the establishment of *ad hoc* specialist groups reflects, to some extent, a response to constantly changing market needs. As new technology is developed, new issues are generated and new alliances may be required to press their case. Likewise, changes in alliance patterns reflect quite clearly changes in the overall structure of the industry. Hence, the increasing involvement of IT users in strategic alliances is unsurprising when the general shift in the IT industry towards a concentration on IT *services* is taken into account. IT producers are, of course, keen to hear precisely what their users require.

Overall, however, it appears that in the IT field cooperation itself breeds further cooperation. Firms collaborating in EU-funded programmes, such as ESPRIT, in the work of the standards bodies, or in the various federations and direct membership fora are increasingly in an informed position to make strategic decisions about their choice of allies on particular political issues. Likewise, the growing trend towards establishing a base in Brussels appears to be encouraging closer contact between the various actors. Those established so far appear to be successful and others seem likely to follow. In part too, the alliance strategies of the various firms reflect the impact of EU institutional incentives. Apart from the knock-on effect of programmes such as ESPRIT and the critical role which the EU played in establishing the ERT and the European IT Roundtable, the importance of participation in the various collective fora connected with the EU in generating a technological community of individuals who know and trust one another should not be underestimated (Sharp, 1990).

Notes

1. I would like to thank the officials in the European Commission, CEN, CENELEC, EWOS, ORGALIME, ECTEL, EUROBIT, EECA, ECIF, BSI and DISC and all those senior industrialists from the IT industry who gave up their time to help me with this research.
2. As the IT sector is dominated by a number of important multinational companies, this case study concentrates on the strategic alliances forged between these firms. While there have been a number of European Commission and national government incentives employed to increase the role of small and medium-sized enterprises in the IT sector, major multinational industries continue to dominate industrial representation in the policy process.
3. ESPRIT – European Strategic Programme for Research and Development in Information Technology; RACE – Research and Development in Advanced Communications Technologies in Europe.
4. This, of course, is not unique to the IT sector – various Directorate-Generals have developed close relationships with their client industries. For example, DG VI and the agriculture industry.
5. Information presented in this section was derived from interviews with senior industrialists in the IT sector.
6. For details on the organization of the telecommunications sector in Europe see Schneider (1992) and Dang-Nguyen *et al.* (1993).
7. For details on the organization of the consumer electronics sector, see Cawson (1992) and Case 3 of this book.

8. As one industrial representative pointed out – this is not always how those paying for such organizations would characterize them. Indeed, there is enormous variation in the levels of resources allocated to sectoral organizations as well as in the levels of staffing. However, it is often the case that a relatively small number of staff are expected to cover a very wide range of issues.
9. As McLaughlin (1994) shows, this phenomenon is not restricted to the IT industry.
10. ICL, GEC and Plessy of the UK; Thomson, Bull and CGE from France; AEG, Nixdorf and Siemens from Germany; Olivetti and STET from Italy; and Philips from the Netherlands.
11. For an overview of the extent of technological concentration in the IT sector in the late 1980s, see Sharp (1993, pp. 217–218).
12. CEN – The European Committee for Standardization, established 1961; CENELEC – Comité Européen de Normalisation Electrotechnique, established 1958.
13. ETSI – European Telecommunications Standards Institute, established 1988.
14. EWOS – European Workshop for Open Systems, established 1987.
15. COSINE – Cooperation for Open Systems Interconnection Networking in Europe; ECMA – European Computer Manufacturers' Association; EMUG European MAP Users' Group; OSITOP – Open Systems Interconnection Technical and Office Protocols; RARE – Réseaux Associés pour la Recherche Européene; SPAG – Standards Promotion and Application Group.
16. For examples, see n. 13 above.
17. See Sharp and Pavitt (1993) for a list of the major EU programmes for promoting new technologies.
18. The approach of Japanese IT firms to the policy process in the EU has been rather different from that pursued by US and European firms and deserves more research. For some insight into the Japanese approach to lobbying in the EC, see McLaughlin (1994).

References

Besen, S. (1990) 'The European Telecommunications Standards Institute', *Telecommunications Policy*, vol. 14, pp. 521–530.

Cawson, A. (1992) 'Interests, groups and public policy-making: the case of the consumer electronics industry', in Greenwood, J., Grote, J. and Ronit, K. (eds) *Organised Interests and the European Community*. London: Sage.

CEN (1993) *Standards for Access to the European Market*. Brussels: CEN.

CEU (1994) *Europe's Way to the Information Society: An Action Plan*. IP/94/683, 20 July 1994.

Collie, L. (1993) 'Business lobbying in the European Community: the Union of Industrial and Employers' Confederations of Europe', in Mazey, S. and Richardson, J. (eds) *Lobbying in the European Community*. Oxford: Oxford University Press.

Dang-Nguyen, G., Schneider, V. and Werle, R. (1993) 'Networks in European policy-making: Europeification of telecommunications policy', in Andersen, A. and Eliassen, K. (eds) *Making Policy in Europe: The Europeification of National Policy-making*. London: Sage.

European Workshop for Open Systems (EWOS) (1993) *General Information on EWOS*. Brussels: EWOS, 21 June 1993.

Grant, W. (1994) *Pressure Groups, Politics and Democracy in Britain* (2nd edn). Hemel Hempstead: Philip Allan.

Green, M. (1993) 'The politics of big business in the single market programme'. Paper presented at the 1993 Biennial International Conference of the European Community Studies Association, Washington, 27–29 May 1993.

Greenwood, J. and Ronit, K. (1992) 'Established and emergent sectors: organised interests at the European level in the pharmaceutical industry and the new biotechnologies', in Greenwood, J., Grote, J. and Ronit, K. (eds) *Organised Interests and the European Community*. London: Sage.

Greenwood, J., Grote, J. and Ronit, K. (1992) (eds) *Organised Interests and the European Community*. London: Sage.

High-Level Group on the Information Society (1994) 'Europe and the global information society: recommendations to the European Council', Brussels, 26 May 1994.

Mazey, S. and Richardson, J. (1993) *Lobbying in the European Community*. Oxford: Oxford University Press.

McLaughlin, A. (1994) 'Outsiders inside? Japanese lobbying in the European Union'. Paper presented to the Conference of Europeanists, Chicago, 31 March–2 April 1994.

McLaughlin, A. and Jordan, G. (1993) 'The rationality of lobbying in Europe: why are Euro-groups so numerous and so weak? Some evidence from the car industry', in Mazey, S. and Richardson, J. (eds) *Lobbying in the European Community*. Oxford: Oxford University Press.

McLaughlin, A., Jordan, G. and Maloney, W. (1993) 'Corporate Lobbying in the European Community', *Journal of Common Market Studies*, vol. 31, pp. 191–212.

Olson, M. (1971) *The Logic of Collective Action* (2nd edn). Cambridge, MA: Harvard University Press.

Peterson, J. (1991) 'Technology policy in Europe: explaining the framework programme and eureka in theory and practice', *Journal of Common Market Studies*, vol. 29, pp. 269–90.

Peterson, J. (1992) 'The European technology community: policy networks in a supranational setting', in Marsh, D. and Rhodes, R. A. W. (eds) *Policy Networks in British Government*. Oxford: Oxford University Press.

Sandholtz, W. (1992a) 'ESPRIT and the politics of international collective action', *Journal of Common Market Studies*, vol. 30, pp. 1–21.

Sandholtz, W. (1992b) *High-tech Europe: The Politics of International Cooperation*, Berkeley CA: University of California Press.

Sandholtz, W. and Zysman, J. (1989) 'Recasting the European bargain', *World Politics*, vol. 42, pp. 92–128.

Schneider, V. (1992) 'Organised interests in the telecommunications sector', in Greenwood, J., Grote, J. and Ronit, K. (eds) *Organised Interests and the European Community*. London: Sage.

Sharp, M. (1990) 'The single market and European policies for advanced technologies', in Crouch, C. and Marquand, D. (1990) *The Politics of 1992*. Cambridge: Basil Blackwell.

Sharp, M. (1993) 'The Community and new technologies', in Lodge, J. (ed.) *The European Community and the Challenge of the Future* (2nd edn). London: Pinter.

Sharp, M. and Pavitt, K. (1993) 'Technology policy in the 1990s: old trends and new realities', *Journal of Common Market Studies*, vol. 31, pp. 129-151.

Sharp, M. and Shearman, C. (1987) *European Technological Collaboration*. Chatham House Paper. London: Routledge and Kegan Paul RIIA.

Simon, H. A. (1976) *Administrative Behaviour* (3rd edn). New York: Free Press.

CASE 2

The Pharmaceutical Industry

A European Business Alliance that Works

Justin Greenwood

The selection of the pharmaceutical industry as a case study for this collection is a strategic choice. The industry is represented in Europe by a federation of national federations ('superfederation'): the European Federation of Pharmaceutical Industry Associations (EFPIA). The superfederation type of representational format has been highlighted by a number of authors as problematic, not least because of the difficulties of reaching meaningful agreement, and because of the slow and tortuous processes through which such formats make decisions and take actions (Grant, 1990; Jordan and McLaughlin, 1991). EFPIA is an example of a highly successful Euro federation, and it is therefore important to study it to help us understand the conditions under which European federations of national federations can be successful.

There has been no shortage of literature highlighting the problems faced by super federations. McLaughlin (1992) entitled one of his conference papers 'Underfed Euro feds', while Jordan and McLaughlin (1991) asked 'Why are Euro groups so numerous and so weak?' Grant maintains that the lack of effectiveness of Euro federations makes them useful for little more than fraternal contact (Grant, 1990, 1993). There is certainly evidence of European federations of national federations collapsing on coherence grounds (Grant, 1990), and indeed in some industries such as automobiles (Case 12) the super federated format has been abandoned in favour of a direct firm membership format. There has been a tendency in recent literature to use this type of evidence to assert the ineffectiveness of European business political organization as a whole. Some authors have gone on to argue that effective representation of business interests in Europe must operate through the national level (i.e. through national associations or national governments) (Grant, 1990, 1993). Others have taken the point even further, arguing that Europe resembles more the fragmented

Washington style of competing groups than the very close relationships evident between singular, authoritative representatives of business interests and governments which is evident in some domains in member states (Streeck and Schmitter, 1991; Lewin, 1992, 1994; Hix, 1994). Streeck and Schmitter (1991), in a well known contribution, trumpet a shift 'from national corporatism to transnational pluralism'. The pharmaceutical industry case rather challenges some of these assumptions. What makes it effective as a business alliance in Europe?

Organized Interests and the Single Market: the Regulation of the Pharmaceutical Industry in Europe

A variety of similarities have been noted across national boundaries in the regulation of the pharmaceutical industry in western Europe (Hancher, 1990; Greenwood and Ronit, 1991a). This is because the issues are in essence the same throughout member states. On the one hand, national governments like a pharmaceutical industry presence because the industry has consistently proved a first-class economic performer whose high-technology nature promises to keep on delivering the goods. On the other hand, all national governments worry about issues of medicine prices (as purchasers), industry salesmanship to prescribers (in inflating costs and impacting on rational drug use), and safety (as consumer protectors). Consequently, the regulatory style is a preference for negotiated settlement between government and industry and is characterized by delegation of regulatory authority to the pharmaceutical industry in return for compliance-seeking among members. Organized interests play a considerable and important role in styling relationships between the industry and the state, and, in the case of the pharmaceutical industry, sector associations both have long histories of establishment and provide one of the earliest modern examples of neo-corporatist policy partnerships (involving a unit of government and a producer interest association organizing an industry for compliance and taking on public functions through mechanisms such as self-regulation). In a comparative study of Denmark and the UK, Greenwood and Ronit (1991b) found classic examples of 'private interest government', where state legislation lies dormant in favour of industry self-regulation administered with the agreement of all parties by a sector association. These similarities have assisted the reproduction of national-level arrangements at the transnational level. An additional key factor has been the multinational character of the pharmaceutical industry, which has developed experiences across national boundaries. The industry has used this accumulated experience in transnational regulatory environments since the 1970s, when the International Federation of Pharmaceutical Industry Associations (IFPMA) was created to confront a regulatory threat from the World Health Organization (WHO). A key feature in meeting this threat was the establishment of a code of self-regulatory practice as a means of confronting WHO concerns about unethical selling practices (Greenwood, 1988). Such experiences assisted the industry when it came to engaging the EC-level of authority.

The European Federation of Pharmaceutical Industry Associations (EFPIA) was formed in 1978. Although this appears somewhat late for a multinational industry to form its own European interest association, it in fact emerged from an amalgamation of associations covering different European territories. In its short life, influence upon European policymaking in the pharmaceutical sector has been considerable, turning the threat of transnational regulation expressed in EC proposals into agreement for the use of itself as a self-regulatory agency to implement policy on drug information, in the creation of Commission proposals for patent law harmonization (Burstall, 1990) and in using the EC to challenge established national pricing arrangements in the European court (Greenwood and Ronit, 1991b).

EFPIA records its aim as to ensure that 'the conditions relating to the supply of medicines are appropriate to the production and development of medicines' (EFPIA, 1988, p.16). A ten-year review reflected that:

> the ten years of EFPIA have demonstrated the ability of a highly competitive industrial sector, with widely differing types and sizes of national industries and companies, to operate in a coherent manner on matters of common concern. The great achievement of EFPIA has been to catalyse discussions, coordinate views, assure contacts, and create conditions for consensus and common positions in the sector in Europe. This achievement demonstrates the spirit of collaboration, cooperation and pragmatic compromise of the pharmaceutical industry within EFPIA. It is to be saluted, and its reinforcement over the next ten years is not to be doubted, since it springs from a common conviction of the worth of the pharmaceutical industry in Europe.
>
> *(EFPIA, 1988, p. 13)*

EFPIA sees itself as a 'unique interface between one of Europe's most dynamic industries and the broader processes of European policy determination' (EFPIA, 1988, p. 16).

EFPIA is well resourced in comparison with many other Euro associations. It employs twenty staff, and receives membership fees from sixteen national associations across EC and EFTA countries, the majority of which are themselves well resourced by individual firms, and who complement EFPIA's resources. All of these are members of the general assembly of EFPIA. The executive committee consists of five permanent members, these being the main producer nations (UK, France, Germany, Italy and Switzerland), and alternating members who are subdivided into more (including the Netherlands and Denmark) and less (including Greece and Portugal) active members, and who hold membership on a biannual basis. One important factor beyond common national experiences which helps explain EFPIA's coherence is that the major national associations pay the greatest fees and in return enjoy the most influence. At the same time, smaller national associations have a voice both in the executive committee and general assembly, where votes are not weighted. The blend of interests is successful; although the distribution of influence is highly asymmetrical, the practice is not to vote. As far as possible a consensus is sought, although, if necessary, majority decisions are taken. Another important factor in coherence-building is the extent of delegation to the Brussels secretariat, which acts with a high degree of delegated authority in finding appropriate and common platforms among member associations or in handling relations with the EC. EFPIA thus has a 'fast track' decision-making process – a key feature of its success both in appealing to its constituency and in its influence with the Commission. As might be expected, there are highly developed symbiotic relations with the Commission, and in particular with DG III (internal market and industrial affairs) and DG XI (environmental affairs).

EFPIA is widely admired within the pharmaceutical industry and the Brussels business representation community for its organization and effectiveness. While there are structural features of the industry, described below, which are largely responsible for this, the role of leadership should not be ignored. Outgoing Director-General Nelly Baudrihaye was widely recognized for her ability to lead from the front, to build an effective organization, to establish credibility in the Commission, and to find ways of balancing the interests of her constituency; much the same is likely to apply with incoming Director Brian Ager. While it is true that the pharmaceutical industry's European alliance is harmonious, there are tensions, and in particular those surrounding American versus European firms. In some countries (e.g the UK), American firms are represented through national associations, while in others (e.g. Denmark), domestic associations exclude non-European firms. A number of American firms have taken non-EFPIA channels as a route to the Commission, sometimes arguing for positions which disagree with those put forward by EFPIA. Consensus-building at the European level in the pharmaceutical industry does therefore have to be managed, and effective representation is not automatic. EFPIA also has to cope with national organization which has become turbulent in recent years.

For instance, in the summer of 1993 the German pharmaceutical industry association collapsed because of its inability to balance the interests of large and small firms. EFPIA has been able to avoid these problems through both effective leadership and organizational design, and also because of factors which are favourable to good European organization. These are reviewed below.

European Regulation of the Pharmaceutical Industry

A key feature of regulation of the European pharmaceutical industry is a consideration of its contribution to the economies of western Europe. Around two thousand firms employ nearly half a million people, with production totals of ECU 70 billion (30 per cent of world production), a world market share of 42 per cent, and a collective trade surplus of ECU 7.7 billion. The value of its exports is three times that of the US pharmaceutical industry, and fifteen times that of Japan's. Its positive trade balance is equivalent to 12 per cent of total production, which compares with a negative trade balance in Europe for all sectors of -0.67 per cent, i.e. $-$ECU 21 billion (EFPIA, 1993; Commission, 1994). The European pharmaceutical industry has a proud record of innovation (58 per cent of all new chemical entities launched worldwide over the past twenty-five years), and stands in the forefront of new technology development. It is a key strategic player for the European Union in world competition of today and the future. These key resources have been used in bargaining exchanges with regulatory authority.

Until 1984/85, the pharmaceutical industry faced the possibility of a restrictive European pricing directive. EFPIA instead proposed an alternative scheme, which the Commission accepted, based upon member states publishing transparent criteria for their medicine pricing decisions. EFPIA has in effect persuaded the Commission that its task should be to worry not about prices but about the overall health of the industry. Thus, an explanatory memorandum to a Commission proposal for a Council directive on pricing records that:

> the single-minded pursuit of short-term financial economies will effectively undermine the research capacity of the pharmaceutical industry . . . the maintenance of a high level of public health within the Community will to a large extent depend upon the activities of the Community's own pharmaceutical industry.
>
> *(EFPIA, 1988)*

Another notable success has been EFPIA's campaign for the incremental erosion of patent life (caused by diminishing research returns) to be addressed. Although the Commission once (1984) regarded this as too difficult to undertake, EFPIA's representational efforts had been rewarded by 1991 with an enhanced protection period. Significantly, EFPIA also persuaded the Commission to take the governments of Italy and Belgium to the European Court of Justice over pricing issues to which the industries in those countries had once been a party. Thus, the transnational interest association had achieved more for its industry as a collective federation than had once been possible by single national associations. This is a far cry from a recent portrait of transnational interest groups as ineffective and incoherent, and whose use is restricted to fraternal contact.

The greatest testimony to EFPIA's influence has been in the field of regulating medicine selling. Here, it successfully established industry-wide compliance for a new self-regulatory code of practice, modelled on that of the UK and elsewhere, as a means of safeguarding the activities of its medical representatives, key actors to the success of pharmaceutical industry selling strategies (Greenwood, 1988). Although the code operates with Commission blessing, the price of this has been to concede a directive on advertising, effective from January 1993, which is far more encompassing than the industry would have liked. Nevertheless, the code does emphasize the way in which the industry has been able to reproduce national strategies in a transnational context as a result of its common experiences. In effect, a neo-corporatist European 'private interest government' relationship has been established as a result of the organizing capacity of a European federation of national federations. This capacity has recently been further demonstrated through the passage of the 'rational use package' (Directives 25–28, adopted in 1992), where EFPIA made a significant impact upon issues of wholesale distribution, classification, labelling and advertising. This included undertaking a number of information studies on behalf of the Commission to establish the appropriate type of regulatory detail. This practice has continued, and in November 1992 the Commission again asked EFPIA to undertake study on medicine codification.

It is not suggested that the industry has had its own way in every instance; recent revisions to national pricing transparency directives, for instance, have irked the research-based industry. Nor is it claimed that all parties in the industry always agree on everything; for example, internal disagreements have surfaced over the remit for the European Agency for the Evaluation of Medicinal Products, a single market measure adopted in November 1992 (for a 1995 start), aimed at speeding up product registrations across the member states. Similarly, American firms have sometimes sought policy initiatives from the Commission which run counter to EFPIA's own positions. Nevertheless, on the whole, EFPIA has been able to protect and promote industry-wide interests through effective platform-building among its members, and by using the industrial strength of the industry to build a close, symbiotic relationship with DG III in the Commission. This relationship has developed into an effective mechanism of sectoral governance. The cases described illustrate the extent to which the presence of particular variables and dynamics (such as common national experiences) shape political relationships. This rather confirms Lowi's concept that 'policies make politics', i.e. that the type of policy influences the underlying politics. The logic of this is to suggest the need to examine arrangements in each sector or domain as they arise, rather than to seek to characterize EC/ interest group relations as a whole. In some sectors the prevailing issues and factors at work will lend themselves to the development of relationships between producer interests and Community institutions which are close enough to be mechanisms of policy formulation and implementation.

What Does the Pharmaceutical Industry Tell Us About European Business Alliances?

Evidence presented here from the pharmaceuticals sector provides a challenge to the generalization of Euro associations, as federations of national federations, being under-resourced, unable to act cohesively, and whose importance is seen as largely restricted to fraternal contact. The difficulty for such outlets in achieving representativeness and acting beyond the 'lowest common denominator' has been held to be disabling to the development of neo-corporatist structures at the European level. The example provided by EFPIA suggests that such a generalization cannot be sustained. Where a sector has some experience of transnational political action, and where it faces common regulatory experiences in member states, the effectiveness of a Euro superfederation seems at least to be possible.

Single case study research is highly valuable for developing hypotheses for testing and confirming with other types of case study evidence. These cases can be strategically selected by choosing most and least likely scenarios for the issue under investigation to occur – what Eckstein (1992) calls a 'crucial case'. The following hypotheses about European business alliances emerge from this study of the pharmaceutical industry.

1. *Industries engaged in broadly similar national regulatory styles are more likely to be able to work effectively in collective formats at the European level than industries operating in highly diverse regulatory environments across the member states.*

The pharmaceutical industry faces broadly the same types of issue wherever it operates in Europe. All governments like to provide a base for a highly successful industry which brings in export earnings, but worry about medicine prices, standards of selling to medical practitioners and safety issues. These factors tend to involve governments and industry in intense regulatory and promotional dialogue, with a single industry association forming part of a closely integrated policy network. Across member states, typically, such a network provides a mechanism for both formulation and implementation of policy, such as self-regulation of selling or price control schemes. Because the issues are in essence the same at national levels, so the industry has been able to act coherently at the European level on the basis of its common experiences.

> 2. *Industries containing a significant number of global multinational firms with experience of working in a number of different regulatory environments are more likely to be able to work effectively in collective formats at the European level.*

Multinational industries such as the pharmaceutical industry have experience in working in each of the regulatory environments of the member states. They are therefore unlikely to face surprises at the European level with a wholly alien environment, and are likely to have developed adaptability in coping with European regulation. Indeed, the Commission may prefer firms with such experiences because they represent expertise which can be drawn upon in designing regulatory and promotional policies.

> 3. *Industries with prior experience of transnational collective action will find the transition to working collectively at the European level smoother than will industries new to collective action beyond national boundaries.*

The pharmaceutical industry's experience in confronting the regulatory threat from the World Health Organization by setting up an international association assisted it in working at the European level. The tactics it adopted in both cases were identical. When confronted with the regulation of its key selling strategy, the medical representative's visits to medical practitioners (Greenwood, 1988), it responded with a self-regulatory code. This is an attractive arrangement to governmental authority because of the spirit of self-discipline involved, and because such instruments are flexible and represent virtually nil cost in time and money resources to state machinery.

> 4. *High-status industries of strategic importance to the European Union are more likely to develop effective collective action formats at the European level than are other industries.*

These factors give the pharmaceutical industry a special place with the Commission. High-technology industries rather match the self-image of the Commission as the force of the future. The pharmaceutical industry is among Europe's three top export earners, and is privileged by European regulation and promotion policies. This attention is a key dynamic in developing European-level collective action: if there are rewards and benefits on offer in Brussels then the industry needs to organize effectively. If there are few, as is the case with tourism, so there is less incentive to develop European-level collective action structures.

> 5. *Industries requiring a high degree of regulation for public safety are more likely to develop effective collective action formats at the European level than are other industries.*

The pharmaceutical industry in Europe has been highly regulated ever since the thalidomide tragedy of the 1960s. Unlike a domain such as tourism, there is no option but to regulate where industrial activity so significantly impacts upon public safety, as is the case with medicines. Indeed, EC regulation of the pharmaceutical industry dates back to Directive 65 of 1965, dealing with safety issues. This degree of Euro competencies in turn encourages the development of European collective action structures. Although EFPIA was formed in 1978, a predecessor organization (based on member state national organizations rather than the more encompassing EC/EFTA states covered by EFPIA), engaged in dialogue with the Commission for safety issues. Crudely, a well defined reason to be in Brussels acts as a key encouragement to the development of European collective action structures.

> 6. *There will be a preference for taking the 'Brussels strategy' where European-level collective action outlets for the interest concerned have developed a track record of success.*

European-level representation in the pharmaceuticals sector takes place mainly through the European level of organization rather than through national associations or national governments because EFPIA has developed a track record of success. Where European-level organization is weak, representation may occur more through national channels.

> 7. *European federations of national federations will be most likely to work where the interests of large firms are given precedence over those of medium/small ones, but where medium/small firms agree to the settlement.*

EFPIA's success is partly due to this balance, detailed in the sections above.

8. *To be effective, a European federation of national federations need a 'fast-track' decision-making procedure.*

This is the case both with EFPIA, as described above, and EuroCommerce (Case 8). Associations with cumbersome and slow decision-making procedures do not tend to last very long (see the case of cars, in Case 12).

9. *Well defined and relatively concentrated sectors have a head start in organizing at the European level.*

Despite the efforts of some commentators to classify pharmaceuticals as a subsector of the chemicals industry (see, for instance, de Ghellinck, 1992), the pharmaceuticals industry is fairly well defined. It produces medicines for human and animal consumption, the majority of which is sold through prescription access. Typically, production is based in large firms, and a degree of concentration has been evident in the industry in recent years (e.g. Smith Kline French and Beecham; Bristol Myers and Squibb; Roche and Genentech). The advantages in organizing are obvious for an industry of this kind when compared with a highly fragmented domain such as tourism (Case 9). Much the same is true of the highly concentrated consumer electronics sector (Case 3).

If comparable cases are chosen, these hypotheses can be probed such that they provide candidate theories of collective action at the European level. The pharmaceutical industry is an important case because the type of alliance under question – a European federation of national federations – works well. Key factors in its effectiveness concern the similarity of national regulatory styles, the strategic place of the industry in the European economy of today and tomorrow, and its fairly concentrated and well defined sectoral nature. Yet on their own these factors may not be sufficient for a super federation (rather than another type of organizational format) to work. A superfederation needs an effective balance between large and medium/small firms, such that the large firm interests are given precedence yet incentives still exist for medium/small firms to retain membership and not to break away to form a rival association. It is also important that the federation is well resourced, with a considerable degree of autonomy delegated to the secretariat such that decisions can be made quickly. In turn, the secretariat needs to develop an effective style of leadership. All of these factors are present in the case of the European Federation of Pharmaceutical Industry Associations.

References

Burstall, M. L. (1990) *1992 and the Regulation of the Pharmaceutical Industry*. London: IEA.

Commission of the European Communities (1994) *Communication from the Commission to the Council and the European Parliament on the Outlines of an Industrial Policy for the Pharmaceutical Sector in the European Community*. COM (93) 718 final, 2 March 1994.

de Ghellinck, E. (1992) 'The chemical and pharmaceutical industries', in Mayes, D. G. (ed.) *The European Challenge*. London: Harvester Wheatsheaf.

Eckstein, H. (1992) 'Case study and theory in political science', in Greenstein, F. and Polsby, N. W. (eds) *Strategies of Inquiry*. Reading, MA: Addison Wesley.

EFPIA (1988) *Ten Years of EFPIA*. Brussels: EFPIA.

EFPIA (1990) *A Brief Guide to the EEC Directives Concerning Medicines*. Brussels: EFPIA.

EFPIA (1993) Annual Report. Brussels: EFPIA.

Grant, W. (1990) Organized Interests and the European Community'. Paper presented at the 6th International Colloquium of the Feltrinelli Foundation, Corton, 29–31 May 1990.

Grant, W. (1993) 'Pressure groups and the European Community: an overview', in Mazey, S. and Richardson, J. (eds) *Lobbying in the European Community*. Oxford: Oxford University Press, pp. 27–46.

Greenwood, J. (1988) The market and the state: the pharmaceutical representative and general medical practice'. PhD thesis submitted to the University of Nottingham, May 1988.

Greenwood, J. and Ronit, K. (1991a) 'Medicine regulation in Denmark and the UK: reformulating interest representation to the transnational level', *European Journal of Political Research*, vol. 19, pp. 327–359.

Greenwood, J. and Ronit, K. (1991b) 'Organized interests and the European internal market', *Government and Policy*, vol. 9, pp. 467–484.

Hancher, L. (1990) *Government, Law and the Pharmaceutical Industry in the UK and France*. Oxford: Clarendon Press.

Hix, S. (1994) 'The study of the European Community: the challenge to comparative politics', *West European Politics*, vol. 17, pp. 1–30.

Jordan, A. G. and McLaughlin, A. (1991) 'The rationality of lobbying in Europe: why are Euro groups so numerous and so weak?', Paper presented to Euro Lobbying Conference, Nuffield College, Oxford, 17 May 1991.

Lewin, L. (1992) *Samhallet och be Organiserade Intressena*. Stockholm: Norstedts.

Lewin. L. (1994) Talk to Centre for Public Organization and Management, Copenhagen Business School, 25 February 1994.

McLaughlin, A. (1992) 'Underfed Euro feds', Paper presented to the Annual Conference of the Political Studies Association, Belfast, April 1992.

Streeck, W. and Schmitter, P. C. (1991) 'From national corporatism to transnational pluralism', *Politics and Society*, vol. 19, pp. 133–64.

Public Policies and Private Interests

The Role of Business Interests in Determining Europe's Future Television System

Alan Cawson[1]

Introduction

For six years the two leading European consumer electronics firms, Philips and Thomson, were at the heart of a collaborative R&D project under the Eureka programme to develop a high definition television (HDTV) technology to compete against the Japanese Hi-Vision system. The project cost over one billion ECUs, both private investment (mainly from Philips, since Thomson is owned by the French government) and public money (almost all from national governments), and, although no direct EC funding was involved, it was enthusiastically supported by the European Commission. The system which was developed, HD-MAC, was officially abandoned by the Commission in January 1993 in favour of a new Digital Video Broadcasting (DVB) technology which the Commission hopes will be introduced in 1996. Eighty-seven private and public organisations in Europe (including some from outside the EU) have signed a Memorandum of Understanding which pledges support for the DVB project. HD-MAC is dead! Long live DVB!

This chapter analyses the process in which European Community policy for new television technology was shaped from 1985 onwards, paying particular attention to the role of business interests in both making and implementing policy. It analyses the privileged position accorded to Philips and Thomson by (some) national governments and the European Commission (especially DG XIII) in determining the HDTV strategy, and explains why this relatively closed process was opened up to participation by a wider range of interests in 1992. The chapter concludes with an assessment of the strength of the coalition behind DVB, and the problems of sustaining collective action in a complex innovation process.

The Formation of the HD-MAC Strategy

In the mid-1980s there was a growing perception amongst European elites of the competitive threat to its indigenous Information Technology and electronics industries (Sharp and Shearman, 1987). The trade deficit in IT and consumer electronics products had grown precipitously, especially following the failure of Europe's home-grown video recorder technology, the Philips-Grundig V2000, against the Japanese VHS system. The Japanese electronics industry had just caught up in VLSI semiconductor technology, thanks to a successful R&D collaboration between the major firms, orchestrated by Ministry of International Trade and Industry (MITI).[2] To follow that, the Japanese state broadcasting organisation, NHK, was leading an apparently similar collaborative effort involving Sony, Matsushita, Hitachi, Toshiba and others, to develop an entirely new television technology, called Hi-Vision. The Japanese had asked the world's regulatory body for television, the CCIR, to consider adopting its 1125/60 production standard as the official world standard for HDTV production.[3] This move caused a panic reaction in Europe, where the major firms feared that the Japanese HDTV system would provide a repeat performance of the VHS saga, and that they would lose their one impressive stronghold in consumer electronics.

The policy response was rapid, and took advantage of the civil R&D-oriented Eureka initiative inspired by President Mitterrand as a response to the Reagan Strategic Defense Initiative (or Star Wars). Just two months after European governments had successfully blocked the Japanese proposals at the CCIR meeting in Dubrovnik in May 1986, the Eureka-95 project on a Compatible High Definition Television System was launched with the aim of producing a European system by the time of the next CCIR meeting in 1990. The core firms, led from a directorate situated in the Philips head-quarters in Eindhoven in Holland, comprised Philips, Thomson, Robert Bosch of Germany, and Thorn EMI of the United Kingdom.[4] Unlike in Japan, the broadcasters (including the major state broadcasters such as the BBC, ZDF and RTF) were excluded from the inner group which determined policy, so that their contribution (within EU-95) was confined to technical matters.

The difference in the nature of the membership of the coalitions in Japan and Europe can be explained by the urgency of the timetable, and the fact that the immediate threat was perceived by the set manufacturers rather than by the broadcasters, whose interest in a specifically *European* HDTV technology would come mainly from pressures from national governments. The issue was defined as an industrial issue, with the industry at risk being the consumer electronics industry and not the broadcasting industry. The picture in 1994 is rather different, with many more private broadcasters operating in Europe, a growing cable television industry, and a thriving satellite television industry. In the situation of the mid-1980s, however, it was a technological solution which was chosen to address what was seen as a problem of industrial competitiveness.

The European HDTV strategy was risky on a number of counts:

1. The leading firms, Philips and Thomson, had no history of industrial collaboration; indeed, up to 1986 their relationships had often been antagonistic as in the struggle to acquire Grundig, and in the refusal of Thomson to manufacture either V2000-format VCRs or CD players when the digital audio format was just beginning to win consumer acceptance (Cawson *et al*. 1990).

2. It was deemed necessary to use a new distribution technology, direct broadcasting by satellite (DBS), because in order to carry high quality images, high-definition television (HDTV) required more bandwidth than is available in a current terrestrial channel. Because of the urgency, the firms decided to adapt a new satellite technology pioneered by the Independent Broadcasting Authority in the UK, which was known as MAC – Multiplex Analogue Component.[5]

3. There was no DBS service in Europe in 1986, so the adoption of MAC would depend on existing broadcasters starting new services (as happened with DBS in Japan) or new broadcasters entering the market. In either case, consumers would have to buy dishes and set-top decoders (to convert from MAC to the existing PAL/SECAM format) in order to receive the signals at all, and entirely new television sets if they wanted to view them in improved quality as MAC pictures or in high definition as HD-MAC pictures.

4. The strategy depended on national broadcasters taking up the DBS frequencies that had been allocated to each country in 1977, and using MAC technology rather than the PAL or SECAM technology of existing receivers. To this end the Council of Ministers adopted a directive in 1986 which made the use of MAC compulsory for all direct-to-home satellite broadcasting using high-power satellite transponders.[6]

Given the apparently greater risks in doing nothing, however, there were few who doubted the wisdom of the strategy at its outset, and many, such as President Mitterrand and the industry commissioner, Vicomte Davignon, gave the strategy powerful political support. This support helped to protect the privileged position of the leading firms, Philips and Thomson, as architects as well as builders of the new high-definition edifice. It was these two firms that decided to develop the MAC system into HD-MAC, and the firms that were responsible for delivering this flagship technology policy. Interventionist industrial and technology policies of this kind can only be successful if producer interests can be co-opted into the process, forming meso-corporatist partnerships such as the one which had successfully introduced Teletext services in Britain (Cawson, 1985, 1986). These are negotiated agreements where policy is formed and implemented through firm (but not legally binding) commitments undertaken by the partners. Innovation can only be successful in consumer technologies if customers can be persuaded to buy the products which embody the technologies. It is, therefore, not surprising that in both Japan and Europe, business interests and governments codetermined HDTV policies, leaving out consumer interests. Even in Japan, however, the risks of this kind of policy-making are becoming apparent since despite having been on the market for three years, fewer than forty thousand sets have been sold.[7]

Collapse of the Strategy

At a technical level, the collaboration between Philips and Thomson within EU-95 worked better than anyone could have foreseen. The four-year deadline was met, and the 1990 CCIR again declined to endorse the Japanese standard, leaving open the probability of multiple standards as had happened in the 1960s with colour television being adopted across the world in three different versions.[8] Once cameras and video recorders for HD-MAC had been developed, the European Commission set up and subsidized a European Economic Interest Group (EEIG) called Vision 1250, to which broadcasters could belong in order to get low-cost access to the very expensive HDTV equipment. The EU-95 firms were acutely conscious that sets could not be sold without services provided by broadcasters, and that services required programmes. However, given political support from the Commission, and from most EC member governments (except the UK and later Denmark and Germany), and the tight regulatory framework provided by the 1986 MAC directive, it looked for a time as if HD-MAC in Europe would succeed as long as the new DBS services using MAC could find a mass audience.

Any successful innovation requires a combination of effective politics (regulation), appropriate technology and a market which takes off. Unfortunately for the European HDTV strategy, the regulatory framework was flawed, the technology was overtaken, and the market for DBS took off in a way which relegated MAC to the sidelines.

The Regulatory Loophole and a Market Failure

The World Administrative Radio Conference (WARC) is the international body under the auspices of the United Nations which regulates international radio and television frequencies. WARC distinguished between communications satellites (which use medium power to cover a very large footprint, and so can be used for telephone calls and for beaming television pictures around the world) and broadcasting satellites which use high power in a narrower beam more suitable for national DBS services to small dishes mounted on homes. It allocated five DBS frequencies to each nation within a series of geostationary slots above the middle of the earth. The EC Council of Ministers adopted a directive which was worded to mandate MAC only for high-power DBS services.[9] In Britain, after a couple of false starts involving the BBC and others, the government awarded the first DBS frequencies to a new venture called British Satellite Broadcasting (BSB). The BSB licence required it to use MAC, in conformity with the 1986 directive.

Since 1977, however, DBS technology had improved to the extent that it became possible to receive DBS broadcasts on an 80 centimetre or 1 metre dish from medium-powered telecommunications satellites. Spotting the potential for a new market, the Luxembourg-based Société Européene des Satellites (SES) launched the world's first privately-owned communications satellite Astra, and leased several transponders to Rupert Murdoch's News International company for his new Sky satellite venture. Murdoch decided to try to get to market ahead of BSB, and his lawyers told him that the 1986 MAC directive would not apply to the Astra satellite. Teaming up with Amstrad, Murdoch announced that Sky would use the normal PAL system, initially with Amstrad-badged equipment manufactured in the Far East. Meanwhile, BSB tried to make a virtue out of the MAC technology (and an untested square dish it called the 'squarial') in an effort to persuade consumers to wait for the new (and, it argued, better) technology which BSB would use. Consumers, however, want programmes rather than technologies, and cost,[10] benefit and availability are important factors in the adoption of new technologies. BSB was late, appearing fourteen months after Sky, in April 1990.[11] By the end of the year, Sky had taken over BSB to form British Sky Broadcasting (BSkyB), and Murdoch had announced that the merged service would continue to broadcast in PAL from the Astra satellite. That the demise of BSB and the first commercial MAC service was a hole in the Eureka flagship was not in doubt; the Eureka partners, however, claimed that it was above the waterline, and there was no danger of the ship sinking.

Technical Obsolescence

It may well be that the Eureka partners were right, and that HD-MAC could have survived the BSB débâcle, since there were eleven other EC countries which might later have launched a MAC service. Consumer electronics is a global industry, and governments and policy-makers (as well as firms) cannot ignore what is happening in other major markets. It is ironic that, in this case, the European-owned multinationals Philips and Thomson were also major television manufacturers in the USA and were partners with NBC in a consortium to develop a new standard for advanced television in the USA.

In 1986 the USA had supported the Japanese HDTV proposals, but after EU-95 was established in Europe, the Bush administration reopened the question. It ruled out a Japanese or European approach involving interfirm collaboration, and decided to ask the Federal Communications Commission (FCC) to organize a competition between contending technologies. The most important policy difference between the US case and Japan and Europe was that, in recognition of the political power of the broadcast networks in Congress, the FCC ruled that all proposed systems would have to be compatible with existing terrestrial transmissions (i.e. there would be no reliance on satellite broadcasting). One of the proposals from NHK of Japan was a version of its HDTV satellite transmission standard MUSE re-engineered to fit within a normal television channel. Just before the June 1990 deadline to enter the competition, one of the contenders, General Instrument, announced that it had developed an all-digital technology, DigiCipher, which compressed the high-definition signal sufficiently to fit within the 6 megahertz of a normal terrestrial channel. This announcement had an immediate effect on the US competition, so that by the end of 1992 there were only five of the original 21 systems left, and four of these were all-digital. It also ignited a fuse which smouldered away beneath the European HD-MAC technology over the next two years. Philips and Thomson switched their offer from a version of the European HD-MAC system to an all-digital system during the course of technical testing supervised by the FCC (Prentiss, 1994).

By the end of the test period, in May 1993, it was clear that there was very little to choose between the four remaining systems (NHK had pulled narrow-MUSE when it was clear that a digital system would be chosen). In order to avoid another round of expensive testing, and on the invitation of the chairman of the FCC's advisory committee for advanced television, the competitors came together to form the Grand Alliance of seven organizations (including Philips and Thomson) which would agree a single common format to propose to the FCC as the US HDTV standard. Thus, in the end, all three major television markets have opted for interfirm collaboration as the *modus operandi*. The difference, however, between the American approach and that taken in Japan and Europe was that technological choice was not handed to the firms at the outset of the process. It was this initial competition (and, by accident, the Americans may have stumbled on a paradigm for innovation in complex technologies) which provided the stimulus for technical progress, and which produced a major technological breakthrough in the application of digital compression technology to broadcasting. Following the General Instrument announcement of June 1990, the Motion Picture Experts Group of the International Standards Association has adopted a refinement of the underlying compression technology as the MPEG-2 standard for compressed digital video for broadcasting (up to and including HDTV quality). Both the Grand Alliance and the European Digital Video Group have embraced the MPEG-2 standard, and it is likely that Japan will eventually follow suit.

The Fall-out in Europe

At first the Eureka partners carried on as if events in the USA had changed nothing. Philips and Thomson continued to press the European Commission to adopt a new, tougher version of the 1986 MAC directive, which would have closed the loophole and would have required set-makers to build MAC circuitry into every large-screen television set sold in Europe, regardless of whether it would be used to receive MAC satellite broadcasts. The two major firms had put themselves into a difficult, and eventually impossible, position. In the USA they argued that fully digital technology could be developed quickly for deployment in 1996; in Europe they argued that digital television was a long way off, and that Europe should close ranks behind MAC. It proved more and more difficult to maintain this position as major European broadcasters, consumer groups, members of the European Parliament, and above all the British government began to oppose the HDTV strategy.

Despite allocating about £100 million in subsidies to the EU-95 programme, the British government began to speak out against the strategy. In the course of 1991/92, technology commissioner Filippo Pandolfi was trying to win support for an ECU 850 million programme to subsidize the making of HDTV programmes in order to pave the way for the introduction of wide-screen MAC and HD-MAC services. Britain initially opposed this using its familiar neo-liberal arguments, which failed to carry much conviction among its EC partners. The discussion became overheated when Jacques Delors accused John Major of reneging on an agreement to endorse the subsidy package at the Edinburgh summit of December 1992. In fact it was the Department of Trade and Industry's argument against the HDTV strategy on *technical* grounds which began to swing opinion against MAC. Under pressure from its own broadcasters, the German Research Ministry began to endorse a shift of tack for Europe, and was instrumental together with the DTI in setting up the European Launch Group for Digital Video Broadcasting (later shortened to the DVB group). Early in 1993, after a rearrangement of portfolios in the European Commission had given Martin Bangemann responsibility for HDTV, he announced that Europe would explore the options for an all-digital television technology and would no longer pursue its HD-MAC strategy.

Finally, in June 1993 Britain eventually agreed to a watered-down package of ECU 228 million for the making of programmes in any wide-screen format. A condition of this agreement was that the Commission would be asked to report to Council and Parliament on digital technologies later that year. The apparently unbreakable grip of Philips and Thomson (backed by the Dutch and French governments) on policy-making for advanced television in Europe had been loosened.

Digital Video Broadcasting: An Inclusive Coalition?

The campaign against HD-MAC was in some respects a broadcasters' revolt at being left out of the inner circle of policy-makers. The grouping around digital video broadcasting, which formally came together with the signing of a Memorandum of Understanding in November 1993, is a much more extensive and inevitably looser coalition of producer interests. Including both Rupert Murdoch's BSkyB and the French private channel Canal+, as well as the major European public broadcasters and the set-makers, the DVB group offers the possibility that Europe will be able to coordinate investments and regulation in a way which will lead to the development of a new market in digital broadcast television.[12]

Digital broadcasting offers a number of advantages over existing analogue technology, or the hybrid systems such as HD-MAC and Hi-Vision. Eliminating redundant information through digital coding and compression enables a single television channel to carry either high-definition pictures or several standard definition pictures, or some combination of the two which can be chosen by the broadcaster. Thus it offers considerable economies to broadcasters (e.g. up to ten digital channels on a single satellite transponder) and in principle reduces the entry barriers to the television industry. However, it is also possible that the first entrants to the market could use proprietary versions of the technology to lock-in consumers to their services and make it difficult for new entrants to have access to the installed base of equipment. It is becoming increasingly clear that one of the major economic assets held by satellite broadcasters such as BSkyB and Canal+ is the computerized database of customers which can be made available to advertisers and merchandisers. The use of smart card technology for encryption of pay-TV channels (known as conditional access) gives satellite and cable operators a wealth of information about their customers which is not available to conventional terrestrial broadcasters.

Hence the policy debate has moved from the industrial policy concerns of creating new technologies to protect Europes high-tech industry, to the competition policy issues of how to regulate the new digital technology to prevent unfair discrimination against new market entrants by the established channels. In making this shift, the European Commission has changed its role from that of guarantor of the Philips/Thomson position to that of facilitator and broker. Other directorates besides DG XIII are now making the running, including DG X which has responsibility for audiovisual policy, and DG IV which covers competition policy. During the lifetime of EU-95, DG IV determined that the strategic importance of HDTV overrode the competition issues. Now, however, with the change of focus away from consumer electronics manufacture to the issue of broadcasting services, competition issues are very much to the fore. In the current world of analogue PAL TV, incompatible *de facto* standards have developed around the encryption technologies chosen by BSkyB and Canal+. In effect, if a new entrant (on, say, the Astra satellite) wishes to charge consumers for watching its programmes, it has to adopt the Videocrypt system chosen by Sky and now used in all the set-top boxes designed for Astra. One of the objectives of the European Commission in the current discussion[13] is to ensure that there is a standard common interface built into the new digital terminals so that new entrants can have access to services without being forced to adopt the technologies chosen by the first movers.

New television services using new technologies present a complex innovation problem, with the ever-present danger of market failure where the perceived risks to entrepreneurs outweigh the perceived advantages. It is possible that advanced television will be seen as part of the information infrastructure, and thus a focus for further interventionist policies. It is more likely, however, that most of the initiative will be left to the private sector (with some EU subsidies), leaving the European Commission in the role of helping to sustain the consensus within the DVB in order to reduce uncertainty and to coordinate the investments in hardware and software required for successful innovation. In this role, the Commission will go well beyond the purely regulatory function of the FCC, and there is no equivalent in the USA to the DVB. The Grand Alliance is concerned solely with proposing an HDTV standard and does not include the broadcasting networks. The European policy focus on wide-screen as well as digital television is not matched in the USA where, despite the Grand Alliance, it is likely that the economics of broadcasting will mean that the new digital technologies will be deployed to proliferate standard definition channels rather than bring in wide-screen services.

Conclusions

The television market in Europe is becoming more pluralistic, and new satellite channels and cable systems challenge the established positions of the older (mainly public) broadcasters. Had Europe, like Japan, forged a business coalition which gave established broadcasters a key role in determining HDTV policy within a watertight regulatory framework, then it is possible that the MAC strategy would have worked. However, even in Japan, where these conditions were present, there is considerable (if as yet muted) opposition to the Hi-Vision system. In Japan, as in Europe, analogue television technology is being deemed obsolete, and close attention is being paid to the claims of the American industry and the White House that the swift adoption of fully digital television will accelerate the journey down the information superhighway. The convergence of digital technologies around compression standards such as MPEG appears to lend weight to these arguments, with telecommunications companies such as BT, AT&T and Bell Atlantic making use of it to test systems which will offer video on demand to individual consumers using the existing telephone network.

　　Some of these claims about convergence are exaggerated, and some of the technical claims made for the universal superiority of digital technologies over analogue are simply spurious. Nevertheless, the events in Europe of 1991–93 suggest that the term 'digital' carries a powerful symbolic meaning which becomes an important part of the political debate. The headlong rush into the bright new technological future offered by seamless digital information infrastructures does appear to have influenced the debate over policy choices. The equivocation of Philips and Thomson did considerably weaken their position, and that of DG XIII which championed the MAC strategy. New faces are now at the television policy table, and the television marketplace is becoming more fragmented as the mass audiences disintegrate. The consumer electronics industry, however, remains highly concentrated and just as much dominated by Philips and Thomson in 1994 as it was in 1986. If digital television does have a bright future in Europe, it will be these firms that manufacture and sell the chips and the boxes and the new wide-screen televisions. The need for an effective meso-corporatist coalition to bring digital television to market is as pressing as ever, and the responsibilities of the European Commission in helping to broker the DVB coalition are considerable.

This case shows that informal alliances between producer interests to open up markets for new technologies are unlikely to suceed unless the basis of collective action can be made sufficiently inclusive to incorporate the key players. In the case of Eureka-95 project, policy-makers privileged an exclusive alliance between Philips and Thomson; mobilization by excluded broadcasters helped to bring about its failure. In the case of the new DVB coalition, the basis of collective action is sufficiently inclusive, but it remains to be seen whether the interests of the different parties converge sufficiently for voluntary agreements to stick, and for self-regulation to reduce or even make unnecessary the kinds of directive which failed to mandate the innovation of the MAC television standard.

Notes

1. I would like to thank the Economic and Social Research Council and the Department of Trade and Industry for supporting the research on which this chapter is based, and the MZES for providing me with the opportunity to write it.
2. According to Peter Drucker (1993), this is the only example of a successful MITI project. Its efforts in orchestrating the car industry were ignored by Honda and Suzuki, and its policies for pharmaceuticals, steel and telecommunications have been expensive failures. There are, of course, opposing views, notably that of Johnson (1982).
3. To understand television technology, it is important to distinguish among production, transmission and reception, since the three aspects can be, to some extent, decoupled. The Japanese system uses 1,125 lines at 60 Hz to record HDTV images at a bandwidth of 32 Mhz. This bandwidth is too great, even for satellite transmission. The images are digitized and compressed to around 8 Mhz using a technology called MUSE, and transmitted as analogue waveforms. The receiver decodes the MUSE-encoded signal

and displays it in wide-screen (16×9) high definition (1,125/60), and the (European) 1,250/50 production standards can still be used to make programmes, even if the transmission and reception technologies are changed.

4. Thorn EMI's television interests were bought by Thomson when it acquired Ferguson in 1987. Philips and Bosch merged their professional television equipment interests in a 50/50 joint venture, BTS, which is now wholly-owned by Philips.

5. MAC provided clearer pictures than PAL or SECAM, and was optimized for satellite transmissions. It carried multiple digital sound channels, useful for multilingual pan-European broadcasting.

6. Some consumers were already using large dishes to receive television pictures beamed down from medium-powered telecommunications satellites. These pictures were either feeds (such as news and sporting events) between terrestrial broadcasts, or pictures transacted to the head-ends of cable systems for rediffusion to households.

7. Perhaps not surprising when one considers that the initial price of a Hi-Vision set was the equivalent of US$30,000 and the current price is US$6,000.

8. Thanks to semiconductor technology it now costs very little to convert between NTSC, PAL and SECAM standards, and adds very little to the price of a set to have multi-standard televisions, as, for example, are all the sets sold in Greece, which now uses both SECAM and PAL. NHK developed such a converter between HD-MAC and MUSE so that 1,250/50 pictures of Wimbledon 1993 and the 1994 Winter Olympics could be shown in Japan in 1,125/60. At the time that EU-95 was set up, it was strongly argued by Philips, for example, that 60 Hz to 50 Hz conversion from 1,125 lines would be expensive, technically difficult and would degrade picture quality. It has been expensive, and even difficult, but picture quality is excellent.

9. Britain and Luxembourg apparently vetoed a clause which would also have mandated MAC for medium-power satellites.

10. The profligacy of the BSB operation is described in detail in Chippindale and Franks (1991). To launch their service, BSB spent £1 billion against Sky's £200,000, largely because BSB had to have its own satellites to use the official British frequencies.

11. Part of the delay was due to problems with chip design. BSB used D-MAC, with multiple audio channels which could be used for other purposes, such as datacasting business information, whereas continental broadcasters were to use D2-MAC with only two audio channels so it could fit the bandwidth of European cable systems.

12. The first digital video television service offered direct to consumers was launched by DIRECTV in the USA in June 1994. This Hughes-backed venture is the third attempt to launch a DBS service in the USA, and requires consumers to rent or buy a small dish and a digital set-top decoder in order to receive an eventual total of over one hundred and fifty television channels.

13. The new television technology directive (to replace the MAC derivative was adopted on 17 November 1994. It embodies the position adopted at the Council of Ministers in June 1994 that the industry rather than the EU should determine appropriate technologies.

References

Cawson, A. (ed.) (1985) *Organized Interests and the State: Studies in Meso-corporatism.* London: Sage.

Cawson, A. (1986) 'Meso-corporatism and industrial policy: the anatomy of a successful initiative', *ESRC Corporatism and Accountability Newsletter*, November 1986.

Cawson, A., Morgan, K., Webber, D., Holmes, P. and Stevens, A. (1990) *Hostile Brothers: Competition and Closure in the European Electronics Industry*. Oxford: Clarendon Press.

Chippindale, P. and Franks, S. (1991) *Dished! The Rise and Fall of British Satellite Broadcasting*. London: Simon and Schuster.

Drucker, P. (1993) Interview in *Wired*, vol. 1, no. 3, July/August.

Johnson, C. (1982) *MITI and the Japanese Miracle: The Growth of Industrial Policy 1925–1975*. Stanford: Stanford University Press.

Prentiss, S. (1994) *HDTV: High Definition Television* (2nd· edn). Blue Ridge Summit, PA: Tab Books.

Sharp, M. and Shearman, C. (1987) *European Technological Collaboration*. Chatham House Papers No. 36. London: Routledge/RIIA.

Political Organization in the European Aerospace Industry

The Case of Airbus Industrie

Desmond Hickie

Airbus Industrie – A European High-technology Alliance

Airbus Industrie is a major European business alliance, probably Europe's biggest and arguably its most successful. This case study analyses the Airbus Industrie in order to explain the preconditions necessary for the creation of Europe's major civil aerospace alliance; the strategies, operating structures and procedures that have enabled the alliance to grow and develop over a quarter of a century; the public policy issues which have come to bear upon the alliance, in particular those at a European Union level; and the processes through which the alliance has attempted to influence the policy process.

Airbus Industrie is a strategic alliance of four major European aerospace companies. It was set up in 1969 to design, build, sell and maintain airliners with over one hundred seats. Its partners are: Aerospatiale (a 37.8 per cent shareholder) from France; Deutsche Aerospace, a Daimler Benz subsidiary (also 37.8 per cent) from Germany; British Aerospace (20 per cent) from Britain; and Construcciones Aeronauticas (4 per cent) from Spain. The alliance currently produces five aircraft varying from the short-to-medium range 150-seater A320 to the 290-seater, long-range A340. Two more, the A319 and A330, will shortly enter production.

The alliance's formal structure is a French one, a Groupement d'Intérêt Économique (GIE), formed in 1970. The structure has the advantage of being a formal legal entity, but one which allows companies to come together to collaborate for a range of common purposes whilst allowing them to remain wholly independent for the remainder of their activities. The GIE structure allows for a central management structure to act as decision-maker for the alliance's joint activities and to provide a focal point for customer relations and marketing. This feature is particularly important for Airbus Industrie because the design and manufacturing of a complex aircraft require a high level of coordination, and because customer airlines wish to have a single relationship with a single airframe supplier, not a series of parallel relationships with a group of collaborating partners.

How successful has this alliance been? Airbus Industrie is the only manufacturer of large airlines in the European Union. Boeing and McDonnell Douglas are its only significant competitors worldwide. In 1992 its turnover was US$7.6 billion. In its first fifteen years to 1989 the alliance sold five hundred aircraft. It achieved its one thousandth sale in 1993, only four years later. By any reckoning this performance makes Airbus Industrie the only major non-American player in the world airliner market.

Why Was It Necessary to Form Airbus Industrie?

The need to create the Airbus Industrie partnership, indeed the existence of only three major players in the world airliner market, reflects the combination of technological risks, financial risks and uncertain demand which characterize that market. Richard Welch, a former Boeing executive has claimed that 'the risks are greater in this business than in any other compared to the returns' (quoted in Newhouse, 1982).

A large, modern airliner incorporates advances from a range of technologies, including aerodynamics, materials, avionics and jet engines. To sell an airliner, the product must not only be offered at a competitive price, it must also be attractive to passengers and economical to operate. Such advantages are derived primarily from its technological features which give the aircraft its structural weight, payload, range, cruising speed, fuel economy, maintenance costs, and so on. The R&D necessary to give an aircraft a technological 'edge' is enormously costly. A new airliner costs several billion dollars to develop (two billion in the case of the A320). This sum will be spent over four or five years before the new aircraft is ready to bring to market. If the aircraft is popular, it will then be sold steadily for about ten years before the project begins to show a profit. However, technological success alone cannot guarantee an airliner's profitability. As the recession of the early 1990s has shown, air-ticket sales (and thus the demand for new airliners) fluctuate markedly with general levels of economic activity.

From a European point of view, the world civil aircraft market in the 1960s and 1970s looked even less promising. About 60 per cent of world demand for airliners lay in the USA, whose domestic market was protected by tariff barriers, and 94 per cent of world production was in the hands of three American manufacturers: Boeing, McDonnell Douglas and Lockheed (Airbus Industrie, 1986). Furthermore, European civil aircraft manufacturers had proved incapable of building airliners that could threaten American market leadership, with the sole exception of the Vickers Viscount. (Even in the 1990s the US market is likely to account for 30–40 per cent of world demand; the European share being perhaps 25–30 per cent.)

In these market conditions it was clear by the mid-1960s that no European aircraft manufacturer had the technological base, the funds or the domestic market to mount a meaningful challenge to the American 'Big Three'. Equally, even Sud Aviation (of France), whose finances and technology made it the best placed of the original Airbus partners, was not sufficiently strong to take the lead on any new airliner project and force its potential partners to take a subordinate, subcontractor's role. Thus in 1969 Sud Aviation, Hawker Siddeley and Deutsche Airbus came together to form Airbus Industrie, and were joined by Construcciones Aeronauticas (CASA) the following year.

However, the creation of Airbus Industrie was not simply the product of market forces, impelling the aircraft manufacturers into an alliance. It was also very much a matter of public policy. Given the extent, nature and time-span of the risks faced by airliner manufacturers, none was able to undertake new aircraft development projects without significant government support, financial and otherwise. For their part, the governments of Britain and France were unwilling (in the light of previous failures) to fund further national airliner projects. This was not even an option in the German case as its aviation industry lacked the technological knowledge to develop a major new airliner without substantial foreign participation. Nevertheless, all three governments wished to encourage the growth of a healthy aviation industry which offered prospects of well paid employment and 'technology pull' from other high-technology sectors (e.g. new materials), as well as having great strategic importance. Hence, they too were drawn towards the idea of an international collaborative project which would both be less risky and reduce the extent of their financial commitment. (In the event, the British government had an attack of 'cold feet' and left the project in April 1969, only to return in 1978. Hawker Siddeley remained in the project with the support of its French and German partners, both private and public). The two primary forms of assistance that the partner governments have given to Airbus Industrie have been launch aid and 'soft' loans to purchasers. Launch aid is a payment made by a government to a manufacturer to pay for the research and development necessary to build a new aircraft. Normally it is expected that the aid will be repaid via a levy on the eventual sales of the aircraft. The US Department of Commerce has estimated that by 1990 Airbus Industrie had received $26 billion in launch aid (at 1990 prices). More recently the consortium's sales success have allowed it to pay off $600 million in 1991 and $700 million in 1992. Having assisted the development of the aircraft, supportive governments have then increased its attractiveness to potential customers by enabling Airbus Industrie to offer cheap loans, extended repayments schemes and advantageous leasing arrangements.

For twenty-five years Airbus Industrie has been seen as a flagship of successful European technological and industrial collaboration. However, until the mid-1980s the European Commission was very much a bystander in matters concerning the partnership. Article 223 of the Treaty of Rome reserves to member states policy-making issues concerning defence industries, which has been taken to include civil aerospace because of its strategic potential. Directorate-General III (DG III), with responsibility for the internal Community market, had one official responsible for all transport industries. DG IV's aerospace policy input was inhibited because matters such as acquisitions, mergers and state aid in aerospace were inevitably interpreted as impinging on the defence interest of member states. DG XII, with responsibility for R&D, did develop a concrete aerospace interest, there being an aerospace element to the BRITE-Euram programme worth $65 million per annum. However, it was within the responsibilities of DG I, for external affairs, that the first really significant Commission breakthrough into civil aerospace policy-making occurred. During the Uruguay Round GATT negotiations, DG I came to assume an increasingly prominent role in drawing up European negotiating positions, especially as the talks moved towards a conclusion in 1993. Civil aerospace subsidies were one of the two or three most contentious issues in the negotiations, with the US objecting to subsidies for Airbus Industrie in particular, and the Europeans counterclaiming that Boeing and McDonnell Douglas were indirectly subsidized by US Department of Defense and NASA research projects. Furthermore, the ending of the Cold War made national governments less willing to spend heavily on aerospace R&D and implied an increasing tendency towards transnational mergers and acquisitions in the industry. Hence DG XII and DG III have come under pressure, notably from AECMA, the European aerospace industry's umbrella body, to take more interest and provide more support for civil aerospace.

Competitive Advantage at Airbus Industrie

Airbus Industrie's ambition has always been to become one of the handful of major players in world civil aerospace. In the early 1970s this was interpreted as taking a 30 per cent share of the market for wide-bodied jets. This was a high ambition, given that in 1973 the three major US manufacturers had a 94 per cent market share (of which Boeing's was 60 per cent). By the late 1980s, however, the alliance's ambitions had grown much further, so that they aimed to achieve a 30 per cent share of the world market for large jet airliners of all kinds. Between 1987 and 1991 its order book rose from 20 per cent to 30 per cent of all large airliners on order, so that its managing director, Jean Pierson, could suggest that over the next fifteen years the consortium should achieve a 40 per cent market share, provided that it made no serious mistakes (*Flight International*, 15–21 May 1991).

Airbus Industrie has been able to achieve a measure of competitive advantage with a long-term strategy based upon two fundamentals: the building of a range or 'family' of aircraft, and lower operating costs for its aircraft, achieved by using the most advanced technologies available. Had Airbus Industrie produced only the A300 and derivatives of it, it could not have obtained a large and sustained market share. An aircraft manufacturer needs to build a family of aircraft with common features capable of serving a wide range of its customer airlines' service requirements (e.g. for short-range, high-density services and for longer-range, low-density services). Such a family offers the airline the prospect of reduced operating costs (e.g. common cockpit layouts mean lower crew training costs, common component parts mean lower spares inventories). Technological advances have been achieved in many aspects of Airbus design (e.g. the increasing use of weight-saving carbon-fibre-reinforced plastics for parts of aircraft structures), but most significantly in the use of fly-by-wire technology.

Organizing the Alliance

The design and manufacture of advanced aircraft within a strategic alliance is not an unalloyed good. There are diseconomies of collaboration that must be overcome: the time taken to agree major decisions (e.g. the launch of a new aircraft); compromises in agreeing what design to pursue; agreeing who does what; and even more prosaic matters such as travel and translation costs (Hickie, 1991). It has been estimated that these contributed to Boeing's costs being 30 per cent below Airbus' in 1986 (*Sunday Times*, 2 March 1986).

Good organization has a key role in overcoming such diseconomies and in making such an alliance viable. International take-overs or mergers are very difficult in the aerospace industry, given the strategic significance of companies to national governments. Equally, for each of the partners, Airbus work is only a part of its portfolio of aerospace activities. A jointly-owned public limited company was inappropriate as the partners would not have endowed it with a sufficient capital base to allow potential customers to feel secure. Hence the attraction of the GIE structure which allows for collaborative management of projects and for each partner to be liable to the full extent of its assets for the joint activity.

Within the GIE structure, formal control rests with a General Meeting of Members, in which each of the partners has voting rights proportionate to its investment in the alliance. Any decisions require an 81 per cent majority ensuring that only CASA among the partners can be outvoted. In practice, key strategic decisions, such as the launch of a new aircraft, are taken by a supervisory board of very senior executives from the boards of the partner companies. Initially it had seventeen members, but this proved increasingly unwieldy, and in 1989 was reduced to five (Airbus Industrie, 1989). Day-to-day decision-making is dealt with by an executive board of seven members which meets monthly and is chaired by Jean Pierson. The executive board is crucial to the successful functioning of the alliance because it: prepares the ground for the strategic decisions to be taken by the supervisory board, whose function should be somewhat formal if the partners are in agreement; makes key decisions in pursuit of the strategy agreed by the supervisory board; and provides oversight of the management of the consortium's programmes. Within this decision-making framework, Airbus managers run the consortium's programmes and supervise the work of the partner companies. In this context each partner's position is akin to that of a subcontractor having to produce work to an Airbus specification.

To understand how this formal system works in practice, it is best to see how it functions at three key stages of the alliance's work: launching new products, dividing work on projects, and after-sales servicing. If a possible niche for a new aircraft is perceived by the partners, the niche will be analysed and defined on the basis of marketing studies both by Airbus Industrie itself and by its partner companies, who then pool their thoughts to arrive at an agreed outline specification for the aircraft. This process is both duplicatory and time-consuming but has been a considerable area of success for Airbus, notably because the consortium has enabled it to design aircraft to meet the needs of growing sectors of the world market (e.g. the A340 for long distance routes with low passenger density) not well provided for by aircraft designed to meet the needs of the US domestic market. On the basis of this brief, each of the partner companies and Airbus itself produces competitive design studies for the new aircraft. Again this is duplicatory and time-consuming, but it is defended because it allows a pooling of ideas from which to arrive at an agreed outline design for the aircraft. Once a market niche and outline design have been defined to the satisfaction of the executive board, the supervisory board agrees the project. Finance has then to be sought from partner governments and from banks.

The precise division of the work of designing and building the new aircraft is both a vitally important and contentious one. It determines the quality of the final product and the extent of partners' benefits from it. The division is agreed by the executive board and generally accords to the proportions to which the partners agree to finance the project. To a significant extent, partners have come to specialize in particular areas of work (e.g. British Aerospace in wings, CASA in carbon-fibre structures). Nevertheless, disputes arise because different areas of work generate different revenues, some areas of work can develop a partner's technological capability, others do not; and some areas of work (notably final assembly of the aircraft) attract more prestige. Until the development of the A321 and the A330/340, final assembly had always been done by Aerospatiale in Toulouse, with the customization to meet particular airlines' needs being done by DASA in Hamburg. German determination to obtain the prestige, experience and revenues associated with the final assembly of the A321 has led to a new division of work in which the final assembly and customization can both take place on the same site (Hamburg for the A321 and Toulouse for the A330/340).

Customer relations are managed in a significantly different manner from earlier aspects of production. Purchasing airlines find it essential to deal with a single supplier, not four partners. Hence Airbus Industrie itself deals with all aspects of marketing, sales, contracts, crew training and the supply of spares.

The GIE form of organization has proved very successful in allowing the alliance to develop in an atmosphere of considerable mutual trust. However, by 1987 it was clear that its precise interpretation at Airbus was too slow, cumbersome and lacked financial clarity. This led to the appointment of 'four wise men' (bankers and industrialists) who produced recommendations for streamlining reforms, which led in 1989 to: the reduction in the size of the supervisory board; a redefinition of Pierson's role to give him more authority; an increased role for the executive board, and the appointment of a finance director. This latter change was an attempt to ensure better cost control over the Airbus work of the partner companies. As a GIE, Airbus Industrie does not have to produce full accounts – its detailed financial results are incorporated within the accounts of each of its partner companies. This led to a situation in which it was felt that partner companies sometimes overcharged the consortium for work done and in which the American manufacturers and government became increasingly suspicious that Airbus Industrie was receiving subsidies illegal under the 1979 GATT agreement.

Public Policy and Government Affairs

The most significant recurring public policy decision to affect Airbus Industrie during its first twenty-five years has been the need to receive the approval of the partners' governments for the financing necessary to fund the R&D for successive new aircraft. This has been a matter for the national governments acting in consultation, as it is they who provide the money. However, the European Commission's increasingly prominent role in the GATT negotiations on civil aircraft subsidies since the mid-1980s has given Airbus Industrie's public policy-making concerns a specifically EU dimension.

Because of their continuing commitment to Airbus Industrie, the partner governments established their own intergovernmental structure to monitor its work. In many respects this shadows the alliance's own formal structure. Ministerial meetings take place largely to give formal approval to changes in intergovernmental agreements concerning Airbus, though by the late 1980s such meetings had become somewhat more businesslike, reflecting growing government concerns about the cost of Airbus projects and deteriorating relations with the USA in the GATT negotiations. The British government showed great reluctance to join the A320 project until the approach of a general election and the presence of British Aerospace factories in or near marginal seats concentrated its mind. Equally, Airbus Industrie's capacity to develop the A321 without launch aid was a great relief to all the partner governments, both in terms of the public finances and European/US relations. An intergovernmental committee of senior civil servants, representing national government departments responsible for civil aerospace (e.g. the Air Division of the DTI), meets formally to agree advice to ministers on key public policy issues but, as with Airbus Industrie's own executive board, these senior officials are in regular contact and have considerable command of the details of policy, and so are in a strong position to influence the stance taken by ministers. An Airbus executive committee of more junior national civil servants meets monthly to monitor progress on the detailed implementation of Airbus programmes (Hickie,

1991). Normally, Airbus Industrie leaves its partners to deal directly with their own national governments, though it does attempt to ensure consultation and collaboration on significant issues coming before the intergovernmental machinery (Hickie, 1991; Hayward, 1986). The Airbus partners have their own government affairs structures and specialists who are engaged in multifunctional relationships with their governments covering a range of issues broader than Airbus alone.

In the key area of obtaining government approval for the launch of new aircraft projects, lobbying was essentially a matter for partner company/ national government discussions. Each of the partner companies has a long-standing and multifaceted relationship with its national government. It requires government help not only to launch and sell Airbus aircraft, but also to launch and sell many of its other civil aircraft, to support the development of and to purchase its military aircraft, and to provide more general R&D support. Furthermore, these company/government relationships stretch back over many decades, more than eighty years in the British case. As a consequence, many company officials have relationships with government officials at a similar level in appropriate government departments, such as the Department of Trade and Industry and Ministry of Defence in Britain. Given the strength and sensitivity of these relationships and the importance of new aircraft launches to the Airbus partners, they have preferred to lobby their national governments directly and have been sensitive to Airbus officials going 'over their heads' in such matters. In general, Airbus officials' role has been to present a well developed marketing and technical case for the launch of a new aircraft, which the Airbus partners would use to help persuade their governments to finance the project. Hence the lobbying before important ministerial and inter-governmental committee meetings was essentially national. In France, Airbus officials, in particular Jean Pierson, have achieved access to ministers on some issues, but this is primarily because Pierson is well connected and French, and because the consortium's headquarters is at Toulouse.

In general, the companies take steps to coordinate their lobbying activities, but some issues are contentious between them, such as the division of work on particular Airbus aircraft, and hence can give rise to intergovernmental disagreements during the negotiating process. For example, the decision to locate assembly of the A321 in Germany instead of at Toulouse (like all other Airbus aircraft) was the result of lengthy and contentious negotiations, mainly between the French and German governments. National and European aviation industry representative organizations, such as the Society of British Aerospace Contractors (SBAC), tend not to be greatly involved in the lobbying process even though many of their members are significantly affected by the outcomes of the political decision-making. The issues concerned are too sensitive to the main contractors, whilst the membership of bodies like the SBAC is too diffuse to allow them to draw up the clear and precise positions needed to intervene effectively in such negotiations. For example, some members (e.g. Rolls-Royce) may be major suppliers to Boeing as well as to Airbus. As a consequence, the process is in essence one of company/national government lobbying, and of international negotiation.

European Community relations with the USA worsened markedly from about 1988, as Airbus Industrie's market share showed steady improvement, not least in the USA itself, and as aerospace industries worldwide began to suffer with the end of the Cold War and the onset of a major recession. In July 1992, a European/US bilateral agreement on civil aerospace products (the Large Civil Aircraft Agreement) was announced. Although initially it was quite well received in Europe, not least by Airbus (Airbus Industrie, 1993), it soon became clear that the accord controlled launch aid (which was limited to 33 per cent of development costs) better than it did the more indirect R&D subsidies provided by the US government to Boeing and McDonnell Douglas. Hence, when broader negotiations took place in 1993 to draw up an agreement of civil aerospace subsidiaries that would cover all GATT signatory nations, DG I, as the EC's spokesperson, took a much firmer line. In this it was assisted by: the appointment of the pugnacious Leon Brittan as EC Trade Commissioner; the adoption of a firmer line by the national governments, in particular the French; and a significantly better lobbying performance by Airbus Industrie and its partner companies. The outcome, when the GATT talks were concluded in December 1993, was a stalemate. At the last minute the US trade representative Mickey Kantor refused to sign a draft that would both have restricted launch aid and have dealt far more firmly with US indirect subsidies.

Boeing and McDonnell Douglas were initially pleased at having avoided tighter controls over their government subsidies, whilst the Airbus partners were somewhat disappointed. However, there are some grounds for believing that both American optimism and European pessimism may well prove misplaced. The American refusal to sign both widely antagonized other GATT members and illustrated the validity of the European case that American civil aerospace was heavily dependent upon hidden subsidies (which had previously been hotly denied). Both factors augur well for the European side should talks resume (Hickie, 1994). More broadly, the stronger Commission line taken after July 1992 has helped to create a greater confidence and a stronger impetus in the EU as a focus for European aerospace policy-making. The industry has begun to call more loudly for a radical expansion of the EU financial support for civil aerospace R&D begun under the EU industrial materials research programme BRITE-Euram Area 5. This both reflects a wish to copy the Americans and to avoid GATT restrictions on launch aid, and an awareness that the fiscal problems faced by national governments are making them less willing to provide support to their national champion companies.

Recession also brings European competition policy to the fore, as the prospects for a spate of industrial restructuring rise, bringing with it the possibility of transnational mergers and take-overs. On a different front, the industry is calling for a European aerospace standards authority so that the industry is less reliant on the American Federal Aviation Authority. Taken together, these developments reflect the growing incapacity of European states to develop satisfactory civil aerospace policies and have led to a growing call from within the industry for a European civil aerospace policy. Almost inevitably the needs of Airbus Industrie would be at the heart of any such policy.

At present, it can be argued, the Commission is not well placed to develop a more proactive policy-making role. Article 223 restricts its powers, whilst its present responsibilities are divided between four directorates-general. Its policy-making activities have been criticized as incoherent, ineffectual and on too small a scale. For example, it is said that the Commission wants European aerospace companies to compete with the US but is reluctant to approve mergers that might enable them so to do. Equally, the Commission was unable to prevent both the rival A319 and Regioloner aircraft projects proceeding, arguably duplicating European effort and wasting scarce technological resources (Hickie, 1994). Significant constitutional and organizational changes are likely to be necessary if the EU is to take greater responsibility for European civil aerospace policy.

The GATT affair has encouraged Airbus Industrie, its partner companies and the European aerospace industry at large to become more professional in its dealings with the EU. Prior to 1991 only DASA and Aerospatiale were directly represented in Brussels, and the Aerospatiale representative was more concerned with NATO matters than the EC. In 1991, as the GATT issue rose to prominence, British Aerospace set up a small office in Brussels specifically to deal with the Community, whilst the balance of the Aerospatiale representative's work has shifted significantly towards civil work. Airbus itself is not directly represented in Brussels, but liaison with the EU is a key part of the work of Michel Dechelotte, its director of international affairs. Significantly, Dechelotte's government affairs function was only separated organizationally, from public affairs more broadly, in 1990 as the GATT issue became more salient. Following the perceived failure to have the Airbus case put convincingly and forcefully enough during the 1992 bilateral negotiations with the USA, the Airbus partners came to rely less upon their national governments to put their case for them to DG I. More emphasis has been placed on dealing directly with DG I officials through the coordinated efforts of Dechelotte and the partners' Brussels offices. It is important to note here the more prominent and proactive role allowed by the partner companies to Airbus officials in this matter. In these dealings with the Commission, Dechelotte and his colleagues are being allowed a more significant part than in relations with national governments. Equally, more effort has been put into collecting and collating the data necessary to give DG I officials a strong case to present in international negotiations. Although these improvements have been made primarily *vis-à-vis* DG I and the GATT talks, the lessons have not been lost on those concerned and one would expect them to be applied to the broader spectrum of Airbus/Commission relations.

Parallel developments have also taken place at an industry-wide level. AECMA set-up a taskforce to develop and present the industry's case during the GATT negotiations, and its two reports had a significant influence upon the Commission's negotiating stance. More interestingly, some AECMA members, including Europe's leading airframe manufacturers, came to perceive the association as being too broadly based to represent their particular views and so created the European Aerospace Industries Council (EAIC) in February 1993. EAIC representation is very senior – chief executive or deputy chief executive. This, and the coherence and authority of the views the council can express gave it significant influence with the Commission in the GATT talks, and is expected to give it a more wide-ranging influence in future (Hickie, 1994).

Conclusions

Despite its alleged $26 billion of subsidy and its low returns to investors, Airbus Industrie can still be judged a major European industrial and technological success. It has moved from a 0 per cent to a 30 per cent or so market share since 1973, in the face of severe competition from heavily subsidized, well established rivals with a huge domestic market. It is truly a long-run, strategic investment. How can its experience be summarized?

1. No doubt in 1969 each of the Airbus partner companies would have preferred to retain or develop an independent capacity to build large airliners, but the risks and resources required were too great either for them or their governments acting nationally.

2. To be successful the Airbus alliance needed a clear long-term strategy to build its competitive advantage, as well as effective structures and processes. Competitive advantage has been built via the development of a closely integrated family of technologically advanced aircraft. The GIE organization form has allowed the building of structures and procedures within which collaboration and mutual confidence has been fostered and in which inevitable tensions have been ameliorated. However, it has also proved cumbersome at times and may not be the most effective mechanism for controlling the alliance's costs. As Airbus Industrie has moved into an era of lower subsidies and, it hopes, of consistent profitability, it may be that significant organizational developments need to take place.

3. Throughout its lifetime Airbus Industrie has been a public policy concern. The key issues to which it has given rise have had their roots in its need for successive injections of launch aid and 'soft' loans. These subsidies and the alliance's success in the marketplace pushed civil aerospace to the forefront of the GATT negotiations. Whilst the international regulation of civil aerospace subsidies remains unresolved, the GATT negotiations have played a key role in emphasizing the need for European civil aerospace policy and the crucial part the EU must play in its development.

4. Airbus Industrie and its partner companies have always been heavily involved in government affairs activities but, again largely because of the GATT negotiation, these activities have both become more professionalized and have developed a much stronger EU focus.

References

Airbus Industrie (1986) *Airbus Industrie Briefing*, Toulouse.
Airbus Industrie (1989) *Airbus Letter*, Toulouse, July 1989.
Airbus Industrie (1993) *Airbus Letter*, Toulouse, January 1993.
Hayward, K. (1986) *International Collaboration in Civil Aerospace*. London: Pinter.
Hickie, D. (1991) 'Airbus Industrie: a case study in European high technology cooperation', in Hilpert, U. (ed). *Techno-industrial Innovation and the State*. London: Routledge.
Hickie, D. (1994) 'Airbus Industrie: the struggle in the GATT', in Pedlar, R. and van Schendelen, M. P. C. M. (eds) *Lobbying the European Union*. Aldershot: Dartmouth.
Newhouse, R. (1982) *The Sporty Game*. New York: Alfred Knopf.

European Bioindustry

Justin Greenwood and **Karsten Ronit**

The New Bioindustry in Europe

Productive applications of biological organisms have been used for centuries in the manufacture of everyday products such as cheeses and beer. In the twentieth century, the invention of penicillin manifested an important medical breakthrough. Modern 'third generation' bioindustry, however, is characterized by the application of advanced gene-splicing technology (recombinant DNA techniques), developed from the late 1970s. Within the past twenty years this has led to a considerable expansion and change of the European landscape in bioindustry. New small and medium-sized firms dedicated to biotechnology have been added to leading transnational corporations interested in the contribution of biotechnology to their industrial products. A cluster of producer branches has evolved from the diversification of the chemical, pharmaceutical and food processing industries and forms the backbone of the 'new bioindustries'. Indeed, bioindustry is not an 'industry' but an industrial technology with applications across a number of different sectors. These features have been important issues in the emerging pattern of interest representation, together with the emphasis placed upon bioindustry by the European Commission as a competitive technology for the twenty-first century, and the environmental consequences of gene-splicing activities. Established industry associations in contributory sectors have not always kept pace with all of these developments.

Bioindustry is unquestionably a strategic asset for the European Union in its quest for global competitiveness in the next century. A recent consultancy report for the Commission predicted that the European biotechnology market would grow fifteen fold to reach £63 billion by the year 2000, and provide two million new jobs (Cookson, 1994). This potential makes it a favoured child of European public policy. Most recently, the strategic position of bioindustry as a twenty-first century technology with

75

which to compete on a global basis has been reiterated in the White Paper *Growth, Competitiveness and Employment* agreed at the heads of summit in December 1993 (Commission, 1993). Biotechnology bristles with all the high-tech glamour, mystery and promise needed to make it attractive to European public policy-makers, and, despite a number of false dawns throughout the 1980s, is ensured highly favoured status through the range of policy initiatives available to the Commission. The Commission is always pleased to be associated with the status of high-technology producer sectors: it fits well with its self-perception as a growing force of today and the inevitable shape of tomorrow. This partly explains the intense activity of the Commission in high technology areas. It is worth contrasting this with the case of tourism (Case 9): the absence of European Union competencies in this cross-sectoral area might in part be because tourism lacks the status appeal of biotechnology. To some extent, the range of Euro competencies in bioindustry may reflect more bioindustry's appeal to public policy-makers than it does the efforts of private interest representation.

The strategic position of bioindustry in the EU means that it is essential for meaningful channels of communication to operate among the range of interests involved, be they public policy, scientific or producer. The Commission's policies today need to be the right ones, and of sound technical quality, if bioindustry is to fulfil its promise tomorrow. It has therefore shown more than a passing interest in seeking to ensure the presence of coherent, encompassing and authoritative interest associations, and on previous occasions has taken the unusual step of publicly criticizing producer interest structures it found ineffective (EBIS, 1991). Indeed, the pattern of interest representation is quite diverse at the European level, both because it is specialized into a variety of sectors, and because it has been difficult to find a single outlet coordinating different branches, national interests and firm sizes. Producer interest representation in bioindustry at the national level therefore takes the form of established sectoral interest associations where members have interests in bioindustry (such as pharmaceuticals, chemicals and food-processing), and bioindustry umbrella associations seeking both to coordinate cross-sectorally and to represent the new, dedicated biotechnology firms which have emerged in the 1980s and 1990s.

Different National Conditions for European Action

Much of bioindustry's interest representation has developed in Brussels rather than in the national capitals of the member states. This contrasts with the pattern which is evident in a number of other domains, where European interest representation is conducted mainly from associations in the member states via their own governments, sometimes because of the inability of their European federations to thrash out worthwhile agreements among constituents. Nevertheless, there is a recognisable tier of organization in most (though not all) member states, and in some of these effective, symbiotic relationships between governments and producer interests in bioindustry operate via channels involving established industrial sectors, or have emerged centred upon dedicated associations for bioindustry.

The importance attached by bioindustry to European interest organizations in Brussels arises from three main factors. One is a reflection of the attention that the European Commission has lavished on bioindustry as a strategy for global competitiveness, while another is a function of the time at which gene-splicing technologies have been maturing, coincident with the development of the European single market through the 1980s and 1990s. A third important factor is the multinational character of the scientific and commercial operations by leading companies and their desire to rationalize the conditions of marketing and political activities. As a large part of the show has been centred on Brussels, partly encouraged by producer preferences for Europe-wide solutions, so bioindustry focused its political representation there. Bioindustry did not have to move headquarters and staff to Brussels from national centres, like so many other industries where a shift of political centres could be observed. To leading transnational corporations, representing the bulk of bioindustry, the familiarity with international political environments like that in Brussels also made this choice easier.

Under these conditions, single bioindustry associations with an established representational monopoly had not matured in the member states. Rather, a number of fora had developed in just some of the member states, hosting a smaller or larger subset of the industry, and with different ambitions to cover the entire industry. In a number of cases no national association has been founded to date, partly because no larger biocommunity exists as, for example, in Ireland, Luxembourg, Portugal and Greece. In some European countries where substantial biotechnology commercial interests do exist, a representative industrial association has not emerged either. Most remarkable, perhaps, is the case of Germany, where it has been seen as too problematic to form such an association. This is in part as a result of the politicization of environmental interests: interests are hosted instead from the screen of the chemical industry by the trade association, VCI. Outside the EU, in Switzerland, almost the same model has been applied. Here, the SGCI is an even more encompassing association, representing the pharmaceutical and chemical industries and a number of specialized branches within the chemical industry, which in other countries often have dedicated associations. Bioindustry is also represented from its premises.

The first national bioindustry association proper was in France (Organibio, 1984), followed by Belgium (Belgian Bioindustries Association, 1986), Italy (ASSOBIOTEC, 1986), Denmark (FBID, 1987), Netherlands (NIABA, 1988), the UK (BIA, 1989) and finally Spain (Asociaciónde Bioindustrias, 1990). The development of national associations in part coincided with the formation of European outlets. They reflected: the points of development of new bioindustry firms (and in particular the distillation of these into recognizable producer interests from technical laboratories); pressures from large-firm interests for dedicated producer representation, and responses to European developments in Brussels, including the desire for organizational compatibility across different countries in the hope of easing Europe-wide coordination. Most started out as recognizable industrial interest groups, such as those in France and Denmark, where non-industrial interests were deliberately excluded. In the UK an association started life as a coalition of scientists, service companies, large firms and small enterprises.

National associations also differ widely in their membership base. The French and Dutch associations have the most comprehensive sectoral coverage. Typically, membership in these associations is only for individual firms seeking dedicated representation of bioindustry interests. Most national associations host a significant number of small and medium-sized enterprises, whose interests are often not represented elsewhere. Large firms differ in their membership strategies. Some join and continue; others sign up and then leave; while others never join. All of these categories have alternative representational options through other associations or via their own resources. Undoubtedly, some use the channel as an additional 'listening post'.

The national level in Europe does not therefore display coherent, singular and encompassing bioindustry associations. Rather, national interest representation in bioindustry is characterized by the presence of sectoral interest associations whose members have an interest in gene-splicing technologies and organizations which attempt umbrella representation and which provide an outlet for small-firm representation. As with all umbrella-type associations, achieving common positions is often problematic, as is evident later in this case study.

The European Channels: Sector Associations and Coordinating Fora

In one sense, European biotechnology interests had the advantage of starting from scratch, i.e. by forming brand new associations at the European level rather than reorganizing a collection of national systems for Brussels representation. However, new associations were, in reality, never in a position to take advantage of a 'fresh start' as a result of cleavages by sector and firm size and the different traditions of national arrangements which soon emerged.

In European bioindustry interest representation, there has always been a will to tackle sectoral differences where these have arisen because of the involvement of large firms whose activities span sectors and that may have experience of networking across sectors and nations. These factors may have assisted intersectoral coordination, but reconciling different national organizational landscapes of interests is not always unproblematical. Neither is the reconciliation of interests of large and small firms.

European sector associations with biotechnology interests include the Association of Microbial Food Enzyme Producers in Western Europe (AMFEP), European Chemical Industry Council (CEFIC), Confederation of the Food and Drink Industries (CIAA), Association of Plant Breeders (COMASSO), European Crop Protection Association (ECPA), European Diagnostic Manufacturers' Association (EDMA), European Federation of Pharmaceutical Industry Associations (EFPIA), European Federation of Animal Health (FEDESA) and European Federation of Animal Feed Additives (FEFANA). Typically, these are federations of national associations whose members tend to be large firms. To these we can add a further number of 'industry platforms', such as the Yeast Industry Platform (YIP), which have been formed in relation to concrete EU programmes. A further specialist clutch of these has recently located in the Hague, such as the In Vitro Testing Industry Platform (IVTIP) and the Animal Cell Technology Industrial Platform (ACTIP), all operating from the same premises.

European biotechnology interest representation evolved from the Frankfurt-based scientists association, the European Federation of Biotechnology (EFB), reflecting the importance of the academic science base in European biotechnology development. Formed in 1978, the EFB performed some coordinating functions before the emergence of coordinated industry action, without in any way representing distinct commercial interests. It was particularly active in relation to the EU research framework support programmes for the life sciences. Stronger incentives for sectoral and industrial interest concertation were provided by the development of EU competence in biotechnology in attempts to regulate bioindustry, and to encourage particular sectors via more targeted programmes. Industrial interests have responded to these, including the 1986 Commission communication on the regulatory framework for biotechnology, the communication in 1991 on the promotion of the competitive environment, and the three directives in the domain: 219 (contained use), 220 (deliberate release) and 679 (worker safety) of 1990. Contacts are manifold and formalized through, for example, the Commission's Biotechnology Coordination Committee formed in 1991, a type of roundtable with industrial interests.

Attempts at industrial coordination first occurred through the European Biotechnology Coordinating Group (EBCG) established in 1985. This forum included the various interested European industrial federations and the existing national associations. It lacked a secretariat and premises with which to reconcile the diverse range of interests across sectors and different sized firms. Perhaps unsurprisingly, the EBCG collapsed in 1991. Two straws broke the camel's back in that year. One was the unusual step of public criticism of the coherence of EBCG by the exasperated CUBE (Concertation Unit for Biotechnology) in DG XII (EBIS, 1991). Another was an incident in which the European chemicals association, CEFIC, was not invited to one of the meetings. Whether this was by accident or design, CEFIC took its ball away and invested instead in the formation of the Senior Advisory Group Biotechnology (SAGB). SAGB learnt the lessons of other Euro groups, and started life in a direct firm membership format. This meant that sector associations and the national bioindustry associations, where the small and medium-sized firms have a stronger foothold, were excluded.

Initially, SAGB membership was by invitation only to the large (mainly chemical firm) players. Some of these have a GDP value higher than certain member states and are influential players in their own right. This pattern is perhaps part of a wider trend in European interest representation seen in other industries such as cars (Case 12) and tourism (Case 9), towards exclusive 'rich clubs' of the big operators. During 1991, SAGB steered clear of the smaller-firm representative structures. For instance, it did not attend a meeting aimed at all bioindustry which DG XI (environment) and the national biotechnology associations, most of them having a strong commitment to the small-firm constituency, had organized.

More recently, SAGB has developed into an open membership format and now includes some of the dedicated biotechnology firms which have grown from small into medium-sized industrial players. Thus, membership has grown from seven at the outset in 1989 to twenty-nine firms by 1994, where membership has stabilized. Although a greater concern now lies with dedicated, new biotechnology firms, it does not represent the constituency of these – rather, just the few which have made it to the top. The Senior Advisory Group Biotechnology (SAGB) remains a large-firm representative outlet. In turn, this has assisted it in developing a track record of effectiveness, such that the outgoing president of the Commission, Jacques

Delors, once described SAGB as the most influential Euro group. SAGB has attempted to formulate policies for bioindustry as a whole, most recently in responding to the White Paper of December 1993 (*Biotechnology Policy in the European Union, 1994*). Interestingly, it has encouraged the coordination of different parts of the Commission whose work deals with biotechnology (DG III industry, DG VI agriculture, DG XI environment, DG XII science, research and technology). However, officials in DG III and DG XII are acutely aware of SAGB's privileged access and the partial nature of the constituency it represents.

There is a concern throughout the Commission to ensure that smaller biotechnology firms also have adequate access to the European corridors of power, and awareness of the need to hear what such firms have to say. In a recent newsletter, the Commission's biotechnology unit (DG XII) put on record its desire both for transparency in its dealings and for dialogue with a wide variety of biotechnology interests (EBIS, 1993, p. 1). This made it one of the first Commission units to respond to Commissioner Pinheiro's new policy on transparency and openness, emphasizing its concern for dialogue beyond large-firm interests.

Coordination of National Associations

The national associations have their own European forum: the European Secretariat of National Biotechnology Associations (ESNBA). This represents the member interests of the seven national bioindustry associations. Formed in December 1991, it rents floorspace from a Brussels consultancy and employs a small staff to perform secretariat functions, assisted by the additional resources of the national associations by rotation.

Although early indications in 1992 were that SAGB and ESNBA might communicate sufficiently to form a working partnership, in practice relationships have not matured to such a degree that labour has been divided or any other agreement has been reached. In March 1993, SAGB took the initiative in forming the Federation of European Biotechnology Coordination (FEBC) and providing the secretariat, aiming to coordinate once again the different sectors in biotechnology and their Euro associations listed above (but not the national biotechnology associations (NBAS)/ ESNBA, who have not been invited). The lessons from the disbanded EBCG were that the inclusion of national associations was unsuccessful at the European level, and that the foci of SAGB and ESNBA were apparently seen as too different in many circles, particularly in some of the sector associations.

SAGB and ESNBA are quite different animals. Where SAGB has direct company membership, ESNBA is an umbrella association; where SAGB has very good relations with DG III, ESNBA has a good accord with DG XI. SAGB is established; ESNBA is more of a newcomer. Where SAGB coordinates across sectors, ESNBA coordinates primarily across nations. SAGB is a European and global forum; ESNBA is a national and European actor, although important bioindustries such as the German, Swiss and Swedish are not organized into this forum, but instead through the SAGB via direct membership.

It is these sorts of difference which may sustain ESNBA in the years to come. Although not completely assured, it would certainly not be accurate to say that the future of ESNBA lies in the balance as a result of the formation of the FEBC. Admittedly, ESNBA is not the best endowed Euro association. Nevertheless as long as it is excluded from SAGB-led activities, ESNBA has a role to play in at least representing the interests of small firms which do not enjoy representation through other channels – a role the Commission has signalled it wishes to see remain. Additionally, a number of large-firm players, for instance Akzo and Novo Nordisk, have carefully kept a foot in both camps. As long as these large players have a use for the ESNBA channel, whose pattern of Commission contacts differs from that of SAGB, then ESNBA will remain. The formation of FEBC does not therefore necessarily spell the beginning of the process of reorganizing the entire bioindustry Euro lobby into one channel – not until SAGB/ESNBA differences are resolved.

Future Forms of Associability

The present difficulties which exist at the European level are heavily influenced by the different, yet slightly overlapping, memberships (the interests of firm size, sectors and national biocommunities) and functions (the national and European focus) of SAGB and ESNBA. Difficulties have also arisen from the nature of the organizations which have emerged, the resources (including personnel) which have been significant in their development, their political styles and the historical baggage of interrelationships. More than anything, these factors seem to be the obstacle to a unified bioindustry representation in the European Union. Given the nature of these factors, it would seem unlikely that such difficulties will prevail for anything beyond the medium term. Cleavages are there, and in some instances they are very strong, but it would be wrong to overdramatize conflicts which may be based on little more than personality disputes between some of the main players. As ever, much depends upon the will of constituent members of the organizations to find solutions. Here, firms who hold membership of both SAGB and ESNBA routes could be key players and pave the way for compromise.

Sector association might also give some encouragement. The track record of SAGB seems to have convinced most at the European level of the sense of working together. Indeed, one less tangible role the SAGB has played has been to demonstrate to sceptics that a bioindustry-wide body can co-exist with Euro federations such as CEFIC (chemicals) and EFPIA (pharmaceuticals). There will always remain an important role for both the sectoral and bioindustry-wide routes. Very successful Euro federations such as EFPIA will always be able both to represent the biotechnology interests of pharmaceutical firms effectively and to engage in meaningful coordination with SAGB. No matter how the coordinating fora manage to divide labour or perhaps even merge, the sector associations are not likely to wither away.

A decisive role of the European Commission in the development of bioindustry representation is imaginable. Once before it has expressed its opinion of the organization of the industry. At present, the Commission is keen to stress its even-handedness in talking to both SAGB and ESNBA (EBIS, 1993, p. 50). Patience may eventually wear thin, particularly as the Commission often reminds groups of the esteem with which it holds those associations which exert a monopoly on industry representation in Europe (SEC(92) 2272 final).

A further incentive in developing bioindustry representation could also be the International Bioindustry Forum, whose members include the United States Bioindustry Organisation, the Japan Bioindustry Association, the Industrial Bioindustry Association of Canada, and the Senior Advisory Group Biotechnology. Representing the ESNBA constituency could strengthen the European arm in this global forum; while for ESNBA, alliance with the SAGB could give those parts of the ESNBA constituency which are not already affiliated with the SAGB access to such a forum.

The solutions to the working relationships of the co-ordinating fora should not be seen in simple terms as an issue of merger, take-over or collapse. As testified by firms who hold dual membership, there has been an independent role for ESNBA. ESNBA has developed its own strengths, such as its links with DG XI (environment), and it is possible that it could co-exist happily alongside the SAGB and the new looser mechanism of FEBC. Besides the valuable working relationships which the national associations have developed inside the Commission, the associations perform a unique role in many of the member states and are able to influence EU policy by influencing the implementation of EU directives, in some cases simultaneously, and in using national governments as a relevant channel. Under these circumstances it is evident that some forum of exchange between national associations is needed, but the more important the stage in Brussels becomes, the greater is the incentive to concentrate resources at the European level. Such appears to be the trend, although moves are more slow and interrupted than both the Commission and industrial interests may wish them to be.

A number of broader hypotheses emerge from the study of European bioindustry. One hypothesis concerns the orientation of a newly industrial activity towards Brussels rather than towards the difficult task of rearranging national-level organization. Perhaps unusually, it is the European levels of organization which are stronger than the totality of the national levels. A second hypothesis is the choice for a direct firm membership format, supplemented by a federated structure. A third is the impact which exclusive large-firm clubs may have upon organizing other types of interests; these may attract competitive representational formats. A fourth factor concerns the attention lavished on bioindustry by the Commission, despite the fragmented nature of contributory industrial interests. It is possible that this arises from the industry's high-tech status and the promise of gene-splicing technologies – factors likely to attract the attention of public policy-makers. In turn, this signifies a fifth factor of significance: the active stance taken by the Commission in organizing industrial interests in Europe which have strategic importance. This is because the Commission needs effective representational structures to support promotional public policies. This in turn emphasizes the importance of meaningful alliances at the European level to industrial success.

References

Commission of the European Communities (1986) *A Community Framework for the Regulation of Biotechnology*. COM(86) 573.
Commission of the European Communities (1991) *Promoting the Competitive Environment for the Industrial Activities based on Biotechnology within the Community*. SEC(91) 629.
Commission of the European Communities (1993) *Growth, Competitiveness and Employment. The Challenges and Ways Forward into the 21st Century*. Brussels: CEC.
Cookson, C. (1994) 'Moving on to the fast track', *Financial Times*. 9 May 1994, p. 12.
Council of the European Communities (1990) *Directive on the Contained Use of Genetically Modified Micro-organisms*. 90/219/EEC.
Council of the European Communities (1990) *Directive on the Deliberate Release into the Environment of Genetically Modified Organisms*. 90/220/EEC.
Council of the European Communities (1990) *Directive on the Protection of Workers from Risks Related to Exposure to Biological Agents at Work*. 90/679/EEC.

EBIS (European Biotechnology Information Service) (1991) *Newsletter*, no. 4, July 1991.

EBIS (European Biotechnology Information Service) (1993) *Newsletter*, vol. 3, no. 4, p. 1.

Senior Advisory Group Biotechnology (SAGB) (1994) *Biotechnology Policy in the European Union, Prescriptions for Growth, Competitiveness and Employment: A response to the Union's 1993 White Paper on Growth, Competitiveness and Employment*. Brussels: SAGB.

Secretariat of the European Commission (1992) *An Open and Structured Dialógue Between the Commission and Special Interest Groups*. SEC(92) 2272 final. Brussels: SEC.

PART 2

'Mid' Technology

The Cement Industry

Joaquim Molins

General Characteristics of the Sector

The European and world cement industry has a number of characteristics that differentiate it from other industrial sectors and which serve to make it unusual. It is included among the sectors studied in this volume as a 'mid-technology' industry, because the product can be considered as classical and the technology of the fabrication process is in reach of all the possible producers, yet technological advances have considerably influenced the production process. Some 40 per cent of production costs are accounted for by energy, which has led to a search for alternative sources. In efforts to reduce fabrication costs, European industry installations have multicombustible alternatives and experiment with unconventional combustibles as well as the use of certain scraps (trash, tyres).

Cement is an industry directly related to the existence of primary products, in particular limestone. Industrial installations are complex and extremely capital-intensive. Even though the product is used around the world, markets are fundamentally local due to high costs of transportation. The centres of production are located mainly in large consumer zones, provided that appropriate primary products exist. The evolution of the sector is directly related to the construction industry: public works, housing and civil engineering. They are the big consumers, as well as concrete-makers and producers of cement prefabrication products. The consumption of cement by the concrete industry varies from 45 per cent of the industry's total consumption in Denmark to 11 per cent in Spain (Gual, 1991).

European cement production (excluding the former USSR) was 250 million tons in 1993. As is revealed by *Exhibit 6.1*, the main European producer is Italy, followed by Turkey, Germany, Spain and France. If we look at the figures for imports, exports and consumption, Greece, Spain, Turkey and Poland are the more active exporters and Germany the most

Exhibit 6.1 *Production, imports, exports and consumption of cement (000 tonnes). (*Source*: CEMBUREAU, 1994a)*

Countries	Production	Imports	Exports	Consumption
Benelux	11,899	3,584	4,020	10,935
France	20,464	1,507	1,739	19,465
Germany	32,481	7,502	1,731	36,811
Greece	13,925	30	6,920	7,167
Italy	34,771	2,938	255	37,357
Portugal	7,617	–	71	7,506
Spain	23,928	2,466	3,736	22,652
UK, Ireland, Denmark	14,608	1,919	1,691	14,797
European Union	158,203	19,946	20,163	156,690
European Economic Area	9,679	803	1,402	9,015
Switzerland	4,042	344	42	4,257
Turkey	32,679	245	3,202	29,778
CEMBUREAU	204,446	21,338	24,809	199,740
Czech Rep.	5,423	76	1,798	3,678
Slovak Rep.	2,610	–	1,091	1,506
Hungary	2,533	153	145	2,481
Poland	13,040	–	3,275	9,811

important import country. Joos (1992) has recently predicted a decrease in consumption in all CEMBUREAU countries except Turkey and Poland.

From the perspective of the size of enterprises, the European scene was rather diverse in the early 1980s: large industrial groups in the Nordic countries, Germany and France, and fragmentation in Italy and Spain. In recent years, the scene has changed, with the consolidation of large groups present in different European countries. In the late 1980s, the five most important European groups controlled 65 per cent of the production (Mendez, 1992).

European Business Alliances

Since 1947 the European cement producers have had their own organization, CEMBUREAU. Propelled by the Nordic countries and the UK, CEMBUREAU developed in the 1950s and 1960s throughout Europe. Currently, the membership includes nineteen countries of western Europe, with four eastern European countries as associates (Czech Republic,

Hungary, Poland and Slovakia). Members comprise both national associations (Austria, Belgium, France, Germany, Greece, Netherlands, Portugal, Spain, Switzerland, Turkey, and the UK) and individual firms (Denmark, Finland, Iceland, Ireland, Italy, Luxembourg, Norway, Sweden). From the associative point of view, the diversity of membership reflects from the beginning of the organization the characteristics of the productive structure of the different countries.

The governing body of the association is a board of directors council. This consists of a president, a vice-president, a representative of each of the nineteen country members, the president of the Liaison Committee of the Cement Industries in the European Union, the presidents of the two permanent committees (industry and marketing), and the general director of the association, who is *ex officio*. The staff of the association includes three directors (technical, information and communication, and general secretary).

The history of CEMBUREAU could be divided in three main stages, paralleling the three geographical locations of the association: Malmo (until 1966), Paris and Brussels (since 1986). Whilst the central objective throughout the association's life has been to promote the interest of producers, these stages were marked by different phases of development. The first stage was fundamentally one of coordination, centred on trade affairs and the production of statistics. With the progressive incorporation of other European countries, the organization became more complex and technical aspects acquired importance. As the association points out:

> The responsibility of CEMBUREAU in the promotion and technical fields was first to ensure for Members a rapid access to information about the markets for cement, the relevant technologies, and related developments of importance, and secondly to provide the base for possible joint actions in matters of a promotional or technical nature where it is clearly in the economic interest of Members to cooperate at the international level.
>
> *(CEMBUREAU, 1975, p. 26)*

A Promotion Policy Committee was formed, and developed its work with the main consumers of the product and their European organizations. The use of the product in pavements for roads has been one of the mainstay activities, including the cosponsoring of an international conference in 1977. Those associations that have worked with CEMBUREAU in promoting activities include the International Federation of European Contractors of Buildings and Public Works (FIEEBTP, now FIEC), the International Federation of the Precast Concrete Industry (BIBM), the ready-mixed concrete producers (ERMCO), and the International Commission on

Agricultural Engineering (CIGR). CEMBUREAU, ERMCO and BIBM established a permanent coordinating committee in 1988.

Technical activities include, among others, a manual of good practice for strength testing, the publication of a procedure for the measurement of the heat of hydration of cement, and a review of measuring methods for the mineralogical composition of clinkers. All these works were related to rules for the standardization of the product. CEMBUREAU has therefore played a key role in technical harmonization of the industry as well as its political representation. This suggests that it is an effective European association.

The Cement Industry and the European Institutions

Early in the 1970s a liaison committee was formed with the EEC with the objective of becoming the intermediary with European authorities. The organization needed to face a new situation, as the 1976 annual report states:

> it is evident that due to economic and other pressures the resources of the
> Cement Industry for participating in development work on new markets for
> cement and in defending existing markets will in the future be strictly limited.
> For this reason it will be necessary to explore all possible forms of cooperation
> between members so as to obtain the maximum return on this form of
> investment. It is the intention that the new organization will be flexible and
> responsive to the changes which can occur in the priorities for common action.
> *(CEMBUREAU, 1976, p. 22)*

At first, the relations with the Community institutions were mainly with the Commission (DG III) at the Liaison Committee initiative and at their invitation. Relations with the European Parliament and the Economic and Social Committee began when these institutions examined a proposal for a directive relating to construction products (COM(78) 449 final). Major concerns for the sector were the nature of decision-taking (unanimity versus qualified majority), and the consideration of cement on the list of priority products. Joint work with the Commission was initiated at the very early stages of a proposal for a directive on Eurocodes, concerning the common rules for all types of structures and specifically concrete structures. A third objective was the discussion of the rules for the European standardization of cements, which obliged all CEMBUREAU members to reach internal agreement. This is illustrative of the way in which a European-level agenda serves to develop collective action amongst business interests.

In the early 1990s CEMBUREAU proposed a scheme for European cement certification which was submitted to the EC Advisory Committee on

Cement, with the support of the Committee for European Normalization (CEN) and the major clients of the cement industry represented by ERMCO and BIBM. Approval in 1994 represented a great success for the association. Besides the work on legislation, the committee also makes an effort to promote the product, following the report of the European Parliament which pointed to the need for Community action to boost the construction sector through the implementation of a programme for housing improvement and a programme for substructure works of interest at the European level.

Environmental Policy

Concern for environmental problems appeared in the mid-1970s, coinciding with a draft report prepared by the Industry and Environment Department of the United Nations Environment Program (report on environmental aspects of the cement industry', 1978). The contents were considered unacceptable for the cement sector, and CEMBUREAU prepared some remarks in response, and agreed with the authors of the draft to prepare a new one. From this experience the association put the environmental issue on their own agenda. However, the experience of having to address global regimes rather than European ones in the 1970s was not an uncommon experience for many transnational associations organizing European interests.

The next issue which arose in environmental affairs to confront cement interests was a Council directive on the combating of air pollution from industrial plants (84/360/EEC, *Official Journal*, L188). CEMBUREAU's concern was how to adapt a broad set of issues to the specific characteristics of the cement industry. Negotiations with the Commission included the specific case of cement kilns and quantification of the emissions of pollutants. This assessment demonstrated the low impact of the emissions from the cement industry into the air, and the Commission Services decided to withdraw the cement industry from the scope of the proposal for a new directive relating to large combustion plants. A specific regulation for the cement sector was to be prepared by a consultant, in joint work between the Commission and CEMBUREAU.

New problems for the sector arose from waste policies: the extension of the concept (the distinction between product and waste), transboundary transfers, and civil liability for damage from waste to the environment. Negotiations have developed in recent years with different levels of success from the point of view of CEMBUREAU. A recent decision (1994) of the Commission establishing a list of wastes (75/442/EEC, *Official Journal*, L5) excludes some used by the cement and concrete industries. In the same way, the EC regulation on the shipments of wastes followed closely in matters of classification the line of CEMBUREAU proposals. On the other hand, the Council directive on hazardous waste (91/689/EEC, *Official Journal*, L377) and the connected draft list of materials could be of critical importance for the sector.

The gradual taxation of energy based on the specific carbon content of various energy sources, proposed by the Commission (COM(92) 226 final, *Official Journal*, C196) have concerned all industrial sectors including the European cement industry. The reaction includes negotiations with the Commission on voluntary agreements in order to curb emissions of carbon dioxide (i.e. a cooperative approach), and have been complemented with contacts with national governments and their delegations in Brussels, in order to lobby against a number of specific issues. These include the very principle of an energy/carbon tax and other referred principles; the method of calculating graduated reductions in the tax paid by energy-intensive industries; and the high impact of the tax on such industries. The importation of cement from eastern countries, sometimes in dumping conditions, and with high-polluting installations was put on the agenda by CEMBUREAU.

The draft framework directive on integrated pollution prevention and control (COM(93) 423 final, *Official Journal*, C311) prompted CEMBUREAU to work with UNICE. The main concerns for the cement industry were the definition of the 'best available technologies' (Report EUR 13005 EN, 1990); the timetable for upgrading of existing installations and reviewing of permits; and the balance between the use of emission limit values based on environmental quality standards. Due to the application by the EU of the principle of subsidiarity, final negotiations on air quality emissions will include not only the Commission and the Council but also negotiations inside the member states.

In 1992 the document *European Cement Industry's Approach to the Environment* was published by CEMBUREAU to provide a structured and coherent statement of the industry's position on all matters where the manufacturing and distribution of cement have an impact on the environment. It reflects the difficulties which European business associations often face in responding to a wide agenda:

> The environmental context in which the cement industry is situated, and the environmental effect of its operations involve a number of different issues of a technical, economic and public relations nature. The tendency is to react to each one separately which creates a risk of concentrating on a few high profile individual issues, and perhaps devoting too many resources to them, at the expense of achieving the best overall environmental balance.
>
> *(CEMBUREAU, 1991, p. 12)*

Annual reports in the 1990s show that the environmental policy has become the most active area for external representation by CEMBUREAU:

> A continuous dialogue has now been established with the Commission and with the European Parliament (EP) in order for the cement industry's views to be known and taken into consideration at every stage of the European legislative process. If this activity is to be successful, however, it must be systematically complemented by high-level contacts at the national level also.
>
> *(CEMBUREAU 1993)*

In 1994, the technical director of CEMBUREAU published a report entitled *Environmental Trends and Developments in Europe* that reflects all the issues concerning the cement industry in Europe. Its more important conclusion states:

> It is strategically important for industry to closely monitor and influence both framework and particular legislation at the drafting stage and participate fully in ongoing dialogue with the authorities, the legislators and the public. To ensure that the active representation of industry's views in this dialogue has the desired outcome, it will be necessary to ensure that representative activities at Member State level and at European level are at all times complementary.
>
> *(CEMBUREAU, 1994b)*

With a vast range of new issues to respond to, it is not surprising that in the late 1980s the organization of the association was again restructured. A new standing committee – Political and Public Affairs – was created for external matters influencing the industry's operations and its business environment. European public opinion about the image of cement became a new objective for the association, because of the high degree of politicization of environmental issues. As the 1991 annual report states:

> The numerous contacts which have been established with European Institutions have shown that here also, as with other influential sections of the general public, the image of the cement industry is frequently at variance with reality. The presentation in Cologne sought to introduce the idea of a communications strategy which would correct the situation so that legislators, in particular, would understand and accept the real issues. The basic elements of a communications strategy were discussed, and an action plan outlined, which would take into account the need to coordinate the messages at different levels.
>
> *(CEMBUREAU, 1991, p. 28)*

This new stage in CEMBUREAU's development suggests the inadequacy of relying on closed 'policy communities' where issues have become widely politicized. In environmental affairs it may now no longer be possible for industry/bureaucracy interfaces to be a legitimate, sole means to govern public affairs because a range of other interests have secured a means of access to public policy-making. In turn, this requires new public affairs strategies to be developed by private industrial interests, and suggests the dynamic nature of 'policy communities' which at one time were relatively closed entities.

Conclusion

The European association of the cement industry (CEMBUREAU) has been an important actor in the collective defence of the interests of the sector, adapting itself to a changing environment. In the past forty-five years CEMBUREAU has achieved the integration of all western European countries (with a particular organization in relation to the EEC), and now in association with the new countries in eastern Europe.

The organization model has been adapted to the peculiarities of the cement industry. It has an interesting mixture of firm and national association membership and has been able to coordinate the common interests, yet different characteristics, of the industry in several countries. Some similarities are evident with chemicals and its organization (CEFIC), and in particular the mix of direct firm and national association membership (Grant, 1993). At the same time, though, the organization has always had a specific character that was not necessarily shaped as a result of the evolution of the sector. However, the impact of new technologies has clearly fostered collective action among members.

Collective action has been built around the promotion of the product, in close contact with the consumers and their European associations (FIEC, BIBM and ERMCO). The technical aspects in particular environmental regulatory issues, have constituted the other main objectives of the association. Its performance has not only been reactive towards the different initiatives at the European level, but also anticipative in order to resolve common problems, particularly those concerning the environment.

The organization model of CEMBUREAU has helped to reach common positions for all members: representatives of all countries ruled the association with the support of a well resourced central secretariat. Senior managers of firms have participated in common work, and individual experts have worked in small *ad hoc* committees with well defined tasks, embracing the principle of equal opportunity for all members to participate in the activities of CEMBUREAU. In its work CEMBUREAU has taken into account the different conditions of firms and countries, but at the same time created the conditions for activities of a cooperative nature. Such factors have been vital in sustaining a coherent, effective and representative association, and are also to be found in the cases of pharmaceuticals (Case 2) and EuroCommerce (Case 8).

As a European business alliance, CEMBUREAU has worked with most European institutions: the Commission, in particular DG III, DG XI and DG XVII; the European Parliament and the Social and Economic Council. However, CEMBUREAU's origins as a trade association pre-date the more recent phases of European integration, and it has had to adapt its structures and activities to a changing environment. It has built an intensive relationship with European institutions, in particular with the Commission, but a neo-corporatist style is not evident.

Regarding the choice of routes for lobbying, CEMBUREAU prefers the representative role of the association. This does not exclude joint work with other associations, such as UNICE, especially when the issue has a general impact in all industrial sectors (as the directive relating to health hazards for workers exposed to noise). As has been pointed in other studies (Greenwood *et al*, 1992) national routes (governments and permanent representatives) have been also a target in CEMBUREAU orientations, and developed by national associations and firms. It will be an interesting research task for the future to see if the principle of subsidiarity will encourage the national route, as we have observed in recent (as yet, unpublished) research on air quality emissions. At this point what is notable, however, is the lack of competitive firm-level lobbying where industry-wide interests are present, and the corresponding ability of CEMBUREAU to coordinate such interests.

As a general strategy for European associations, negotiations with the European institutions have shown again the necessity of finding allies in other sectors and developing a common position in each issue (van Schendelen, 1993). The establishment of a permanent coordination among cement, ready-mixed concrete and precast concrete sectors is a good example. Throughout, the collective action of the cement industry confirms the necessity of establishing permanent contact with public European institutions.

References

CEMBUREAU (1975) Annual Report 1975. Paris: CEMBUREAU.
CEMBUREAU (1976) Annual Report 1976. Paris: CEMBUREAU.
CEMBUREAU (1991) Annual Report 1991. Brussels: CEMBUREAU.
CEMBUREAU (1993) Annual Report 1992-93. Brussels: CEMBUREAU.

CEMBUREAU (1993) *European Cement Industry's Approach to the Environment*. Brussels: CEMBUREAU.

CEMBUREAU (1994a) Annual Report 1993–94. Brussels: CEMBUREAU.

CEMBUREAU (1994b) *Environmental Trends and Developments in Europe*. Brussels: CEMBUREAU.

Grant, W. (1993) 'Pressure groups and the European Community: an overview', in Mazey, S. and Richardson, J. (eds) *Lobbying in the European Community*. Oxford: Oxford University Press.

Greenwood, J., Grote, J. and Ronit, K. (1992) *Organised Interests and the European Community*. London: Sage.

Gual, J. (1991) *La industria catalana als anys 90*. Barcelona: Ariel.

Joos, M. G. (1992) 'Long term trend in cement consumption', *International Cement Review*, August.

Mendez, J. (1992) *La liquidacion del patrimonio industrial. El caso del cemento*. Barcelona: VCA.

van Schendelen, M.P.C.M. (1993) *National Public and Private EC Lobbying*. Aldershot: Dartmouth.

PART 3

Service

European Banking and Insurance

Business Alliances and Corporate Strategies

Peter Vipond

Introduction

Banks and insurance companies based within the European Union face changing national markets as well as the emergence of a European market and, in some areas, the development of global markets for financial services. The business environment in which they function has become characterized by change, both in terms of the geographical linkages between various markets and because of changing regulatory and competitive conditions within each market (Vipond, 1994).

Although competition and market reregulation are not entirely new phenomena to financial institutions such as banks and insurance companies, it is worth stressing that well into the 1980s many European countries had tight controls over financial services. These extended from the price of the products (price regulation), through controls over the range of products that financial firms could provide (functional regulation) to the areas within which they could provide them (geographical regulation). As if this were not enough, a significant proportion of banks and insurance companies, nearly half of Europe's top one hundred banks for example, were state-owned (Bisignano, 1992). Competition has not, therefore, always been a core feature of financial service markets.

The driving forces for change are much discussed and include the effects of national deregulation as well as the single market programme; the development of new information technology; and competitive pressures from other parts of the world economy. From the firm's perspective, however, this discussion is less important than addressing the consequences of change. The individual firm faces an uncertain environment for business, and within that will be subject to many forces for change over which it has little control. In this situation, rational action by the firm is manifested in the making of strategic choices. It is through these strategic choices that the firm achieves efficiency, manages the risks of its environment and develops through innovation and adaptation (Ghoshal, 1987). A crucial aspect of those strategic choices are the various alliances that the firm makes.

In proposing this approach, two issues are raised which merit further comment. The first concerns the use of strategic management concepts as a basis for the analysis of rational decision-making by financial firms; and the second concerns a focus on the kinds of alliance firms may make as part of that strategic decision-making. What is being claimed is that alliances, be they with other firms or collective actions through industry associations, are explicable in terms of the attempt by firms to make strategic business choices, some of which will involve anticipating or even shaping changes to market conditions.

The language of management theory, especially strategic management theory, provides a rational choice model at the level of the firm and allows an expansion of the notion of an alliance. Strategic management theory is less strong, however, in explaining the internal operation of national and European-level associations which are responsible for collective action. In order to explain these, the empirical cases of the British Bankers' Association (BBA) and the Association of British Insurers (ABI), as well as the European associations to which they belong, are considered. Examining the firm as a rational actor seeking to maximize its market position through strategic choices, and looking at the institutional framework through which financial institutions seek collective action, allow a fuller appreciation of the role of banks and insurance companies within the European market. More importantly, they will allow us to disaggregate the concept of alliances within the industries in order to analyse and gain a fuller understanding of them. A core distinction drawn here is between market alliances which firms enter into usually with one (but occasionally more) institutions and the institutional alliances they enter into through membership of industry associations at the national or European level. While there are linkages between the two, they are fundamentally different when viewed from the perspective of what the firm seeks to achieve through them.

To develop these points the following two sections examine the institutional alliances that are made in the banking and insurance industries respectively. The nature of market alliances is then examined in terms of the strategic choices made by financial institutions, and the final section concludes the case by drawing out some of the differences between the two industries.

Banking Alliances and Institutional Representation

As with other industries, the basic organization of banking firms in Europe is through national associations such as the Association Française des Banques (AFB) or the Bundesverband deutscher Banken (BDB). The peak association, composed of national members, is the European Banking Federation (EBF). Within the UK, the key national organization is the British Bankers' Association (BBA), though there are other organizations such as the recently renamed London Investment Banking Association (LIBA) which provides additional representation for banks that specialize in the capital markets and corporate finance areas (LIBA, 1994). Although LIBA and similarly specialized associations make their own representations as appropriate, they are directly represented within the BBA and sit on major committees.

An important feature of banking associations is that while they may have national titles, that does not necessarily mean they have entirely national memberships. Although the BBA is exceptional, in that London is a major international financial centre, it is worth citing that out of more than three hundred members only 16 per cent are UK-based banks. In fact, 24.5 per cent of the BBA's membership is from other EU states, while 11 per cent and 12 per cent respectively come from North America and Japan (BBA, 1994).

Given the international nature of much in the field of international finance, this is not surprising, though a corrective to an overly internationalist view of the BBA can be found in its funding. More than half of its £4.76 million income for 1993/94 came from the 'major British banks' (BBA, 1994). However, this too must be held in context because there are a number of high-cost activities undertaken by the BBA which concern UK banks alone. Very few non-UK banks have a serious interest, as yet, in retail banking, yet this is precisely where the BBA has to deploy resources in public and media relations. For example, a great deal of effort has been expended in developing a second edition of the Code of Banking Practice in the UK. It was introduced recently, informed by careful Parliamentary lobbying and soundings taken at party political conferences. Yet its contents were focused primarily at the retail level and were irrelevant to major institutional lenders. Such work has a high public profile and is linked to politically sensitive issues from a Parliamentary perspective. Yet within the industry, it does not, of itself, threaten the balance of competitive advantage between firms, and nothing much hangs on the outcomes for strategic decision-making at the level of the firm. Indeed, the advantage of collective action on the part of the banks may well lie in making sure that Parliamentary proposals for legislation, backed by unelected consumer interests, do not create a statutory framework that would be inflexible and unsuited to a fast-changing industry. Collective action serves a collective goal for UK banks, to state the obvious, but it does so in a way that is unlikely to disadvantage one institution with respect to another. Also, collective action, from the firm's perspective, may be more appropriate for market environment issues (such as rules, taxes or financial reporting conventions) where a competitor firm will be affected in much the same way.

The EBF is recognized by the European Commission and actively consulted in the process of developing new directives. Along with some national associations it is now actively involved in seeking to work more extensively with the European Parliament (EP), given the EP's role, through co-decision, in amending new legislative proposals.

Within the EBF as much as within key national organizations, individual firms play a necessary role. This is not a case of individual firms seeking to dominate policy for company-specific advantages, nor even of forcing through a lowest common denominator policy so as to prevent any adverse collective decisions rebounding on the firm. Rather it focuses on aspects of collective decision-making that political science literature tends to play down or ignore. In general terms, the issues are better highlighted through a tradition of policy-making literature that has its origins in writers such as Lindblom (1968), and more recently Majone (1989). The specific point here is that many of the collective rules affecting banks (and other financial institutions) are technical, industry-specific and require agreed implementation procedures. Debates about them may divide to an extent on national lines, and the cause of the divide may be political/economic. This has been the case with recent debates and directives on capital adequacy where one group has polarized around the deregulatory and liberal view of the British and Dutch. Even here, however, the complexity of policy-making – the practical issues of how different assets should be rated and what kind of capital in what sorts of ratio should be held against a bank's (or credit institution's) assets – is not a wholly political question. Politics is not always part of a broader policy debate within industries such as banking, and at times that policy debate becomes determined by a series of technical issues which have involved industry representatives as well as national and Commission staff in trying to find workable solutions.

Insurance Alliances and Institutional Representation

Representation of insurance firms within the European market has, as may be expected, both national and European-level dimensions. It is worth noting that at both levels, the collective action of firms is as much directed to technical problems as to differences of political position. In insurance, more than many industries, debates about and analysis of the minimum conditions of contracts or the physical properties of equipment, such as fire doors, are of great importance. A distinctly political input is often limited to helping provide some additional dynamic, usually at an EU ministerial level, when the parties are unable to reach an agreement.

The European-level representation of the insurance industry is through the Comité Européen des Assurances (CEA) which represents dominant national industry groups from throughout the EU (CEA, 1994). In addition, the EFTA countries, with one exception (Iceland), are members, as are Turkey, Cyprus and Malta. Associate membership, no doubt to be upgraded in time, has been awarded to the Visegraad states (Hungary, Poland, the Czech Republic and Slovenia). With a total staff of thirty, the secretariat is clearly dependent on its national member associations to staff the various committees and do much of the work, especially on technical issues. These associations in turn rely heavily on member firms to provide committee members and advisors who have the appropriate technical skills.

In broad terms, the CEA has two main areas of operation. One is the policy area and concerns matters such as proposed EU directives and implementation issues as well as related matters. The second area is often known as the technical issues area, and work here is undertaken through specialist committees. Whereas the policy area work focuses on wide-ranging insurance directives, the technical areas focus on developing a position on specific issues. This can be seen from some of the committees which exist under the CEA: everything from legal expenses to computer risks; from motor risks to an arson working group. While both policy and technical matters can lead to divides along national or regional political lines, this is not inevitable, and does not constitute the basis of discussion within committee.

The CEA pre-dates the EU, or even the original Common Market. An organization has existed since 1953, partly because of the international aspects of much insurance, including the need to provide cross-frontier cover, and the serious technical issues that this industry needs to address. As such, the CEA has a mission and a purpose outside the EU. Nevertheless the single most important function of the organization is to work through its 'Common Market Committee' which is officially recognized by the EU and through which all insurance directives pass. In recent years, however, although the financial services aspects of insurance have grown in importance, so too have other issues. As large employers, many insurance companies have been caught up in the moves towards compulsory worker representation. Issues concerning pensions have also been taken up by DG V. DG XI has been important because of continuing debates about the insurance of nuclear risk; while DG XXI has become of much greater importance given the tax aspects of cross-border insurance sales.

The interest of DG IV in insurance is relatively long-standing, not least because of 'block exemption agreements'. These have allowed insurance companies, particularly in Germany, to fix both insurance contract terms and charges, and hence are 'exemptions' from standard market competition. The Commission has used the power of Regulation No. 1534/91, which is based on Article 85(3) of the Treaty of Rome, to allow widespread cooperation between firms in the insurance area. The right of exemption is itself within the power of the Commission and it has made it clear that:

> the Commission reserves the right to withdraw the benefit of exemption when it finds the common standard policy conditions contain clauses which create, to the detriment of the policy holder, a significant imbalance between rights and obligations.
>
> *(Commission, 1993)*

This is a particular example of an industry collectively negotiating with a part of the European Commission, itself working under delegated legislative powers as well as considerable executive ones.

The block exemption issue is a specific policy case, one which has been created because of distinctive national legislation (in this case German rules on compulsory citizen membership of private insurance schemes). At a broader level, most of the major single market directives for insurance will have been extensively discussed and amended through the Common Market Committee. Given that such directives constitute a second layer of European regulation, harmonizing in certain areas but providing mutual recognition in others, firms rarely pursue firm-specific interests at this level. Their two main aims tend to be gaining information about proposed changes to market conditions, and (usually) supporting a national policy position which they will have developed at a domestic level. It tends to be larger firms which participate and which, in any case, are more interested in cross-border operations. However, as with banking, national differences have been apparent, with Britain and the Netherlands pursuing a much more liberal and open market approach, as opposed to the Germans and Mediterranean countries. This latter group tends to seek much less liberalization and tries to accommodate existing market practices and industry structures even when the lessons of the single market are that competition delivers considerable benefits.

One of the interesting developments regarding interest representation within the CEA has been the changing position of the French industry association in the 1990s. From being less market-oriented, the French association has gradually swung to join the liberalizing elements of the CEA, and its change has helped push through, at the CEA, a position which has supported the European Commission as regards the third life and non-life directives in insurance (92/49/EEC and 92/96/EEC respectively). The changing position of the French insurance industry has thus been a major factor in reorienting the CEA towards an approach more consistent with the principles of the single market. The change in the French industry is partially explicable in terms of a domestic political development as the industry began to restructure and face up to the challenge of privatization. Traditionally, much of the industry in France was state-owned, but this is changing, with market leaders such as Union des Assurances Paris (UAP) now privatized and others, such as Victoire, which were in the private sector, sold to non-French companies. Many French financial firms have both size and significant capital strength. In the past this has been reigned in, and in some cases nationalized, by previous governments. The single market programme provided opportunities for cross-border diversification and growth. This has generally led French firms to forge alliances within insurance markets and within financial services markets more generally. These market alliances in turn came to be echoed in policy changes at the institutional level of the national industry.

Within the UK, the national association is the Association of British Insurers (ABI). The body which actually does much of the representation to the CEA as well as to bodies such as the OECD and even UNCTAD, is the British Insurers' International Committee (BIIC). Within the BIIC, groups such as Lloyds (the insurance market) and the British Insurance (Atomic Energy) Committee have representation. This situation has been modified as of 1993, however, with much of Lloyd's input now going directly to ABI committees and some of the European issues being dealt with by those committees as well. In essence this is because the BIIC is an operational arm of the ABI with additional inputs rather than a competitor with significantly different views.

Relations between the Department of Trade and Industry (DTI), which is the main regulator of insurance companies in the UK (though not necessarily of the investment products they sell or the securities markets in which some of them operate), and the ABI/BIIC are generally good. The DTI is always keen to consult member firms both about new proposals and about the implementation of agreed ones. For example, with reference to the third (framework) directives mentioned above, the DTI circulated the proposed means of transposing them into national legislation via the Companies Act and statutory instruments throughout the early part of 1994. A joint interest in maintaining the size of the British insurance market and in promoting a competitive environment for insurance products has bound the BIIC and DTI together and produced a national position which has won increasing support in European negotiations.

What emerges from this brief analysis of the institutional alliances in the industry sector is a picture not so much of permanent conflict and zero-sum confrontations, but rather cooperation in much of the collective interest representation. The complexity of some issues, from the specification of fire doors to the portfolio of assets that life firms can carry, are not simply political matters. As Majone puts it: 'We miss a great deal if we try to understand policy making solely in terms of power, influence and bargaining, to the exclusion of debate and argument' (1989, p. 2).

National positions can be said to exist both in the congruence found in the British case and in the policy shift at both the political and industry level in France. The policy-making processes within the CEA and within the Commission both share an acceptance of the need to accommodate different national perspectives. In any case, some of the poorer countries do not have the expertise or funds to enforce the highest national standards, and their interests need to be recognized. The deregulatory zeal shared within the UK is only partially found elsewhere, and there are limits to the speed at which deregulation will be accepted. In the area of life assurance policies, for example, the third directive allows a great deal more investment in equities (shares) which carry a greater risk than bonds (and hence a higher return). The new third directive, which is being implemented across the EU and even within the EFTA countries mentioned above, in so far as they are European Economic Area (EEA) members, raises the amount that assurance and pension funds may invest in equities. However, it allows national regimes to set tighter limits so that German firms will invest about 20 per cent of their portfolio in these financial products whereas British firms may invest up to 60 per cent in them.

Firms, particularly those with Europe-wide market strategies, will wish to participate in collective policy formation, whether the subject of these policies be technical issues or the broader framework directives. Participation helps manage the risks of their commercial environment and provides directly and indirectly information flows about competitors. Whatever the firm's role, however, the specific alliances that it forges in the market are also a way of making strategy in the European marketplace, and it is to these alliances to which the next section turns.

Alliances and Market Behaviour

As the above sections have indicated, collective action by firms at a national level and through peak associations at an EU level is an important means of risk management for firms, especially those risks that come from policy-induced changes. There are other fora, not the subject of this case study, which have an important role, such as the G30, a group of private banks, and the Bank for International Settlements (BIS) which is the central bankers' bank. Whereas the G30 is designed to articulate private-sector-led responses to policy problems, such as derivatives risk, the BIS is not accessible to the private sector at all.

Alliances and collective bargaining, discussed above, have importance for financial firms but limited value for banks and insurance companies in terms of their commercial operations. At least as important for any financial firm, in terms of the strategic choices it makes, will be the specific alliances it forms with other firms in the European market. These alliances may fall along a spectrum from limited flows of information to joint marketing and onwards to share swaps, culminating in a merger or take-over that would produce one company. Banks and insurance companies have both been active in this field during and after the single market programme. Research by the Bank of England, covering the period 1987–93 and focusing on financial services groups, provides empirical evidence in a number of areas. There have been over one hundred cases of acquisition or majority share purchase, while there have been nearly eighty cases of minority share-holdings changing hands. Other approaches to business alliances include limited share swaps, such as that between Royal Bank of Scotland and Banco Santander in Spain (fewer than twenty cases) and joint ventures (approximately twenty cases) (BEQB, 1993).

The alliances that firms choose in the market are excellent examples of their rational calculations being turned into strategic choices. Any bank or insurance company has to weigh up the costs of growth and expansion, particularly if that growth is into markets, such as the German domestic ones, which are not very contestable. Further, few firms have the size and strength to 'go it alone', as Deutsche Bank has, and simply buy banks in other countries. The need to form alliances as a means of expanding a role in the European market is above all about getting better information about market conditions. As such, forming alliances is crucial for major firms. Organic growth in Europe's domestic markets is slow and subject to pitfalls precisely because the incoming firm does not have local market knowledge or management expertise. In this framework, alliances have tended to be of limited commitment between equal firms, or of cross-border dominance (usually with a majority stake changing hands) between two unequal firms. The kinds of alliance that firms enter into, therefore, are based on the economic power (a function of size, profitability and managerial expertise) of the firm and its potential partner. Firms with strong domestic (i.e. national) economic power are unlikely voluntarily to surrender that power across national borders:

> In contrast to domestic alliances, there have been no cross-border mergers between institutions with a dominant position in their domestic markets.
> A number of such deals have been proposed – significant examples include the merger of AMRO/Générale de Banque and ING/Bank Bruxelles Lambert – but have failed to be completed.
>
> *(BEQB, 1993, p. 375)*

Where substantial mergers have taken place between 'equals', as the above quote makes clear, this has been at the national level. Particularly in medium-sized or smaller countries, such as the Netherlands or Denmark, firms have made the strategic choice of merger to make themselves larger and better able to compete, including the ability to form European business alliances, from a position of strength. Somewhat ironically, therefore, for those who predicted a small number of pan-European banks emerging out of the single market, there have been many more national alliances formed in order to create financial institutions with the economic power to be Europe-wide players and to form non-national alliances from a position of strength.

A good example of this process at the company level is the Dutch bank ABN-AMRO whose title reveals the two banks that were merged. The combined group had assets of DFl 491,000 million in 1993 (approximately US$276 billion) and made profits after tax of DFl 2.024 billion (approximately US$1.1 billion at July 1994 exchange rates) (ABN-AMRO, 1994). An extremely large and economically powerful institution with a very good credit rating (an assessment of its credit worthiness from ruling agencies) was thus able to expand its European operations, subject only to factors such as the availability of financial institutions. In consequence, ABN-AMRO grew in Europe in 1993/94 not only through subsidiaries but also through a new specialist bank, Banque Odier Bungener Courvoisier (OBC), added to its other French operations. It continued to maintain a participating interest in the International Bank in Poland. The key alliance was very much a domestic one which produced a merger that allowed the resultant institution the economic power and presence to work without the need for any alliances of equals in other parts of the market. While some such involvement (i.e. without total control) was countenanced (as in Poland), the bank was powerful enough to generate strategy from endogenous resources. This contrasts with the Royal Bank of Scotland case where neither partner was economically powerful enough to do that, despite both firms being well run and profitable. This latter route is the more likely option for many banks, while smaller ones face a future as a permanent potential take-over target, protected only by factors such as national take-over rules or mutuality where these both work against a change in ownership.

The process of alliance-building has been undertaken at the same time as fundamental changes have been taking place in the financial services sector, as outlined in the introduction. All these factors have come together to generate a rethinking of the basic economics of the sector and of the production function for financial services at the level of the firm. One of the main consequences is that banking and insurance companies have begun merging and banks have begun to offer their own insurance products. This process, known as Bancassurance or Allfinanz, has meant that the strategic choices of banks and insurance companies have become intertwined. In some cases, such as with Germany's second largest bank, the Dresdner Bank, and the largest German insurance company, Allianz, alliances have been formed, backed by cross shareholdings. In other cases, such as the Internationale Nederland Group (ING), a bank and insurance company were merged into a single firm, though admittedly one which had subsidiaries. In other cases, banks and other credit institutions, such as building societies in Britain, have established, and then subsequently broken, links as their strategy developed. The Halifax Building Society, which counts as a credit institution, established an alliance with Standard Life, a major provider of life insurance. However, by 1994 the Halifax ended this alliance, quite probably because it had gained much of the expertise it needed in this area so that it could at least manage the delivery of these products in the retail market (it is still using outside expertise in areas such as investment analysis).

The pattern of alliances between insurance and banking firms often leads to the latter becoming a dominant partner. Some of the reasons for this are regulatory. Many national bank regulators do not encourage banks to be owned by non-banking firms and some (such as the British) generally do not permit it. Another important factor favouring banks, at the retail level, is that they have better outlets, mainly through high street branches. It would be difficult for insurance companies to justify the sunk costs of a new high street presence, but it makes tremendous sense for banks to try and achieve economies of scope through cross-selling insurance products (Nicholson, 1992). Therefore, given the changing nature of the financial services industry, the rational choices for banking and insurance companies are constrained in different ways, and in the case of insurance companies, to a greater extent.

Conclusion

The analysis of this case indicates that banks and insurance companies make rational choices through the strategies that they develop over time. These strategic choices are conditioned by the economic power of the firm in the market. As part of the process of making strategy, firms enter into alliances. Some of these alliances are to achieve collective decision-making on behalf of the industry at the national and at the European level. Other alliances are made in the marketplace with other firms, and this may result in mergers and take-overs. As regards the institutional alliances in both the EBF and the CEA, there is clear evidence of the continued existence of national positions on some policy questions, especially those connected to the liberalization of markets. When national positions shift, as was the case of the French in the CEA, this shift will alter the overall position of the association and lead to changes in the speed or nature of EU directives. Individual firms play a role in the EBF and CEA, providing skilled committee members and filling leadership roles in capacities such as the president of the association. However, no real evidence or examples have come to light from research of individual companies seeking to use collective decision-making to gain competitive advantage. Rather, participation in institutional alliances is seen more as a means of influencing the general climate for business and for the individual firms to gain the best possible information about changes to market conditions, especially regarding issues such as regulation and taxation. Such information, no doubt, is one factor among several feeding into the corporate planning process of banks and insurance companies as they face an even more competitive European marketplace for financial services in the coming years.

References

ABN-AMRO (1994) Annual Report 1993. Amsterdam: ABN-AMRO.

Bank of England Quarterly Bulletin (BEQB) (1993) 'Cross-border alliances in banking and financial services in the single market', *BEQB*, vol. 33, pp. 372–378.

Bisignano, J. (1992) 'Banking in the European Economic Community: structure, competition and public policy', in Kaufman, G. G. (ed) *Banking Structures in Major Countries*. Boston, MA: Kluwer.

British Bankers' Association (BBA) (1994) Annual Report 1993–1994. London: BBA.

Comité Européen des Assurances (CEA) (1994) *CEA Info*, no. 34, June. Paris: CEA.

Commission of the European Communities (1993) *XXII Report on Competition Policy 1992*. Luxembourg: Office for Official Publications of the EC.

Ghoshal, S. (1987) 'Global strategy: an organizing framework', *Strategic Management Journal*, vol. 8, pp. 425–440.

Lindblom, C.E. (1968) *The Policy Making Process*. Englewood Cliffs, NJ: Prentice Hall.

London Investment Banking Association (LIBA) (1994) Annual Report for 1993. London: LIBA.

Majone, G. (1989) *Evidence Argument and Persuasion in the Policy Process*. Yale: Yale University Press.

Nicholson, G. (1992) 'Competition between banks and insurance companies: the challenge of bancassurance', in Steinherr, A. (ed.) *The New European Financial Market Place*. London: Longman.

Vipond, P. (1994) 'The financial environment', in Nugent, N. and O'Donnell, R. (eds) *The European Business Environment*. London: Macmillan.

CASE 8

The Representation of Retailing in Europe

Grant Jordan and **Anna Wadsworth**

This case study deals primarily with EuroCommerce, the European federation representing retailing and distribution. Commerce is one of the most important sectors of the European economy. The single European market has some 320 million consumers. Retailing accounts for 15 million jobs, of which the wholesale sector provides 4.5 million. The nature of EuroCommerce's work is shown in some of the achievements claimed in publicity material in 1993:

- Participation in Commission and Council level discussions on behalf of the food trade in food law matters such as the removal of a proposed ban on the use of certain packaging gases in the EU additives text;

- Success in the battle over the footwear labelling directive which, prior to the EuroCommerce input, had required pictogram posters to be placed at the point of sale to inform consumers of the components of the footwear.

- Reduction in the quantitative targets regarding recovery of packaging and packaging waste.

- Confirmation from the Commission that commerce was eligible for intervention from structural funds.

EuroCommerce was created on 29 January 1993 by the merger of three separate lobby groups: the Confédération Européene de Commerce (CECD), the Federation of European Wholesale and International Trade Associations (FEWITA) and the Groupment Européene des Enterprise de Distribution Integrée (GEDIS).

EuroCommerce provides a single voice for retailers, wholesalers and traders – both small and medium-size enterprises (SMEs) and major distributors – whether trading in food or non-food sectors (EuroCommerce brochure, 1993). It aims for the cohesion of a very varied membership (EuroCommerce Newsfax, November 1993). EuroCommerce has at least one member in every Community/EFTA country and the Hungarian Chamber of Commerce is the first eastern European member to be affiliated.

The first EuroCommerce Annual Report (1993) claimed that the merger stemmed from the logic of the single European market, 'which saw the need for a strong organization to successfully defend the common interests of commerce. The effects of the Maastricht treaty will make this even more apparent ...'. The British participant in EuroCommerce (the British Retail Consortium) has described the significance of the European dimension as follows:

> with the completion of the Single Market ... the issues addressed by the British Retail Consortium have an increasingly European dimension ... the majority are now directly influenced by events in Brussels.

EuroCommerce has three different types of member. There are *full members* which are 'national associations representing all the retail, wholesale and international trade sectors of the member states of EC and EFTA countries' (Article 4.1 of Internal Regulations). Typical full members are the Belgian participants, Fédération Belge des Enterprises de Distribution and Nationale Christelijk Middenstand Verbond, and the single British member, the British Retail Consortium. There are about thirty-five full members. Subscription levels vary, but one large member pays about £100,000.

There are *affiliated members* who are (1) European associations of branches of commerce, and (2) companies or groups of companies engaged in commerce. (To be admitted to EuroCommerce they must also be a member of a national body already in full membership. See Article 4.3 of the Internal Regulations.)

Affiliated bodies include the European Federation of Electronics Retailers, Confederation of International Trading Houses Associations and individual companies such as Kingfisher, Tesco, Kaufhaus, and Marks and Spencer.

Supporting members are: 'individuals and legal entities whose activities do not meet the definition of commerce but who wish to contribute to its objectives' (Article 4.3).

The merger brought together the existing members of the three parent bodies: all full and associate members of CECD, all members of GEDIS and FEWITA itself. This formula lasts until the end of 1995 at which time FEWITA loses its automatic right to membership and the rights and obligations are taken over by those of its members who so request. They will then individually become members. FEWITA's place in the new organization was also protected by (temporary) veto powers on certain matters (e.g. Articles 9, 11, 12).

Given the wide interests found within EuroCommerce, there is a politics of membership: there is rarely a single national organization that 'fits' the EuroCommerce brief. In the British case there are thought to be advantages for British companies through the single membership of the BRC, but other business groups would be eligible to join (e.g. Association of British Chambers of Commerce). BRC's single representative position is due to an early awareness on its part of the European issue and some entrepreneurial initiative. BRC attempts to ensure that its own category of affiliated membership subsumes other trade or professional groups that are active in the area. From the CBI perspective, the BRC is a sectoral trade association, such as the National Farmers' Union, Society of Motor Manufacturers or Federation of Clearing Banks, all of which lobby separately *and through the CBI*. The BRC has resisted invitations to join. Undoubtedly the BRC sees the CBI as a rival voice for its members: for example, the CBI publishes widely reported retail sales figures. Individual companies such as Kingfisher are prominent members of both the BRC and the CBI.

As a general policy, BRC operates through 'coalition-building'; this helps to ensure that it is not challenged in Europe as the authoritative British voice. However, there is surprisingly little contact between the CBI and BRC at Brussels. The BRC does not participate, for example, in the 'CBI Club in Brussels' though the Brussels representatives of individual retailers are active.

Organization of EuroCommerce

EuroCommerce has a general assembly but is run by three smaller entities: the board of administration, the steering group and, the general secretariat. The board of administration has at least one and a maximum of four members per country, one of whom represents wholesale and international trade. The board is appointed by the general assembly.

Board and assembly votes can only take place on issues that are specified in advance on the agenda. Board and assembly decisions are only valid if half the total votes of EuroCommerce are present or represented. Except for special cases, a simple majority suffices. Internal regulations set out the number of votes held by each full member: this can vary depending on whether the subject matter is general business or budgetary matters.

For decisions on budgetary matters each *country* (sic) has a number of votes (*see **Exhibit 8.1***) depending on its collective subscription: one vote per BFr 300,000 paid, to be reviewed annually, with a maximum of sixteen and a minimum of one vote. For non-budgetary decisions each country is allocated votes in proportion to representation on the EC Council of Minsters (EFTA countries get one vote each). It is up to the national organizations represented on EuroCommerce to share their allocated votes internally.

Exhibit 8.1 *EuroCommerce: allocation of votes in decision-making*

Country	Allocated votes
Austria	1
Belgium	5
Denmark	3
Finland	1
France	10
Germany	10
Greece	5
Iceland	1
Ireland	3
Italy	10
Luxembourg	2
Netherlands	5
Norway	1
Portugal	5
Spain	8
Sweden	1
Switzerland	1
UK	10
Total votes	82

Note: This assumes a budget of BFr 40 million; 30 million from full members and 10 million from other members.

Despite the fairly elaborate voting rules, the working assumption is that EuroCommerce should act through consensus. If a vote is taken, the 'losing' position can insist that its position is 'clearly expressed' in any lobbying by EuroCommerce. This is one reason that unsuccessful member organizations might persist in membership even when they lose on a vote. A more speculative reason is that EuroCommerce is sufficiently broadly based in that if a member leaves, it knows that EuroCommerce will continue to act. The calculation will usually be that it is better to stay inside with a chance of influence than to 'exit' and forfeit all say.

The board of administration decides on the setting up of committees or working groups. The steering group consists of the president, the vice-presidents, the secretary general and the treasurer (Article 12d). The secretary general heads the professional organization; attending and minuting the meetings and assemblies of the association, but without a vote. Currently the secretary general is backed by five political consultants and four support staff. The organization functions largely through a series of committees: social affairs, legal/consumer affairs, fiscal affairs, new methods of payments, food law, environment, logistics, and international trade. The objective of the food law committee (as an example) is to:

> lobby as effectively as possible so that proposed EU legislation will not negatively influence the activities of food retailers. Proposals made by European civil servants often demonstrate a lack of insight into the day to day practicalities of operating a food business.
>
> *(Annual Report 1994, p. 17)*

These committees exist to try to create a consensus within the industry that will influence Commission officials. For example, the food law committee reports that 'several organizations have been invited to participate in the activities of the Food Committee, thus enabling EuroCommerce to speak on behalf of all food trade'.

EuroCommerce is active in the Packaging Chain Forum which is responding to the proposed directive on packaging and packaging waste. EuroCommerce had responsibility providing for the secretariat of the SME Forum from July to December 1993. In 1994 it is attempting to secure a commerce place on the new Consumer Forum. EuroCommerce also acts on its own: for example, meeting Belgian COREPER representatives during the Belgian presidency of the Council.

Even though most EuroCommerce business is with DG XXIII, it will meet other officials as necessary. For example, it met DG XI (environment) in 1993 to discuss ozone layer depletion. On the code of conduct about card-based payment systems when there was stalemate between the banking industry and commerce, EuroCommerce asked for arbitration from the Commission and met the relevant director-generals. These were Claus-Dieter Ehlermenn (DG IV Competition), John Mogg (DG XV financial services – the lead directorate), Heinrich von Moltke (DG XXIII commerce and services) and Dieter Hoffmann, Head of Unit of the CPS (Consumer Policy Service). They lobbied Mr Krenzler, director-general of DG I on EC external trade policy. They also discussed a position paper with Mr Dugimont, coordinator of the steering group on the Uruguay Round, and sent the paper to the Commissioners, the Economic and Social Committee (ESC) and the European Parliament. They participated in the Industrial Group on the Protection of the Ozone Layer (IGPOL), which is the official consultation platform of industry and trade at the Commission. Contacts are also maintained with the Parliament and the ESC. About sixty EC officials attended the annual European Day of Commerce during which Euro-Commerce tries to give commerce a higher profile.

The Commission also functions through committees that act as a link between its directorates and the sectors for which it is responsible. The Commission staff are few in number and rely on outside bodies both for information and building political support. This style presents an opportunity for groups such as EuroCommerce.

The most significant early achievement of EuroCommerce was to obtain recognition from the commissioner for commerce that Euro-Commerce would be accepted as the relevant representative of commerce. For example, in its first year of existence (1993), EuroCommerce participated in exercises on: the company-feedback committee on VAT and excise duties; the pilot group on labelling of cameras, and the consultative forum on the eco-label award scheme (Annual Report 1993, p. 2).

On the Advisory Foodstuffs Committee of DG III EuroCommerce is allowed to determine the retail representatives. National representatives in this case have to brief the selected EuroCommerce participants.

When EuroCommerce feels it is not having success at Commission level, it can use its national members to press their own governments. On personal data protection in 1993, EuroCommerce noted:

> the Commission is not ready to adopt [all EuroCommerce proposals] and the members have been strongly requested to lobby at national level on the basis of the EuroCommerce position paper as the text is being discussed at Council level for adoption of a Common Position.
>
> *(Annual Report 1993, p. 10)*

Fast track Decision-Making

EuroCommerce, like other European organizations such as the European Federation of Pharmaceutical Industry Associations (EFPIA), has intro-duced a 'fast-track' decision-making procedure. This involves the steering committee being able to take responsibility for EuroCommerce decisions thereby relieving members of the difficult task of reaching a compromise (if asked, the members might disagree, but they might be prepared to live with a fast-track decision). Instead, the vice-presidents and the secretary general can come to a decision on a matter. This system can have advantages in meeting opportunities for an input to policy-making where there is often time pressure. However, there is a possibility that SMEs can be ignored as it is the larger companies that typically supply the vice-presidencies. The procedure has to be used with political sensitivity to avoid, in effect, driving some members out of the organization. On the whole, though, even small members believe that the increase in effectiveness is worth some risk to the level of control by members.

Rationale for EuroCommerce Membership

All studies of interest group membership are subject to the argument by Olson which suggests that individuals or companies do not join groups in pursuit of collective benefits:

> Indeed, unless the number of individuals in a group is quite small, or unless there is coercion or some other special device to make individuals act in their common interest, *rational self-interested individuals will not act to achieve their common or group interests*. (1965, p. 2)

In this perspective they would 'free-ride' and assume that they could obtain the benefit without any contribution. EuroCommerce advertising material suggests that its aim is to 'enable the setting up of a single market in which the laws will be flexible and favourable to the growth of one of the most dynamic and innovative sectors in the European economy'. Olson suggested that pursuit of such general objectives is not rational investment by any individual company.

In practice, organizations seem more successful at mobilization of members than Olson anticipated. This is for several reasons. There *are* selective incentives which Olson stressed are available only to those in membership. A EuroCommerce brochure (1993) says:

> Further incentives are: to monitor developments, provide information and support, and influence the crucial players . . . Being a member of EuroCommerce gives access to any information required by decision-makers in the commercial sector . . . Being a member also allows active participation in the decision-making process of the European Community.

However, membership also seems subject to other pressures. There is an 'equity ethic' which induces a 'fair share' style of participation: individuals and groups feel a responsibility to contribute rather than to free-ride. There are non-economic, 'soft' incentives, such as respect, that were discounted by Olson. Thirdly, and a proposition that is particularly relevant, participation within groups can help shape the group agenda. In other words, the *active* member can help determine which collective goods are pursued: the level of activity within the organization may be of more significance in terms of securing benefits than membership *per se*. Membership can be of a 'Trojan Horse' type. The Euro federation can be the means for the company to get its selective ambitions discussed at directorate level.

Consider another example from BRC related to the fitting of speed limiters to goods delivery vehicles:

> The [Distribution] Committee was broadly content with the original UK proposals but strongly opposed to the EC's proposals which will result in a lower speed limit overall. The BRC pursued the issue strongly within [EuroCommerce] and succeeded in obtaining a joint . . . position on the issue . . .

In other words, membership of a Euro group can mean that on matters that particularly affect one country, that country can 'wrap itself in the Euro flag' and talk to the Commission as a legitimate Euro interest rather than as a 'selfish' national interest.

The Euro group membership means that – particularly where there is a strong national interest – the national organization (and through it, its leading member companies) can claim EuroCommerce places in key negotiations and hence parachute into the heart of the discussions in a way that would be more difficult if it were not wearing a Euro label. Indeed, a large company with its own representation in Brussels claimed that its own dealings with officials were made easier because it was also active in the appropriate national and Euro group. They felt that officials could, if necesary, pretend to themseves that they were meeting them as prominent representatives of a Euro organization rather than as self-interested lobbyists. In other words, as argued by McLaughlin *et al*. (1993, p. 202)

> while some companies gain good access, it appears that Euro-groups are more likely to find themselves pushing at an open door in Brussels. Officials seem predisposed to groups making them an attractive lobbying option for major companies. If large companies can shape group positions to suit their particular needs this becomes a crucial channel of influence.

Individual companies will operate through their national organizations or through their own permanent staff in Brussels (e.g. Marks and Spencer), but they might join EuroCommerce as an affiliated member. For example, on the matter of the food claims directive, Tesco affiliated to Euro-Commerce on an individual basis because the BRC place within the relevant committee of EuroCommerce was already taken. Even without a vote on EuroCommerce, participation can help secure the policy preference of affiliated members.

EuroCommerce is the recognized partner for commerce with DG XXIII. The secretary-general of EuroCommerce, Mr Henrik Kroner argued, 'EuroCommerce doesn't need to persuade members to join; we offer membership and if the groups don't join they miss out on member privileges'. Since EuroCommerce has this access to the Commission, free-riding is not very sensible for a national group. It is unlikely to get as good access standing outside the umbrella of EuroCommerce as it does by political action within EuroCommerce.

EuroCommerce and UNICE

Just as there is tension between national-level competitors such as the BRC and the CBI, Brussels-level relations between EuroCommerce and UNICE (Union of Industrial and Employers' Confederations of Europe) are perhaps more competitive than might be imagined. One UNICE activist has conceded that in matters such as the working time directive, UNICE did not reflect commerce's problems, though he claimed that on areas such as the environment and transport UNICE's performance was better. He argued that, nonetheless, 'EuroCommerce has responded by separating itself from UNICE rather than trying to get closer to it'. With regard to the social dialogue (under the Social Protocol of Maastricht), EuroCommerce is claiming a separate seat opposite the ETUC as well as its sectoral dialogue with EUROFIET (European Retail Trade Union Organization). UNICE's reaction has been to set up a European Employer's Network.

Advantage of the Euro Federation in the Policy Process

The rationale for the integrated, single-voice Euro federation is that such a structure of representation is more cost-effective. It is also likely to be particularly effective *vis-à-vis* the Commission when there is group unanimity. Because of the policy-making complexity that would result, individual companies are less likely to be listened to on a one-to-one basis – though there are examples of such influence in special circumstances. The 'legitimacy' of the Euro federations within Community discussions is itself a potential benefit for the member organizations in securing valued outcomes – as long as they are happy with the federation position.

European confederations enjoy a privileged relationship with the Commission (Pryce, 1973). Partly, this is a preference for simpler consultative patterns. In the early Community there was also optimism that by enhancing the access of Community-wide groups the divisive national pressures could be diminished. Mazey and Richardson (1993) argue that the

Single European Act 1986 reinforced the tendency for lobbying by Euro, rather than national, organizations. They say that the 'Luxembourg compromise' of 1966 had in effect given national governments a veto to defend national interests. This was eroded by the Single European Act.

Another reason for Commission support for Euro federation structures is that they help to provide the opportunity for self-regulation that can serve as a simple alternative to EC legislation. Self-regulation means that the Commission avoids the time demands (and political costs) implicit in policy formulation, adaption, adoption and implementation, but knows that the sector is being sufficiently regulated. As EuroCommerce puts the argument, it aims:

> to develop codes of practice as a flexible alternative to European legislation which cannot regulate the multiplicity of ways in which commerce meets consumers' changing attitudes without being binding or too detailed. It is felt codes of practice are voluntary and therefore more motivating and effective than mandatory regulations.
>
> *(EuroCommerce Newsletter, November 1993, p. 1)*

Community institutions have encouraged the self-regulatory approach and have supported the principle of subsidiarity and recommending the wider and more timely consultation with interest groups. It also argued that Community institutions should be more transparent in their activities so that interest groups could be better informed. According to a Commission document *Towards a Single Market in Distribution* (1991) 'formal proposals for Directives and Regulations . . . will be made as a last resort'.

Broadly speaking, there are five main phases in the EC policy-making process: problem definition; formal proposal (from the Commission); amending stage (including European Parliament input); amending (at Council of Ministers stage); and implementation (at national level). An organization such as EuroCommerce will attempt to lobby at all stages, but the most important phases are likely to be earlier rather than later. As Robert Hull, himself a Commission official, has argued:

> The Commission has to be the primary target of any lobbyist or pressure group. The early thinking on any proposal takes place usually in the office of one Commission official who will have the responsibility for drafting legislation. The individual who is responsible for the initial preparation process over a given period of time (first draft, consultations with the Commission, consultations with interested parties, subsequent drafts, navigation through the Commission) will find that when the final proposal is adopted by the Commission it usually contains 80 per cent of his or her proposal.
>
> *(1993, p. 83)*

The role and goal of the lobbying organization is to attempt to get the *problem definition* agreed in ways that suit its members. This can often be done in informal negotiations with Commission staff. Sometimes the function is not to influence Commission policy but to persuade the Commission that it needs to adopt a policy: the group identifies the problem. Hull says (1993, p. 83): 'at the beginning he or she is a very lonely official with a blank sheet of paper, wondering what to put on it. Lobbying at this early stage therefore offers the greatest opportunity to shape thinking and ultimately to shape policy'. The first (1993) annual report of EuroCommerce stressed that its creation in 1993 led to a reinforcing of informal contacts with European institutions.

Nonetheless, for structural reasons a body as broadly constituted as EuroCommerce is likely to be more influential at the second (formal proposal) stage of policy-making than in the early problem definition stages. Defining the 'good' of the organization is much more complex than for the individual company. We might expect individual firms to be able to intervene more effectively in preliminary stages of policy-making. In contrast, the EuroCommerce position tends to be the reactive consensus secured in response to proposals by the Commission.

Pressures within EuroCommerce

A Brussels activist argued that consensus can be reached within Euro-Commerce committees 80 per cent of the time – an example of compromise/harmony was on a proposed directive on footwear labelling. Sometimes EuroCommerce splits into two broad camps (e.g. on packaging and packing waste); at other times one member can be recalictrant (e.g. hallmarking of precious metals) and there is national isolation. In this latter case the BRC came to the table with its own experience. In Britain there was independent third-party hallmarking, but in Germany, for example, the marking was done by manufacturers. Britain tried to work with the Dutch but ended up operating on its own.

Another possible pattern of interests is where the national groups within EuroCommerce reach a compromise but the national governments on the Council of Ministers fail to do so. An example was on the European Works Council. On the one hand, UK commerce backs the Conservative government's opposition to works councils (under the Social Protocol), but there are two good reasons that British companies would want to participate in discussions about such councils. Firstly, British companies operating in other countries will have to comply with local conditions. Secondly, British companies believe that a future Labour government might accept agreements made before they came to office, in which case the British companies will have missed their opportunity for influence.

BRC and its relations with the CBI, and Euro federations such as EuroCommerce, are examples of the pressures in all lobbying organizations between breadth and specialization. The possible lines of cleavage within EuroCommerce are both national and subsectoral.

National Issue: The British Example

In a whole range of domestic areas the BRC offers its cooperation to policy-makers anxious to raise awareness of particular policies (not least a battery of EC directives). Thus, the BRC is represented on departmental committees such as the DTI Monitoring Committee on Misleading Price Indications and the DTI Ad Hoc Committee on Monitoring Green Claims in Advertising and its subcommittee on Animal Welfare Labelling. This sort of 'good citizen' participation may seem minor but the extent to which it establishes goodwill and trust between the group and Whitehall should not be under-estimated.

The civil service (both in Whitehall and Brussels) is organized on a client group basis. Thus the civil servant in a particular division is likely to define his or her job as assisting particular groups. The BRC is usually, if not always, dealing with civil servants who recognize that part of their job description is to act as advocate for particular groups.

On the whole, civil servants are well aware of the likely reactions of establised interests. Thus the European regulations on a system of 'appelation d'origine' for foods (where can a Cornish pasty be made?) were made against the joint opposition of BRC and other interest groups. The Ministry for Agriculture, Fisheries and Food (MAFF), which had no departmental angle itself, checked with its 'constituents' and quickly found there was opposition. The BRC Annual Report 1992 notes: 'The final text reflected MAFF recommendations to minimise the potential scope of application of the regime . . . BRC is assisting MAFF in drawing up the UK's contribution to the list [of generic names excluded, e.g. 'Cheddar' cheese].'

BRC set up a Brussels office in support of its membership of EuroCommerce, but the office also exists as an alternative to Euro-Commerce. BRC has been identified as particulary influential in Brussels and within EuroCommerce for five main reasons. Firstly, the (two-person) BRC office pre-dated the establishment of the EuroCommerce office in January 1993. This meant that strong relationships built up when the BRC staff perhaps had a useful comparative advantage in terms of knowledge of the system. Secondly, the BRC has an informal and proactive style within Brussels that is generally seen as being associated with influence. Thirdly, the physical presence of the BRC two doors down the EuroCommerce corridor means that they may be given the opportunity to comment on rough drafts of documents. Indeed, since the EuroCommerce is undermanned at times, BRC staff can on occasion be delegated the drafting of Euro-Commerce material. Fourthly, the Brussels BRC has maintained a conspicuously close relationship with the London office and with the British government departments. On occasion this means that BRC can pick up information about policy developments before EuroCommerce (e.g. information on the establishment number for dairies and health marks on milk and dairy products came to EuroCommerce via the BRC's national channels). Fifthly, the British also have some advantage in that the BRC serves as one umbrella group for British interests: other countries are represented by up to five separate organizations (but the position is not simply that 'more is bad': German retailers are represented by four full and one associated member, but overall their influence is certainly stronger than that of the two full members from Greece). Overall, the influence of the British in EuroCommerce is not predominantly due to the structural factor of single group membership but to its activist role within committees and in its active response to invitations to comment.

Subsectoral Conflicts

In a group as broadly based as EuroCommerce there are inevitably tensions between the component subsectors. Writing with a US perspective, Heinz *et al.* (1993) in effect declare the peak association dead; even where it still exists its dominance is so reduced that it represents a different phenomenon. They note that 'peak associations cannot always satisfy the policy preferences of their diverse constituencies. Larger associations tend to take positions that minimize internal conflict, thus encouraging specialized interests to develop independent strategies' (p. 376).

Interest groups such as EuroCommerce try to accommodate the internal pressures by systems of committee specialization that attempt to reconcile narrow demands with the advantages of a broad group that might have easier access to officials. This sort of balance is, however, difficult to maintain in the long term. It is perhaps for this sort of reason that bodies like the Confederation of British Industry keep out of sectoral arrangements such as EuroCommerce and prefer to operate through UNICE which acts as a Euro-level umbrella group for national umbrellas: there is perhaps too much potential for conflict within its own membership. Pressures towards simplification of the interest group pattern are liable to be reversed by demands for more specialized representation. The tide is still running towards simplification, but the very success of the strategy may lead to centrifugal tendencies as the lowest common denominator groups that result may be subject to fragmentation.

References

Heinz, J. P., Laumann, E. O., Nelson, R. and Salisbury, R. (1993) *The Hollow Core: Private Interests in National Policy Making*. Cambridge, MA: Harvard University Press.

Hull, R. (1993) 'Lobbying Brussels: a view from within', in Mazey, S. and Richardson, J. J. (eds) *Lobbying in the European Community*. Oxford: Oxford University Press.

Mazey, S. and Richardson, J. J. (1993) *Lobbying in the European Community*. Oxford: Oxford University Press.

McLaughlin, A., Jordan, G. and Maloney, W. (1993) 'Corporate lobbying in the European Community', *Journal of Common Market Studies*, vol. 31, pp. 191–213.

Olson, M. (1965) *The Logic of Collective Action*. Cambridge, MA: Harvard University Press.

Pryce, R. (1973) *The Politics of the European Community*. London: Butterworth.

CASE 9

Tourism

How Well Served, and Organized, is the
'World's Largest Industry' in Europe?

Justin Greenwood

Travel and tourism lays claim to be 'the world's largest industry and the world's largest generator of jobs' (World Travel and Tourism Council, 1994). Europe accounts for 60 per cent of world tourism in terms of numbers of visitors and 53 per cent in terms of revenue, representing an estimated 5.5 per cent of the European Community's gross national product (Commission, 1994). A simple reading of these data might suggest that we would expect to find a range of tourism competencies within the Commission, administered by a well resourced unit; and that there would be a well endowed, encompassing and effective interest association representing the umbrella of tourism interests in Brussels. The reality is somewhat different. The tourism unit housed within DG XXIII consists of five *functionnaires*, and, whilst notoriously overworked, operates with a highly limited set of competencies. Although there is an effective global association with a Brussels branch office – the World Travel and Tourism Council – it is an international organization representing the interests of the largest firms in a domain with a significant small business segment. A Brussels-based tourism-wide interest association dedicated to European representation does not exist; instead, there is a plethora of associations representing different types of interest within tourism, some of which do not have Brussels bases and whose resources are often highly limited. Why should 'the world's largest industry' lack attention and political coordination across its range of activities in Europe?

The answer to this question lies in the fragmented nature of tourism businesses. A relatively well defined sector such as the pharmaceutical industry enjoys a considerable advantage over tourism in seeking to organize itself. Indeed, tourism is more a fragmented service domain than an 'industry'. Tourism consists of a variety of activities, and its very definition is extremely contentious. Package tour holidays are uncontroversial; but

128

should we include under the 'tourism' umbrella activities such as a business trip to a neighbouring town, a meal taken at a distant Indian restaurant, or expenditure incurred by a student in fulfilling a study exchange under the SOCRATES programme?

An increasingly accepted definition, and one used by the Organization for Economic Cooperation and Development (OECD), the World Tourism Organization (WTO) and the European Commission, states that tourism is an activity involving trips away from home exceeding 24 hours. This would include not only all holiday trips, but business and conference travel, visits to friends and relatives, and trips for study and health purposes, although some definitions exclude these last three categories. Nevertheless, including travel for purposes beyond long break (over four days) and short break (more than one but fewer than four days) holidays does rather have the effect of making 'tourism' seem more of a statistical aggregation than an industry. Even if these controversies are put to one side, the issue about diversity of businesses which contribute to 'tourism' remains. Should multinational airlines be classified as 'tourism enterprises', or should they be considered more as transport companies? What of public railway systems? In reality, tourism is a 'domain' which itself consists of many different contributory sectors, including hotels, self-catering establishments, timeshares, caravan and camp sites, tourist attractions and theme parks, museums and historic buildings, entertainment outlets, package and scheduled travel, recreation activity in all its forms which is used by those on 24-hour-plus trips, travel agents, business and conference meetings, retail outlets and restaurants.

Such diversity by sector in part signifies diversity by size, ranging from a concession by a small croft to erect a tent on private land, to a multinational airline. A further cleavage is between the types of organization concerned. These include public sector organizations, such as municipal visitor centres; organizations holding trust, charitable or cooperative status (such as the UK National Trust, or guardians of a local historic attraction); activities of private individuals (such as a public exhibition of model railway artifacts by an enthusiast); and private sector enterprises, such as a hotel and restaurant chain or a multinational enterprise. These cleavages help explain the lack of an all-powerful 'industry unit' in the Commission, or the absence of a large tourism interest association located in the politically fashionable Brussels 1040 district.

Tourism Competencies of the European Union

The marginalized Economic and Social Committee (ESC) has historically been the European institution which has shown most interest in tourism, although this has been matched in recent years by the European Parliament (EP). Although EP activities mainly take the form of an unofficial intergroup, consisting of any MEP with an interest in tourism affairs and a range of interested parties, it does provide an important means of access for tourism interests into public policies, particularly where decisions impacting on tourism are taken by cooperation and codecision mechanisms. The European Commission's activities reflect the diversity of tourism activities. A number of directorates-general (DGs) have remits which affect tourism interests not inconsiderably, such as DG I (external relations), DG III (internal market), DG IV (competition), DG V (employment), DG VII (transport), DG X (culture), DG XI (environment), DG XVI (regional policies), DG XXI (customs union, value added tax) and DG XXIII (small businesses). This latter directorate-general includes the tourism unit, which seeks to coordinate tourism issues across the spectrum of Commission activities and policies, and handles the minimum competencies retained by the Commission in the tourism domain. However, the important regulatory issues arise from the activities of other DGs, where there is no guarantee that the interests of the tourism domain are a top priority. Hence the four most important regulatory events to impact upon tourism in recent years have come from outside DG XXIII. These are:

1. The 1989 Council Regulation 2299/89 on computerized reservation systems, preventing distortion of competition by the order of appearance of airlines' flights on travel agents computer reservation screens.

2. The 1990 package travel directive, giving the consumer a minimalist framework of protection.

3. The 1993 unfair contract terms directive, giving a cooling off period for Timeshare contracts.

4. The 1994 distance selling directive, where tourism interests and DG XXIII had to work hard to ensure that tourism businesses (excluding timeshares), affected by a number of clauses including those concerning reservations, would be excluded from its scope.

Besides representing tourism interests on a 'damage limitation' exercise throughout the range of Commission policies which emerge, the DG XXIII unit attempts to ensure a proactive role where Commission activities do not embrace tourism but could usefully do so; for instance, not one Commission policy is concerned with fairgrounds. However, there is a view among those in the tourism domain that the unit lacks influence, not least because of its small size and the range of functions it needs to undertake.

Policy on tourism is based on a communication submitted to the Council in January 1986, and a small amount of subsequent 'incremental creep'. Its ambitions are limited to:

1. Assisting tourism flows to the EC, particularly from the USA.

2. Improving the seasonal and geographical spread of tourism.

3. Better use of financial aid, such as that available under regional policy initiatives.

4. Better information and protection of tourists.

5. Improving working conditions in tourism enterprises.

6. Increasing awareness of the sector.

7. Preservation of heritage.

8. Developing new forms of tourism such as sports tourism.

9. Promoting tourism opportunities for disadvantaged groups.

10. Promoting quality within the tourism domain.

The limited nature of these activities is emphasized by the fact that the tourism unit in DG XXIII has a budget of only ECU 6 million to fulfil these responsibilities. This money is spent mainly on pilot studies for projects, such as schemes to develop new kinds of tourism. An additional concern is that, while tourism statistics are collected by organizations such as the World Tourism Organisation, there is no regular statistical profile of tourism in Europe. This issue is addressed through the framework research programme, where the task is put out to contract by tender because the DG XXIII tourism unit is too overworked to take on the job itself. Indeed, it is so overworked that it does not have time to enter into meaningful dialogue with tourism interest associations in a way which is evident in other policy domains, such as pharmaceuticals and consumer electronics. The Advisory Committee on Tourism, representing the variety of tourism interests across the EU, has not met for almost two years, and was recently in threat of being disbanded. There are no significant, sustained bilateral exchanges between the unit and any interest groups in the tourism domain, nor any select 'roundtable discussions'. Rather, when the unit needs to consult industry, it holds large, impersonal, one-day meetings in a conference centre where any interest can put forward a view. Around ninety representatives of tourism interests were present, for instance, when the unit held a consultation meeting on the 1994 distance selling directive. Another main form of industry/Commission dialogue is where a Commission official is invited to address a tourism conference. It is a matter of regret to officials in the unit that they do not have sufficient time for more direct exchanges with tourism interests, but their workload does not enable them to do so. Indeed, the unit has not sought to manage its dialogue by playing a more active role in organizing tourism interests into a 'one-stop shop' in a way in which other parts of the Commission have done with their corresponding sectors. In areas such as biotechnology, the Commission has found that playing such a role has also helped it in managing workload and increasing the flow of information relevant to policy.

The workload of the tourism unit also means that the unit does not have the time to attend the Parliament intergroup on tourism, which, unusually, is where there is strongest dialogue between tourism interests as a whole and EU policy-makers. However, tourism interests are fairly well represented through the Council of Ministers, to the extent that most member states, particularly in the south of Europe, recognize national and regional interests in the promotion and development of tourism. Nevertheless, there is a dispute, where the lines are drawn roughly between the northern and the southern countries, about the development of Euro competencies in tourism. Broadly speaking, southern countries seek Euro competencies, whereas northern countries, most notably Germany and then Britain in this case, fret about subsidiarity and national sovereignty. Only at the last minute was a reference to tourism squeezed into the Maastricht Treaty. The tourism unit in DG XXIII is at present working on a Green Paper, to be published in 1995, on the development of Euro tourism competencies. Of interest is that tourism groups will again not have the chance to provide input to the Paper, but rather will have to wait until it is produced. This underlines the rather weak policy relationship between the Commission and tourism interests. Part of this can be attributed to the relative weakness of interest representation structures for tourism as a whole.

European Collective Action in Tourism

While there is a plethora of interest associations across the European Union with some degree of interest in Euro tourism, there is only a limited number of significant associations representing mainly tourism interests which are based in Brussels. None seeks to encompass the diversity of tourism interests. Two have a level of resources to give them more than just a symbolic presence: HOTREC (Confederation of the National Hotel and Restaurant Associations in the European Community) is a federation of national hotel and restaurant associations; and the WTTC (World Travel and Tourism Council) which is a global association looking after the interests of large companies (although some of the issues covered are of relevance to smaller players too). ECTAA (Group of National Travel Agents' and Tour Operators' Associations within the EEC), which one might expect to be significantly resourced, has a staff which the organization describes as 'very limited', such that it needs to request funds from outside its members for operational requirements (ECTAA, 1994). Indeed, none of these associations has the resources to match those of the well organized sector associations such as pharmaceuticals and chemicals, with secretariats of twenty and fifty staff respectively. Moreover, the umbrella association seeking to coordinate all tourism's interests, the European Tourism Action Group (ETAG), is resourced by one executive operating from a private address in London, assisted by administrative help as required from a different organization in Paris. This organization has no ambition to be a 'one-stop shop' tourism representative, but rather exists as a forum for the exchange of views and as an additional voice for its members.

The apparent tourism-wide absence of organization reminds us that we cannot make the mechanical link between the resources of an 'industry', and its patterns of collective action and influence. Firstly, in order to be effective, power resources such as economic 'bargaining chips' need to be organized properly, and organized at the European level by well endowed Brussels-based associations. Secondly, the degree of organization of an interest is dependent upon its cohesiveness. The relative lack of industry-wide organization of tourism interests reflects the diversity of tourism itself. In turn, this is partly responsible for the lack of tourism competencies in the European Union. Given the presence of disagreement at the Council of Ministers on the subject, tourism interests need to have convinced the Commission of the need to invest resources in the promotion, deregulation and reregulation for market purposes of 'the world's largest industry'. It has been unable to do so. In part, the argument has some circularity in that lack of organization contributes to lack of Euro competencies, which in turn does not provide an incentive for industry-wide European organization. Yet there is more to the circularity argument, in that one of the major features responsible for the lack of Europe-wide organization is the diversity of the tourism domain.

The landscape of European tourism interest associations appears in *Exhibit 9.1*. The exhibit provides an overwhelming impression of diversity: hence the difficulty of coordination. However, the diversity is greater in that smaller enterprises, which constitute a substantial part of producer interests in tourism, tend not to be represented by these associations. The World Travel and Tourism Council, for instance, is a dedicated representative of large-firm chief executives, and membership is by invitation only; while

Exhibit 9.1   Landscape of European tourism interest associations

Acronym	Tourism association	Location
AEA	Association of European Airlines	Brussels
HOTREC	Confederation of the National Hotel and Restaurant Associations in the European Community	Brussels
EFC	European Caravan Federation	Amsterdam
ECFED	European Community Federation of Youth Hostel Associations	Brussels
EUROTOQUES	European Community of Cooks	Paris
EFCSO	European Federation of Camping Site Organisations	Gloucester, UK
EFCT	European Federation of Conference Towns	Brussels
FERCO	European Federation of Contract Catering Organisations	Brussels
EUROPARKS	European Federation of Leisure Parks	Eindhoven, NL
EFTGA	European Federation of Tourist Guides Associations	Paris
EHMA	European Hotel Managers' Association	Rome
ELRA	European Leisure and Recreation Association	Reading, UK
ETAG	European Tourism Action Group	London
ETTFA	European Tourism Trade Fair Association	Brussels
ETOA	European Tour Operators' Association	Surrey, UK
ETC	European Travel Commission	Paris
EUTO	European Union of Tourist Officers	Brighton, UK
GEBTA	Guild of European Business Travel Agents	London
ECTAA	Group of National Travel Agents' and Tour Operators' Associations within the EU	Brussels
TDA	Timeshare Developers' Association	London
WTTC	World Travel and Tourism Council	New York, London, Brussels

associations in membership of ETAG do not have a small and medium-sized enterprise (SME) constituency. Typically, SMEs have their own associations, rarely operating beyond national boundaries, sometimes partly subsidized by grants from public sources anxious to ensure that these firms have a voice; these associations nonetheless lack the ability to encompass the interests of the industry (Greenwood, 1993). Other sectors have not developed a European tier of organization but remain instead with international outlets. Some of these have a contribution to make, but others are little more than 'letterhead' associations. Others have Europe-wide remits but operate from bases far from Brussels. Some of these, such as the

European Tour Operators' Association, have developed a reputation for effectiveness, while others are less well recognized, including at least one in *Exhibit 9.1* which is virtually defunct. A particularly telling point, however, is that while tourism is a mainstay of southern European economies, most associations lack southern European members. This emphasizes the lack of coverage and limited range of tourism interest representation in Europe.

It is possible that the diversity of the domain, the presence of a significant group of small producer interests, and in some cases absence of organization, has its benefits for Euro organization in that the domain does not (yet) display evidence of competitive interest representation that is apparent in, for instance, biotechnology (Case 5) and, in part, shipping (Case 13). On the other hand, the case of biotechnology does suggest that exclusive 'rich firm clubs' which exclude smaller producer interests can provide an incentive to SMEs where they get themselves organized. This remains to be seen in the case of tourism, although such tensions may emerge as interest representation structures in tourism mature. Similarly, the potential exists for competitive representation, in that some member firms of the World Travel and Tourism Council have member access to other associations, although as yet there is no evidence that this causes difficulties.

HOTREC only became a dedicated European-level representative outlet in 1991, when it gained independence from the Paris-based International Hotel Association and moved to Brussels. It has three permanent staff, including two *functionnaires*, and supplements these resources by drawing on those of its national member associations. Its membership base does not always lend itself easily to platform-building, in that it represents thirty-two national associations. Member associations are thus multiple within some member states; hence, whilst there is only one British association there are no less than six in France. With the exception of the Netherlands, there is a tendency among such members to specialize in representing medium and large hotels and restaurants, which means that the substantial small-firm category so typical of a number of tourism sectors lacks representation at the European level. Links with other sector associations in tourism is limited, although there are exceptions such as attempts to work with ECTAA on matters concerning the package travel directive.

Established in 1990, the World Travel and Tourism Council is an impressive organization, with bases in New York, London and Brussels. Its *raison d'être* is to obtain recognition among public policy-makers of the economic contribution of travel and tourism, to eliminate barriers to growth, and to promote environmentally compatible development. Its members include chief executives from multinational firms in a number of sectors encompassing the diversity of travel and tourism interests, although it has a particular strength in representing those from air transport firms. These include Airbus Industrie, American Airlines, Amsterdam Airport Schipol, Boeing, British Airports Authority, British Airways, Cathay Pacific, Delta, Iberia, KLM, Qantas, Scandinavian Airlines System, Singapore Airlines, Sky Chefs and United Airlines. Hotel members include Forte, Hilton, Holiday Inn, Hyatt and Marriott. Membership in other sectors includes the chief executives of Alamo, American Express, Avis, Crown Casino, Diners Club International, East Japan Railway Company, Europcar, Hertz, Kuoni Travel, Thomas Cook and Walt Disney (although not EuroDisney). These names emphazise the potential of the organization in interest representation, but also the global (rather than dedicated European) base of operations. Similarly, the names portray the 'rich firm club' nature of membership, and the emphasis upon firms with significant interests in the better defined transport sector.

One of the reasons for the formation of the European Tourism Action Group (ETAG) was the frustration felt by the European Travel Commission, consisting of public sector national tourism offices in Europe, at their inability freely to express their views because of their status as public servants. The European Travel Commission played a key role in the launch of ETAG, and continues to support it by providing administrative help from its Paris base. This support is supplemented by the resources of its members. ETAG's role is rather minimalist in comparison with coordinating groups in other domains (see Case 5 in particular on biotechnology), and it has no ambitions to become the 'spokesperson' of tourism in the EU. Indeed, partly because of the considerable diversity to be found within tourism producer activities, some of ETAG's members see no justification for a Brussels-based umbrella group and would resist expanding its role in sectoral coordination. One respondent pointed out that it may be just as effective to continue to have organizations representing different sectors of the same industry, as long as tourism interests can develop the ability to speak with a common voice on the larger policy issues. There appears not to be enough issues common to the variety of tourism contributory sectors to encourage the industry actively to develop a 'one-stop Brussels shop'. The diversity of tourism is once again the key issue in understanding interest representation in the domain, whether the issues are those of collective action or of influence.

Contribution of Tourism Interests to European Policies

One consequence of living with diversity for a tourism interest group is that it needs to maintain dialogue throughout a range of public policy authorities. HOTREC, for instance, finds itself in regular contact with the Consumer

Protection Service, DG III (internal market), DG IV (competition policy), DG V (social dialogue), DG XI (environment) and DG XXI (taxation). Rather ironically, contact with each of these directorates is greater than that with the tourism unit in DG XXIII – a matter of some regret to HOTREC. Maintaining dialogue with a number of DGs is perhaps typical for most European interest associations, although the issue is more acute for a tourism group than for most others. This diversity is managed both by a series of working groups and by relying on members to engage their respective national ministries for the 'national route to Brussels'. This was used to good effect in the case of the distance selling directive, where tourism interests, including HOTREC, needed to secure their exclusion from its scope to avoid a number of damaging and expensive changes to working practices, such as those concerning reservations. Although both the Commission (with the notable exception of DG XXIII) and the Parliament (both engaged directly by HOTREC) wanted to include tourism businesses within the remit of the directive, national hotel interests, coordinated by HOTREC, worked successfully through the Council of Ministers route (and in particular the Greek presidency) to help secure their exemption in June 1994.

Of note from the distance selling 'campaign' is that HOTREC's main efforts were targeted at the Parliament, where, although ultimately unsuccessful, tourism can always find a sympathetic ear through the guise of the inter-group. Of greater interest, however, is that HOTREC attributes the outcome to the role played by DG XXIII in influencing the response of member states to the Directive. This is an example of a Commission unit performing the role of an interest group *vis-à-vis* other sections of the Commission, emphasizing the role of bureaucratic politics in European public policy-making. This makes the absence of real dialogue between DG XXIII and tourism interests, such as the absence of industry input to the forthcoming Green Paper, rather difficult to understand, although some industry representatives have predicted that meaningful relationships will develop. Given the relative youth of both the DG XXIII unit (formed in 1989) and European tourism interest representation landscapes, it is possible that this will occur. If the November 1994 Green Paper results in a greater inheritance of tourism competencies by the Commission, a more symbiotic relationship is likely to develop between private and public interests. One tangible example of this might be the possible delegation by the Commission to HOTREC of the task to develop and implement a Europe-wide hotel classification scheme. However, the current absence of dialogue and the lack of maturity of industry structures are evident in that the proposals from the distance selling directive emerged and proceeded without consultation with tourism interests. This suggests that the main players involved in the development of Euro competencies will be the member states, and in this respect there is as yet no sign of the northern members being influenced by tourism associations to give up subsidiarity. In short, there is no sign of neo-functionalist processes at work in tourism. On first sight, it is tempting to agree with van Kraay that what has been done so far 'is a good start which gradually paves the way for a Community tourism policy' (van Kraay, 1993, p. 114). Yet in reality the future is much more uncertain, and cannot be predicted by studying the relationship between the Commission and private interests in neo-functionalist terms. The closest relationship between a tourism interest and the Commission is in a sector within its own right – aviation – involving the World Travel and Tourism Council, and the aviation section of DG VII (transport). Where it needs to work on more general 'tourism' issues at the European level, the WTTC relies more on the relationships between itself, its members and the national governments.

The 1990 package travel directive, proposed in 1988, pre-dated much interest group activity in tourism at the European level. It provided a minimalist framework of protection for the consumer, but fell short of what consumer groups like the Brussels-based Bureau Européen des Unions de Consommateurs (BEUC) would have liked. Tour operators and travel agents were able to exert some influence, mainly from national-level organization where self-regulatory agreements between the industry and national governments are common. Indeed, relationships between these parties are fairly well developed, such that industry sources have become policy participants in some member states. These relationships have yet to be repeated at the European level, but were used to good effect as a means of influencing the directive, and the package travel industry came to regard the outcome as highly successful. For instance, it was proposed that a contract price between an agent and the consumer may not be increased within thirty days prior to departure, but industry representation successfully reduced this period to twenty days (van Kraay, 1993).

One further means of tourism interest representation occurs through territorial offices, where European regions have significant interests in tourism. The European Regional Development Fund (ERDF) gave around ECU 2 billion to tourism projects in the period 1989–93. This once again draws attention to the diversity of interests in European tourism, the central issue when seeking to understand European-level collective action and competencies in tourism.

Conclusions

The 'world's largest industry' lacks attention in European public affairs, and the landscape of European interest representation in tourism is still in an adolescent phase of development. Both of these factors can be attributed to the diversity of sectors and types of organisation involved in the supply side of tourism, and to the highly varied demand side of tourism activities. This diversity helps to explain the absence of strong tourism-wide policy communities, involving private interests and the European Commission. Although tourism interests have been able to exert influence upon European public affairs, the means of influence have mainly been through the 'national route'. With the exception of the WTTC, a global forum representing large firms in a domain characterized by small and medium-size enterprises, collective action, where it exists, is largely sectoral with limited attempts at, and indeed ambitions towards coordination. There are few, if any, signs of neo-functionalist spillover mechanisms of integration at work. Taken as a whole, tourism interests are outsider onlookers when it comes to their relationships with the European Commission, particularly when compared with the close relationships that are evident in some of the other domains described in this book.

Students of European business alliances will see a number of messages in this case study. One is the importance of industry definition for both collective action and the development of Euro competencies. Another might be industry status. The European Commission is fascinated by high status, high technology and well defined industrial sectors like information technology and pharmaceuticals. It is less fascinated by a domain with uncertain boundaries comprising a number of activities where the output sometimes lacks glamour. Indeed, the highly seasonal tourism industry has some difficulty in convincing public opinion that the jobs it provides are equal in value to those in manufacturing sectors. The *raison d'être* of the WTTC is to convince public policy-makers, and public opinion, of the value and importance of tourism for the world economy. That in itself suggests an outsider status. However, the role of the DG XXIII tourism unit in defending tourism interests in the case of the distance selling directive is notable, in particular *vis-à-vis* other parts of the Commission and with member state governments. Although the tourism unit is not regarded as influential by a number of industry sources, it does suggest the need to look beyond the focus of the landscape of private interest organization in seeking to understand producer influences exerted upon public policies.

References

Commission of the European Communities (1994) *Report from the Commission to the Council: European Parliament and the Economic and Social Committee on Community*

Measures Affecting Tourism. COM(94) 74 final. Brussels: Commission of the European Communities.

ECTAA (Group of National Travel Agents' and Tour Operators' Associations within the EU) (1994) personal communication, 19 July 1994.

Greenwood, J. (1993) 'Business interests in tourism governance', *Tourism Management*, vol. 14, pp. 335–348.

van Kraay, F. (1993) *Tourism and the Hotel and Catering Industries of the EC*. London: Athlone Press.

World Travel and Tourism Council (WTTC) (1994) *Did You Know? Travel and Tourism. Brussels: WTTC*

PART 4

Utilities

PART
Utilities

CASE 10

Euro Awakenings
Water Supply Representation in Europe

William A. Maloney[1]

Introduction: The Europeanization of Water Policy

> It is no longer possible to understand the policy process in any of the twelve members states of the EU, especially the role of pressure groups in that process, without taking account of the shift in power to Brussels. In this context, the Single European Act (SEA) which significantly extended the scope of EC legislation and reformed the Community's decision-making process marked an important turning-point.
>
> *(Mazey and Richardson, 1993a, p. 191)*

The European Union (EU) plays an increasingly important role in influencing the operating environment of Europe's water industries.[2] In recent years there has been a continuous growth of regulation, particularly in the environmental field.[3] Consequently, the sector has been subject to a wide range of EU directives and regulations covering areas such as drinking water, waste water, water use, discharge of dangerous substances, controls over industry and products, sewage sludge disposal, and public procurement of works and supplies. As one official in a national agency argued, 'the ever-increasing number of EC directives is one of the major challenges facing the industry'. As a result of these developments, the water organizations of Europe have abandoned their traditionally reactive stance towards influencing EU policy, aimed at damage limitation, in favour of a more positive, proactive approach designed to 'minimize their surprises'.

The increasing level of EC intervention in the water sector (and the Europeanization of water policy) was nowhere more forcefully demonstrated than during the privatization of the water industry in England and Wales in the late 1980s. Indeed, so serious was the EC's intervention that the privatization of the water industry was, albeit temporarily, postponed. On no fewer than five occasions the British government was forced to modify its privatization proposals with the most significant change relating to the regulatory regime post-privatization (Maloney, 1993). The EC requires each member state to nominate 'competent authorities' to monitor and enforce the implementation of EC legislation. The British government intended to nominate the privatized regional water authorities (RWAs) as such bodies, but the Commission, however, insisted that the authorities must be public bodies. The British government was then forced to create a publicly controlled competent authority – the National Rivers Authority – as an environmental regulator (see Richardson *et al*. (1992) for a full account of the competent authority issue).

European Water Federations: Aims and Objectives

There are several European federations active in the water sector. Firstly, the European Institute for Water, for Resources, Management and Development (EIW/RMDI) which aims to integrate environmenal and sectoral economic policies and to manage natural, human and financial resources without waste. The EIW/RMDI encourages cooperation between EC and non-EC countries in matters of administration, management science and technology.

Secondly, the European Water Pollution Control Association (EWPCA) whose *raison d'être* is to advance knowledge in water protection, and to encourage further interaction and collaboration between countries in the technical and scientific practice of water management. The EWPCA has four main objectives.

1. To promote the advancement of the science and practice of water pollution control.

2. To foster and promote the common interest of the association members in relation to the constituent bodies and other agencies engaged in the prevention and control of water pollution.

3. To enhance both the profession of water pollution control and its standing and recognition by appropriate agencies.

4. To act as a representative body of water pollution control interests.

The EWPCA was founded in 1981 and now has twenty-nine national member associations and corporate members from twenty European countries. The main incentive for corporate members is to 'influence the EC and CEN [Comité Européene de Normalisation]'.

Thirdly, the European Waste Water Group (EWWG) is an alliance of waste-water operators which seeks an integrated approach to waste management throughout Europe. The EWWG was formed largely because waste-water interests were not effectively represented in Europe and had taken second place to water quality issues. The EWWG has three main objectives:

1. To create a forum for dialogue between operators and the European Commission.
2. To offer constructive views from both the private and public sectors of Europe's waste-water industry.
3. To implement achievable and affordable solutions to waste-water problems.

The EWWG was established in 1991 and has seven members: Britain, France, Greece, Italy, Luxembourg, Portugal and Spain. Membership cost is based on population size and is relatively inexpensive.

The most important (water-related) federation and the main focus of this case study is the Union of European Associations of Water Suppliers (EUREAU) whose main task is to defend the interests of the water suppliers *only* in the EU's decision-making process. EUREAU was formed in 1975 and its creation and development were similar to other sectoral associations. Its origins date back to the 1972–74 period when representatives of the national associations of the six founding countries of the European Community met to discuss a common response to the DG III proposals for a directive on cold water metering. Following their initial ('successful') collaboration, EUREAU was formed. EUREAU represents water supply operators' interests to European Union organizations responsible for formulating directives and European standards, and assesses and monitors both current and future water supply problems in order to attain a consensus among its members on the most effective and efficient way to face these challenges. EUREAU has been concerned with issues such as: drinking water quality; pollution prevention (especially with regard to ground and surface waters); diffuse sources of pollution (specifically from agricultural sources); discharge of dangerous substances into the aquatic environment; the market entry and use of pesticides; and public procurement of supply works and service contracts.

EUREAU has several objectives:

1. To defend the common interest of European water suppliers.
2. To review, discuss and present a common view on prospective and actual legislation proposals with the relevant EU organization involved in the water sector.

3. To analyse existing legislation so that, at the time of revision, EUREAU's views on balancing the politically desirable with the technically achievable can be advanced.

4. To devise a vast standardization programme in the framework of the achievement of the single market objectives, through its membership of the CEN which aims to achieve Europe-wide standards in order to facilitate the exchange of goods and services by eliminating, essentially technical, barriers to trade. EUREAU coordinates the work of its representatives on the two technical committees (TCs) of CEN: TC 164 Water Supply and TC 165 Waste Water Engineering which are drafting some two hundred standards.

EUREAU has two types of member:

1. Members: water associations at the national level which are members of the European Community or of the European Free Trade Association (EFTA).

2. Observer members: national associations of countries outside the European Economic Area.

EUREAU has members from eighteen countries: Austria, Belgium, Denmark, Finland, France, Germany, Greece, Iceland, Ireland, Italy, Luxembourg, Netherlands, Portugal, Spain, Sweden, Switzerland, Turkey and the UK. Its one observer member is Hungary. It has no competitors and has good links with other groups such as the EWWG and the Union of Industrial and Employers' Confederations of Europe (UNICE). EUREAU does not suffer from the collective action problems associated with many interest groups; *de facto* all of its potential members are in membership. The only country which is not a member is Liechtenstein, and this is simply because all members and observer members must be national associations of water suppliers. Liechtenstein does not have a national association.

The successful mobilization of its membership is also fostered by a very low subscription rate which is calculated on the basis of gross national product (GNP) and population size. For example, France, Germany and the UK pay BFr 550,000 (just over £11,000), while Luxembourg pays BFr 55,000 (approximately £1,100). Such cheap membership costs help to take the decision to join to below a threshold of (economic) rationality (Jordan *et al*, 1994; Marsh, 1976). The subscription cost is kept low because the individual members supply the group with the scientific and technical information it requires when dealing with the Commission. Thus, while the permanent secretariat located in Brussels is the professional lobbying arm of EUREAU, the ammunition is supplied by the individual members. For example, country representatives who wish to have a major impact on specific issues attend EUREAU meetings with fully prepared research papers which form (either part or all of) the basis of the discussion and probably set the parameters of the debate. Thus the costs of membership are variable. Those who (have the resources and) wish to influence policy make a greater contribution than those who do not feel strongly about a specific issue. While the costs may be greater for more active participation, the cost of not doing something may be greater still.

EUREAU's activities are managed and directed by a board of management and each member association is entitled to two seats on the board. The board of management has representatives from private companies, local authorities and national trade associations, for example: J. P. Quinio, Directeur General Adjoint, Compagnie Générale des Eaux (France); T. Ward, Managing Director, Yorkshire Water Services (England); J. Fenwick and J. J. O'Sullivan, Dublin and Cork Corporation, respectively (Eire); L. Borges, Associacao Portuguesa dos Distribuidores de Àgua (Portugal); L. Jansson, Swedish Water and Waste Water Association (Sweden). The presidency of the organization is assumed by each member country on a two year rota basis. The board of management has a steering committee below it to make preparations for board meetings and to respond to urgent problems. The board also has three standing commissions with discrete responsibilities and each country is entitled to two seats in each commission. The standing commissions are:

- EU I – water resources, treatment and quality.
- EU II – standardization and certification.
- EU III – legislation and economics.

These commissions consider issues within their broad area of expertise and draft reports which are submitted to the Board for consideration. Once approved by the board the reports are circulated to the member countries.

EUREAU: Internal and External Politics

The Rationale for Membership and Organization

Members join EUREAU for several reasons. Firstly, for early warning of Commission proposals. As one EUREAU board member put it: 'Through EUREAU with its secretariat in Brussels we do obtain advance intelligence'. It is vital for the group to get a copy of working documents as early as possible so that it can have the maximum impact. Successful interest representation in the EU policy process depends to a great extent on the group being able to intervene at the drafting stage in the Commission. As one EUREAU member argued: 'It is evident that it is necessary to influence the decision process in as early a stage as possible, because the further work has advanced, the more difficult it becomes to intervene'. Mazey and Richardson (1993b, p. 112) also point out that advance intelligence is vitally important to groups because 'participation in the [EC] policy process is unpredictable, and policy ideas may appear suddenly and from little known sources. In practice, therefore, keeping track of EC policy initiatives is a major undertaking for groups'. They further maintain that a 'successful' Euro strategy also requires that groups 'stay with the issue at every stage throughout the whole process' (p.123) after getting in early in the first instance.

Secondly, members join because they recognize that the Commission prefers to deal with European federations, and gives greater credence to their claims, as opposed to individual companies or national associations. In general, the Commission is surrounded by a multitude of interests, all of which are attempting to influence policy direction. As one EUREAU member argued: 'If you work through EUREAU you're more likely to get a hearing [because] the Commission finds it irritating if a whole host of national associations are attempting to influence it'.

The Commission however, recognizes that EUREAU represents the views of the whole European water supply industry. The Commission, as Greenwood *et al*. (1992, p. 24) point out, prefers 'encompassing Euro groups' for reasons such as 'expertise, information and cooperation in the formulation and implementation [of policy] with significant economic interests who contribute much to European economic performance'. There are other specific reasons for the Commission's preference. The EC bureaucracy, despite the myth, is quite small.[4] In 1991 there were only '3,500 senior administrators in posts in EC institutions' (Mazey and Richardson, 1991). This makes reciprocal relationships with interests a necessity rather than simply desirable.

Thirdly, members join to ensure that their national interests are taken account of within the European federation, given that the Commission prefers to deal with collective 'encompassing Euro groups'. Members recognize that shaping, or playing a significant part in shaping EUREAU's policy may ultimately lead to greater influence with the Commission than simply making individual representations. As one EUREAU member commented: 'The main advantage of EUREAU is that, with one voice on drinking water matters it can influence and assist the European Parliament and the relevant Commissions, particularly on technical issues and cost'.

While, in theory, the Commission prefers to deal with European federations, in practice it also deals with domestic peak associations, individual companies, consultants, etc. who have tradable resources.

Fourthly, members join because their national governments cannot be counted on to represent their interests on every occasion. As one water industry insider in Britain argued: 'The British government does represent the industry but the expertise of the companies through WSA [Water Services Association] and also through EUREAU *can and does add value*' (emphasis added). Thus in the UK, the Department of the Environment (DOE) is not, and could not be expected to be, the most effective vehicle for representation of the British water industry in Europe. It has to consider the broader national interest. The DOE also has to bargain within the (domestic) governmental machine and has to combat traditionally strong opponents such as the Ministry of Agriculture, Fisheries and Food (MAFF). Though the DOE does its best to coordinate its activities with the water industry there are times when the British government's interests differ from the industry's. For example, the British government has been pushing for a complete relaxation of European legislative standards on pesticides (the government has felt it necessary to respond to the pressures from MAFF and pesticide manufacturers). The water industry, however, wants strict control on the use of pesticides in order to protect water resources. While there are a handful of issues where the industry and the government differ, it is vitally important for the USA that it does not alienate the DOE. As Mazey and Richardson (1993b, pp. 114–115) highlight:

> the European Community . . . is not a sovereign state. Legislative power is divided between national member states and the Community. In consequence, groups must maintain existing national lobbying strategies whilst developing new strategies in response to the growing legislative competence of the EC. They must do this in a way which does not undermine existing relationships at the EC level. Thus, 'playing the Brussels card' against a national administration may work on any given issue, but it may have serious long-term consequences in undermining relationships at the national level which have taken a long time to build'.

The DOE and WSA do their best to agree a common position prior to European negotiations. There is a European group within the DOE which is helping the British government become much more proactive in Europe. Neil Summerton, head of the Water Directorate at the DOE has stated:

> I know that there has been concern that in the past the DOE went to Brussels and acted by its best light without being in touch with the water industry . . . What I am trying to do now is to play a coordinated game in Brussels and talk

to the principal UK players about the forthcoming EC agenda . . . It is
important that all the various people from this country who are trying to
influence the Commission should keep each other informed as far as possible.
(Water Bulletin, no. 559, 28 May 1993)

Finally, EUREAU provides a forum for exchange of ideas, practices and customer issues among water suppliers.

Policy Formulation

Formally, EUREAU policy is decided by the board of management. In practice, however, the recently formed steering committee decides policy and the board of management approves it – a situation analogous with the cabinet and cabinet committee system in the UK. The steering committee comprises Belgium, France, Germany, Italy, Spain, the UK and the country which holds the presidency. Traditionally, the main driving forces behind EUREAU policy have been Germany and France, with the French companies (Compagnie générale des Eaux and Lyonnais des Eaux-Dumez) being particularly influential. The French companies have not found themselves in such an influential position by accident; they have committed the necessary resources to influencing EUREAU policy. They attend committee meetings with fully prepared papers and hence have a head start on the other participants. However, since privatization the UK representatives have devoted more time and resources to shaping EUREAU's policy. For example, the UK's representatives on the various EUREAU committees and sub-committees meet quarterly to exchange information and to decide a coherent and coordinated UK strategy for the various EUREAU committees.

While EUREAU has little difficulty agreeing a common position on policy issues, there are two general areas where conflict, however rare, is most likely to emerge. Firstly, the French and the British have interests in both water supply and waste disposal, whereas the rest of the members are interested only in water supply. At times this can lead to differing perspectives emanating from the two camps. Secondly, with regard to the costs versus quality issue, the Netherlands and the UK find themselves at opposite ends of the spectrum. The Dutch are interested in pushing for the highest achievable environmental standards, and see costs as largely a secondary issue. On the other hand, the British (especially since privatization) are more interested in 'balancing' costs and benefits. Prior to reunification, Germany allied itself more closely with the Dutch position;

since then, the Germans have shown increasing sympathy for the British position and have become more cost-conscious.

EUREAU or Euro Lobbying?

EUREAU's permanent secretariat has fairly good contacts with the Commission because it is a resource-rich group (Maloney *et al*, 1995). As Mazey and Richardson maintain, 'successful' groups usually exhibit several professional characteristics: 'namely resources, advance intelligence, good contact with bureaucrats and politicians, and above all an ability to provide policy-makers with sound information and advice. Reputations for expertise, reliability, and trust are key resources in lobbying in Brussels' (1993b, p. 110).

EUREAU has close and regular contact with the Commission, and its influence derives from the authoritative nature of its scientific and technical data provided by its members. The Commission needs this information in the exchange-based relationship with EUREAU, as well as needing EUREAU's cooperation in the implementation of agreed policy. EUREAU's officials claim that their arguments are sometimes taken on by the Commission and that the Commission has actually used the same language and terminology which was contained in EUREAU's submission. EUREAU's representatives currently meet Commission officials two to three times a month to discuss revisions to the drinking water directive. If we consider the whole gamut of water-supply-related issues then the contact is on a week-to-week basis. Effective groups need to cultivate and maintain links with several directorates-general and not simply their 'home base', in EUREAU's case DG XI (environment, consumer protection and nuclear safety). Groups need to be aware of the impact of the cross-fertilization of policy from other areas outside their 'natural environment'. EUREAU's contact with other directorates-general is not as good as with its home base, but it is dedicating more resources to establishing better contact with other directorates.

Mazey and Richardson highlighted two main implications for interest-group strategies which follow from the distinctive nature of EC policy-making. Firstly, 'EC lobbying is a multilateral operation which requires interest groups to coordinate national and EC-level strategies' (Mazey and Richardson, 1993c, p. 16).

Secondly, EC policy-making also reveals that sectoral interest groups compete both with 'their traditional adversaries' (e.g. water suppliers such as the UK Thames Water plc versus certain environmental groups such as

Greenpeace or Friends of the Earth), as well as 'with their counterparts from other Member States' (Mazey and Richardson, 1993c, p. 17). Following from Mazey and Richardson's first point, effective interest groups, especially Euro groups, need to be active on several fronts: the European Commission, the European Parliament and at the national level. This inevitably means that there must be a degree of integration and cooperation between national and European associations. For example, with regard to the costs and pace of environmental improvements, British interests have found it useful to lobby on several fronts.[5] They have acted as 'own account' actors in Europe, through the European federations (e.g. EUREAU, EWWG) as well as domestic channels (e.g. DOE, Treasury). There is some evidence that the British water industry has had some degree of success. At an EC finance ministers meeting in November 1993, the UK Chancellor of the Exchequer, Kenneth Clarke, called for a delay in complying with the municipal waste-water directive on the grounds that the costs of compliance within the current time limits were 'unacceptable' (*Financial Times*, 23 November 1993), while the UK Secretary of State for the Environment, John Gummer, indicated that he intended to 'sound out EC partners to see if the urban waste water directive could be modified' (*Financial Times*, 5 November 1993). In response to Mr Gummer's statement, environmental groups stated that they were disappointed that the minister has followed the general OFWAT/WSA line. Guy Linley-Adams, a water campaigner at Friends of the Earth (FoE) argued that the government was 'allowing Ian Byatt [Director General of Water Services, i.e. the economic regulator] to dictate policy' (*Water Bulletin*, 29 October 1993, no. 580). Thus it appears that some British policy actors have found it useful to keep the pressure on the British government in pursuit of European objectives. As Mazey and Richardson, (1993c, p. 17) warn 'one should not underestimate the enduring strength of national sentiments and their capacity to undermine the formulation of stable transnational policy communities'. It is because of this that one must be careful not to overemphasize the degree of Europeanization. At times, groups can find it effective to work through domestic channels when attempting to influence European policy. Indeed, Greenwood *et al* (1992) highlight several reasons (some applicable to the water sector) that interest groups 'should use the 'national route' to Europe'. Firstly, the 'reliance upon member states for policy implementation affords considerable possibilities for influence' (Greenwood *et al.*, 1992, p. 22). Much policy is still decided at the national level: he who implements decides. As Neil Summerton, head of the Water Directorate at the DOE, pointed out:

> Many environmental standards which directly affect the water industry are set in a European context and the Department of the Environment has an

inevitable role here as it is the member state which negotiates the standards and is accountable when it comes to meeting them.

(Water Bulletin, 28 May 1993, no. 559)

The second reason that Greenwood *et al.* give for using the 'national route' is that 'large firms will often be valued at the national level as national champions, and can rely upon the support of national governments' (1992, p. 22). Thirdly, 'there may be circumstances where it is easier, and perhaps essential, for national interests to act alone than with others' (Greenwood *et al.* 1992, p. 22). Thus, individual water companies do not tend to act as 'own account' actors in Europe; rather, they work through their domestic trade associations and their representatives on EUREAU committees. Individual national associations can at times, where appropriate, lobby on top of this contact to maximize the pressure. The other occasions when national associations lobby independently is when they wish to supplement the federation position with their own national problems or views. Associations such as the WSA have worked on their own and retain consultants in Brussels to keep them abreast of policy developments as they emerge. However, the WSA contacts the Commission directly, and uses consultants for advance intelligence and information-gathering only. The British and French national associations have enjoyed good access to the Commission despite its preference for European federations, and their national associations have been able to speak authoritatively for the whole sector within their respective countries. Furthermore, they can deliver domestic compliance once agreement is reached. In several other European states, water supply and sewage disposal are disintegrated with hundreds of separate organizations providing the services. Consequently, achieving uniform compliance has proved difficult.

Where possible, EUREAU tries to coordinate the activities of the national associations because, as one EUREAU official pointed out, there is a grave danger that the national associations 'could jeopardize the good contact EUREAU has established over several years with the Commission'. The only occasions when EUREAU does not attempt to coordinate its members' European activities is when an issue relates solely to one country. In this situation representation is best left to the national association.

Drinking Water Directive

EUREAU is currently seeking a revision of the drinking water directive (80/778/EC) which was developed by the Commission in the early 1970s while EUREAU was still in its infancy and was unable to make a substantial contribution to the formulation of policy at the time when it most mattered. EUREAU maintains that at the implementation stage several shortcomings in the directive have emerged. Thus EUREAU's commission EU I (water resources, treatment and quality) prepared the technical argument outlining the need for the revision, while the commission EU III (legislation and economics) drew up the legal arguments for a revision. Their findings were collated in a book which EUREAU maintains was the catalyst for the revision process. EUREAU's board of management recommended that the members hold 'informative meetings' at the national level with government officials and water suppliers in order 'to sensitize a maximum number'. EUREAU organized information campaigns during 1992 and held a European conference in Madrid in 1993 to present the revision proposals in detail. EUREAU learned during the conference of the World Health Organization's (WHO) recommendations on drinking water quality and decided to adapt its report to take account of WHO's interpretation in an attempt to strengthen its technical argument.

Following EUREAU's conference on the drinking water directive, the European Commission organized a conference in Brussels in September 1993 to canvass the opinion of those interested in revising the directive. The conference was attended by representatives of the European Parliament, local authorities, consumer organizations, the environmental movement, as well as the agricultural, chemical and water industries. EUREAU's lobbying activities were rewarded with fifty of the two hundred delegates invited to attend the conference. Subsequently, EUREAU was invited to two meetings with the European Commission to discuss some technical issues in more detail. The consultation process is ongoing in 1995 and EUREAU has geared up to maintain its contacts with DG XI (including the working group on drinking water) and other directorates-general, the European Parliament and the Economic and Social Committee (ESC) to ensure that it has the maximum impact.

Conclusions

The water (hydrological) cycle lends itself to greater EU involvement because the externalities of water use cross not only local but also national boundaries. Consequently, the EU's role in water policy-making has expanded in recent years, and is likely to continue to grow rapidly. EUREAU has responded to this and has developed close and regular contact with the Commission. However, the relative openness of the EU policy-making system with its many 'opportunity structures' (Mazey and

Richardson, 1993a) means that competing interests are, in some instances, likely to represent a significant challenge to EUREAU in the policy making-system.

In European policy-making terms, EUREAU is a *core insider group* (Maloney *et al.* 1995). It has attained such a status for two main reasons: Commission officials see it as an important and authoritative source of scientific and technical data; and the Commission *prefers* to deal with encompassing Euro groups. EUREAU members are well aware of this preference and will continue to focus much of their lobbying activity through the European federation. National associations will also, however, continue to act as own-account actors in Europe as well as lobbying at the domestic level in pursuit of European objectives because, as Key (1956, p. 168) observed: 'Where power rests, there influence is brought to bear'.

Notes

1. I would like to thank Mark McAteer and Andrew McLaughlin for their comments on this chapter.
2. The water industries in Europe comprise various forms of ownership from wholly public (e.g. Scotland and Eire) to the franchise system (e.g. France) to the wholly private (e.g. England and Wales).
3. As Majone (1989) highlights, approximately two hundred 'directives, regulations and decisions were introduced by the Commission' in the environmental field. This, as Mazey and Richardson (1993b, p. 114) point out, 'is despite the fact that environmental protection is not even mentioned in the Treaty of Rome and that the Commission's authority in this area was not recognised until the passage of the Single European Act'.
4. Mazey and Richardson (1993b, p. 115) point out that 'there are approximately 15 staff in DG XI concerned with the control of chemicals yet in the US the Environmental Protection Agency has over 500 staff'.
5. British interests also feel that they have to work much harder in the European arena than some of their continental counterparts because of the prevailing impression of the British (government's) lack of commitment to Europe.

References

Greenwood, J., Grote, J. and Ronit, K. (eds) (1992) *Organised Interests and the European Community*. London: Sage.

Jordan, G., Maloney, W. A. and McLaughlin, A. M. (1994) 'Interest groups as artefacts: supply side influences over group size. Working Paper Series No. 7, British Interest Group Project, Aberdeen University.

Key, V. O. (1956) *Politics, Parties and Pressure Groups*. New York: Cromwell.

Majone, G. (1989) 'Regulating Europe: problems and prospects', in Ellwine, T. *et al.* (eds), *Jarburch zur Staats und Verwaltungswissenschaft*. Baden-Baden: Nomos, pp. 575–596.

Maloney, W. A. (1993) 'The politics and dynamics of organisational and regulatory change in the water industry in England and Wales 1945–1993'. PhD thesis, Department of Government, University of Strathclyde.

Maloney, W. A., Jordan, G. and McLaughlin, A. M. (1995) 'Interest groups and public policy: the insider/outsider model revisited' *Journal of Public Policy*, vol. 14, pp. 17–38.

Marsh, D. (1976) 'On joining interest groups: an empirical consideration of the works of Mancur Olson', *British Journal of Political Science*, vol. 6, pp. 257–271.

Mazey, S. and Richardson, J. J. (1991) 'British pressure groups in the EC: changing lobbying styles?' Paper presented to the Joint Sessions of the European Consortium for Political Research, University of Essex, 22–28 March 1991.

Mazey, S. and Richardson, J. J. (1993a) 'Interest groups in the European Community', in Richardson, J. J. (ed.) *Pressure Groups*. Oxford: Oxford University Press, pp. 191–213.

Mazey, S. and Richardson, J. J. (1993b) 'Environmental groups and the EC: challenges and opportunities', in Judge, D. (ed.) *A Green Dimension for the European Community: Political Issues and Processes*. London: Frank Cass, pp. 109–128.

Mazey, S. and Richardson, J. J. (1993c) 'Introduction: transference of power, decision rules, and rules of the game', in Mazey, S. and Richardson, J. J. (eds) *Lobbying in the European Community*. Oxford: Oxford University Press, pp. 3–26.

Richardson, J. J., Maloney, W. A. and Rudig, W. (1992) 'The dynamics of policy change: lobbying and water privatisation', *Public Administration*, vol. 70, pp. 157–175.

PART 5

Traditional Industries

Lobbying the European Union in the Textiles Industry

Bob Switky

Introduction

Few industrial sectors in Europe are as important in terms of employment and value-added as the textiles industry. Often grouped with the clothing industry, roughly 10 per cent of all European Union manufacturing jobs are generated by the textiles industry. As the Commission reported in 1993, with a turnover of ECU 180 billion and a workforce of some 2.7 million, the textile and clothing industry occupies a key position in the Community's industrial base (Commission, 1993). Over the past fifteen years, however, technological change, international competitive pressures and unfavourable exchange rates have all contributed to a crisis in the European textiles industry. The responses to this crisis from European labour and industry provide the context for this study. With an emphasis on EU trade policy, this chapter explores the ways in which interests in the textiles industry are aggregated to affect policy at the European level. In light of the recent completion of the Uruguay Round and the subsequent enforcement of the final Multifibre Arrangement[1] which manages the global trade in textiles, EU-level policies have had a considerable impact on the behaviour of member states, their firms and their workers. It is suggested that lobbying efforts in the textiles sector have changed in response both to industrial changes and to changes in EU institutional structures. The state remains the main interlocutor of interest groups, as neo-realists would expect, but the EU institutional role must not be ignored. The EU in particular is more than an arena for national action: it is an active player worthy of lobbying attention from firms and workers (Colebatch, 1991). As neo-corporatists would expect, a special relationship has evolved between EU institutions and transnational industry and labour associations. However, the community of interests in this sector suffers not only from internal divisions but also from benign neglect as other industries and other policy domains are given greater priority by both the Commission and national governments.[2]

The first part of this study provides an overview of the nature of the textiles industry. Then the focus is on the relevant players in the EU institutional structure, particularly the Commission, Council and European Parliament (EP). This is followed by a brief look at the European-level textiles lobby organizations. With this background established, the focus moves to the lobbying strategies of industry and labour at the European level. The theoretical ramifications of the findings from the textiles industry are discussed in the final section.

Nature of the Textiles Industry

It is worth reviewing the textiles industry because the sector is composed of many different kinds of enterprise. The political significance of textile companies depends on what is produced and whether the business activity involves production or distribution. As a result, some kinds of textile firm have more influence than others in affecting policy outcomes at national capitals and in Brussels. The differences can also lead to conflicting member state policies as some states are more protectionist or liberal than others.

Products that comprise the textiles industry range from medical sutures to wind-surfing sails, and from exercise tights to neckties. The textiles industry, strictly speaking (that is, excluding clothing) includes the production of natural and synthetic fibres, yarns, fabrics, embroidery, lace and carpets. As a separate category, industrial textiles consist of high-technology textile applications such as static-free and lint-free products for clean rooms in microelectronics manufacturing as well as filters for liquids and gases for environmental equipment. The industry also provides outlets for the producers of dyestuffs and specialty chemicals, and textile and clothing machinery. Goods in the clothing industry (woven and knitted fabrics) are more obvious: trousers, shirts, suits, scarves, and so on. One can analytically separate the clothing industry from the textiles industry, but as is common practice in EU dealings, the two will be considered together in this chapter.

The structural characteristics of the textiles industry go a long way towards explaining the ways in which lobbying is conducted as well as the political tendencies of member states. For the most part, the average textile firm is small or medium-sized. Of the roughly 220,000 firms in the textile industry, 4,000 employ between 100 and 500 workers, 42,000 employ between 10 and 100, and 175,000 firms work with fewer than 10 people. Only about 1,200 firms employ more than 500 people (COMITEXTIL, 1993, table 3). There are several political consequences of this sectoral make-up. Firstly, most company leaders have neither the time nor financial resources to lobby EU institutions directly. As such, reliance on national associations and Euro groups becomes imperative. Secondly, since the number of firms (and opinions) involved is so high, achieving a single, coherent voice capable of influencing EU policy is difficult. Another important structural feature of this sector is its territorial concentration. Labour concentration, for instance, has a reverberating impact on how the national political situation affects EU-level negotiating positions. In Spain, for example, roughly 80 per cent of the industry is concentrated in two regions: Catalonia and Valencia (Galli, 1992). The textiles industry in Portugal accounts for roughly one-third of all exports and one-quarter of all manufacturing employment (Barnes, 1991). Similar problems are found in eastern Germany and Greece. Moreover, as the Commission noted in 1985, the loss of jobs poses particular problems in the traditional textiles areas which are more frequently found near older industries such as shipbuilding, steel and coal mining, themselves in decline. Alternative employment is therefore difficult or impossible to find locally (Commission, 1985). For these regions, protectionist trade policies are critical since their direct competitors are mostly from the Third World. *Exhibit 11.1* illustrates the comparative advantage that Third World countries have over EU member states in terms of labour costs in the textiles industry.

The resulting political spectrum develops into two opposing blocs of EU states. In southern states, such as Spain, Portugal and Greece, where production of low- and medium-scale goods is the norm, national attitudes towards trade policies lean towards protectionism. France and Italy fall somewhere in the middle with successful up-scale manufacturing and less competitive low- and medium-end production. These two countries usually support or lead the protectionist camp within Europe. By contrast, liberal tendencies exist in northern states with high technology, capital-intensive industrial textiles production (such as Germany), in states whose firms have either focused their energies on distribution (the Netherlands), a niche area (carpets in the case of Belgium), or states that have more-or-less abandoned any activity in the sector. These national attitudes confront each other at the European level where important regional and external trade policies are formulated.

Exhibit 11.1 *Wage cost differentials in the EU and with selected non-EU states (ECU 1991)*
(Source: COMITEXTIL, 1993, p. 11)

Country	Total hourly textile cost in EU	Country	Total hourly textile cost, main textile producers
Germany (West)	14.27	USA	101.2
Germany (East)	7.62	EEC average	100.0
Belgium/Denmark	14.68	Taiwan	49.0
Spain	15.49	South Korea	35.3
France	6.49	Hong Kong	33.3
Greece	10.63	Turkey	30.4
Ireland	4.87	Tunisia	27.4
Italy	7.44	Mexico	27.4
Netherlands	14.58	Brazil	14.7
Portugal	15.26	Morocco	13.7
UK	2.63	Hungary	12.7
EEC Average	8.53	Thailand	8.8
		India	5.9
		Pakistan/Sri Lanka	3.9
		China/Indonesia	2.9

EU Institutions Relevant to Textiles

Since a detailed description of the structure of EU institutions is unwarranted for this chapter, brief overviews of the three most relevant institutions for this domain will be provided. These include the Commission, the Council and the European Parliament. In the textiles industry, the role of the European Court of Justice (ECJ) is marginal, or at least indirect. In addition, the ECJ is not the target of lobbying efforts from industry or labour.

The Commission is one of the most important contact points for organized interests in the textiles industry. Both labour and industry lobby the Commission vigorously, either through commissioners directly, their cabinet or the staff at the relevant directorate-general (DG). Depending on the policy area, different DGs come into play. On trade policy matters, for example, DG I (external affairs) and DGIII (internal market) play prominent roles. For 'internal' policy areas, DG XVI (regional policy), DG XXI (customs union), DG XXII (coordination of structural instruments), and increasingly DG XXIII (small- and medium-sized enterprises) are also targeted.

Aside from the usual institutional aspects of the Council, one of the unique features with regards to the textiles industry is the Council's 113 committee. The 113 committee is sanctioned by the Treaty of Rome's Article 113 which covers the EU's Common Commercial Policy; it deals specifically with trade matters affecting non-EU countries. Special 113 committees are responsible for particular trade areas (e.g. textiles). The committees are usually headed by a Commission DG I member and staffed by at least one national representative from ministries of the exterior, trade or industry, for example. Often, heads of firms participate as well. The special 113 textiles committee is designed to provide advice to Council ministers dealing with the textiles dossier, and, although its decisions are not binding, 113 committee 'recommendations' are usually accepted in the Council. In accordance with Article 113, decisions are taken by qualified majority. Sometimes, if the 113 committee cannot reach agreement, the issue may be sent up to the COREPER which may deliberate and decide, or send the issue back to the 113 committee for further review.

The role of the European Parliament in Europe's textiles trade is contingent upon the issue area. In general, the EP's influence in this sector echoes its weakness in other areas. In external trade matters involving Article 113, for example, the EP is in effect locked out of the policy process; EP ratification is not necessary for most agreements with non-EU countries.[3]

Since no change was made to Article 113 under the Single European Act (SEA) or the Maastricht Treaty, the EP's role in trade matters has not changed either. A constant factor in external trade policy is the need for flexibility and timeliness in international discussions. As one Council member noted, in international trade negotiations, the EU needs to act and adapt swiftly. It can not have EP consultations slowing down the process (interview with the Council, 25 November 1993). In areas outside of 113 jurisdiction, such as the Association Agreements with East European states, EP ratification – and hence input – is required.[4]

The real power of the EP concerns aspects involving EU financing. These powers, although limited, do come into play on such issues as regional policy, specific programmes such as RETEX,[5] and anywhere that structural funds are involved. For example, EU structural funds were made available in order to gain the support of obstructionist member states in establishing the Commission's negotiating positions for the MFA. Thanks to the Maastricht treaty, the cooperation procedure gives the EP the ability to voice an opinion that can only be overridden by the Council with a unanimous vote.[6]

Finally, even though the European Parliament has no officially sanctioned committees to handle the textiles industry, an informal 'intergroup' is the focal point for much of the lobbying attention. Neither official nor permanent,[7] this intergroup nevertheless can play an important role if the policy issue falls within the EP's jurisdiction. Behind the efforts of M. Cravinjo, for example, the EP intergroup was instrumental in pressing the Commission to establish the RETEX programme (interview with ETUCTCL, 27 May 1994).

Textiles' Interests Aggregated at the European Level

There are several product-specific textiles federations at the European level. For example, one can find European-level representation for cotton (EUROCOTON), for cellulostic fibres (CIRFS), for synthetic fibres (CIRFS) and for wool (INTERLAIN). Usually, these associations work through superfederations that represent association interests at the EU level. The most well-known and influential is COMITEXTIL, a coordinating body of national textile federations.[8] A similar organization exists for the clothing industry: the Association Industrielle Européenne d'Habillement (ECLA). COMITEXTIL in particular has played an important role as the regional lobby for the textiles industry. For example, in the recently concluded Uruguay Round, direct contacts with Commission officials helped bring EU trade policy in line with mainstream European industrial concerns.

European Largest Textile and Apparel Companies (ELTAC) represents a small and rather élite group of firms, while COMITEXTIL comprises a wide variety of large and small firms represented through their national federations. ELTAC was formed because of the perceived lack of Commission attention given to the largest textiles enterprises. In late 1992, a new coalition between COMITEXTIL, ELTAC and ECLA was formed to provide greater influence on EU policy-making (*Agence Europe*, 1992b). The cooperative venture was rendered more official on 9 June 1994 with the establishment of EURATEX. By forming a united front, the three groups hoped that a clearer message could be sent to the Commission, the EP, other trade associations and the media. ELTAC's success has thus far been limited. The textiles industry is predominantly composed of small and medium-size firms; ELTAC represents only the large firms. The Commission is very aware of this and does not grant ELTAC undue favours. The role of firm alliances in this domain is therefore not significant outside group contexts.

The textile Euro groups are not always well coordinated and coherent entities. Splits exist within the industry because of the wide variations between federations, variations along product lines and differences between the smaller and larger manufacturers. For example, the Belgian textiles federation FEBELTEX must operate within a federal system divided into three regions: Flanders, Wallonia and Brussels. Portugal, by contrast, is so dependent on the textiles industry that significant attention is provided by the national government. In Britain, textiles and clothing are under one roof (the British Apparel and Textiles Confederation), but knitting firms maintained separate representation until 1994. These variations in national styles contribute to the difficulties in overcoming collective action problems, that is, achieving coherence at the European level. Thanks to the importance and timing of MFA discussions in the Uruguay Round, the main groups are closer to institutionalizing a single voice. In practical terms, however, the effects are not yet clear. In spite of the trend towards greater cooperation among Euro groups, the impact has not been significant at the EU level (interview with the Commission, 26 May 1994). Differences within the industry continue to hamper those efforts.

The main labour organization at the European level is the European Trade Union Congress for Textiles, Clothing, and Leather (ETUCTCL). It represents national labour unions in the respective subsectors, although, as with industry, variations across EU national union structures exist.[9] One of the biggest problems facing labour in achieving a coherent European voice is that ETUCTCL members are not convinced that the best way to go is European. In short, nationalism is still strong. The problem has been particularly acute at times of recession (interview with ETUCTCL, 19 November 1992). Furthermore, differences between states such as Germany and Portugal in terms of skills and wages cause added problems for European labour.

Lobbying Paths in the European Textiles Industry

Exhibit 11.2 below provides a simplified version of the lobbying paths that may be taken by industry and labour.[10] In general, direct contact between textiles firms or workers and EU institutions is rare. One exception involves state aids which falls within the jurisdiction of the Commission, particularly DG IV (competition). Due to the small size of most textile and clothing firms, such a direct lobbying approach is beyond their financial and time constraints. As such, most companies prefer to work through organized

Exhibit 11.2   Lobbying paths to EU policy-making for companies and workers

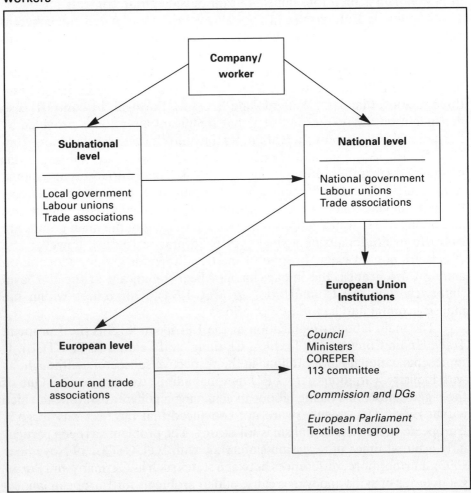

groups at subnational, but especially national and European levels. (The importance of subnational- and national-level organizations varies from country to country.) The locus of lobbying attention in the European institutional structure by textile firms and workers varies according to several factors. These include the type or nature of the issue, the importance of the issue, and the structure of national interest aggregation. In general, the national-level associations play an important role in funnelling the myriad of small and medium-size firms into peak associations. The contact made with the EU, however, is normally indirect, as achieved through Euro groups such as COMITEXTIL.

National efforts at lobbying EU-level policies are not encouraged by the Commission, and they can even backfire. In 1993, for example, France's textiles industry launched a campaign against EU policies perceived to favour Third World producers. On 17 May, ten thousand workers *and* employers in France staged a demonstration against the Commission. Combined with a media advertisement blitz, one would have expected some impact on Brussels.[11] However, due to faulty evidence and unfocused counter-proposals to the Commission, the campaign not only fizzled, but it left the Commission cynical about the French textiles industry.[12] The demonstration was a very unusual event. The French tried to influence EU policy by attacking the Commission. In this particular and unusual case, the French interests may be described as that of outsiders.

When textile lobbying efforts are initiated at the national level, contact at the EU level may occur at several locations. In the Commission, contacts may be made with the appropriate DGs and nationals serving as commissioners. Labour and industry lobbying efforts on national governments also may influence ministers or lower-ranking national civil servants in the Council, the COREPER, and the special 113 textile committee if external trade is involved. The access channels within the EU institutional structure for transnational labour and industry associations are, however, not always helpful. Firstly, open access does not always translate into policy influence. The Commission and EP are fairly open, but this openness extends to most competing interests; there is no real monopoly of access to Brussels bureaucrats. Secondly, some paths, while open, may lead nowhere. In the textiles industry, the Economic and Social Committee (ESC), for example, plays a negligible role. In addition, in terms of external trade policy, the EP intergroup is virtually powerless.

The role of labour is much more restricted at the level of European policy-making. The transnational union movement suffers from the problems of fragmentation and limited resources. Achieving a single voice in textiles is difficult enough at the national level let alone the EU level. In addition, ETUCTCL continues to face a long battle in overcoming limited financial support and national-level thinking from its members.

Theoretical Issues

The ways in which textile interests are aggregated at the European level are a function of several factors. The single market and the Maastricht treaty have had an indirect role in changing trade rules (such as Article 115[13] and the cooperation procedure). In general, however, the market liberalization set in motion by the Single European Act (SEA) has caused much concern in the vulnerable textiles industry by exposing it to further Third World competition. Another important variable determining the lobbying strategies of textile workers and firms is that of industrial structure. The sector is composed of tens of thousands of firms involved in a wide variety of vastly different activities. Often these firms are regionally concentrated in areas that have limited outlets for other business activities. Also, with important exceptions, much of the industry is relatively low-skill, putting it into direct competition with low wage manufacturers in the Third World.

The national route to EU level policy-making continues to play an important role, but it is not the only route. Symbiotic and important links exist between textile Euro groups (especially from industry) and EU institutions. The Commission relies on the input of Euro groups to provide statistical data and technical expertise and to get a better sense of what is going on in the industry. In the case of COMITEXTIL in particular, a symbiotic relationship exists to some extent with the Commission. The two groups maintain constant contact and exchange information regularly. COMITEXTIL may be described as more than just a reactive organization to European-level policy initiatives; it actively tries to – and does – influence the policies formulated by the Commission. One may describe the relationship between the Commission and COMITEXTIL as neo-corporatist in the sense of private interests crossing 'the boundary' and becoming a part of the 'state', i.e. the EU authorities (Greenwood *et al*. 1992).[14] The same can not be said of the European labour lobby. Fragmented by both diversity of individuals (in terms of skills and wages), and by nationalistic attitudes from national unions, European labour has yet to overcome its collective action problem. The situation is exacerbated by national governments and a European Commission that are more sympathetic to industry concerns. These factors are evident in Roethig's study of the European Trade Union Confederation (ETUC) (Case 19).

Industry contacts with the EU, however, do not always translate into positive outcomes for the transnational lobby. In one recent example, the Commission approved a ECU 46 million aid package that the British government plans to give to the Taiwanese firm, Hualon, in Northern Ireland. The British government justified the aid on the grounds that 1,800 jobs would be created in the Belfast area cutting unemployment by 17 per cent. COMITEXTIL worked closely with the Commission studying the impact of the proposed deal. COMITEXTIL concluded that the new factory would create a considerable increase in productive capacity and would put pressure on other European textile manufacturers. The Commission, nevertheless, ignored the COMITEXTIL recommendation (*European Report*, 1994). One reason that the influence of textile Euro groups on EU policy is not secure is that the textiles industry has been sacrificed in at least two larger European games. Firstly, it has been ascribed less importance in the wake of the single market programme. Secondly, to support foreign policy objectives in the Third World and eastern Europe, policies that might have staved off further bankruptcies and job losses in Europe were not accepted by the EU. The picture is thus somewhat mixed. At times, the transnational interest organizations play important roles in influencing the direction of EU policy, but the impact is not always as strong as desired. Because the textiles industry is given a fairly low priority by most member states and the Commission, the demands of industry and labour are not always met.

The case of lobbying in the European textiles industry points to several important issues beyond this sector. Firstly, the relationship between Euro groups and EU institutions depends upon the composition of the sector. In the automobile industry, for example, a similar number of people are employed, but they are concentrated in a dozen or so firms. National governments and the Commission also place a higher priority on this industry than on textiles. The lobbying interests in automobiles thus have greater ease in overcoming collective action problems. Secondly, the evidence from the textiles industry suggests that the links between Euro groups and the EU can be tenuous. Even though contacts between COMITEXTIL and the Commission are constant, formal and often mutually beneficial, COMITEXTIL and the textiles industry as a whole still suffers from lack of attention from most member states as well as the Commission. Without backing from national governments, strong links should not be expected from other industries and EU institutions. Finally, the experiment with EURATEX (the Euro group representing three subsector federations in textiles) might be viewed by other sectors struggling to influence Brussels as an alternative strategy. The jury is still out, however, since the organization was only founded in June 1994.

Notes

1. The Multifibre Arrangement (MFA), under the auspices of GATT, is designed to manage trade between industrial countries and developing states. Roughly 40 per cent of the textiles trade in Europe is subject to protectionist measures such as MFA quotas that limit the quantity of exports to the EU. The quotas are negotiated on a bilateral basis between the developing country and the Commission (on behalf of the entire EU). The MFA does not cover trade among advanced industrial states nor countries covered by special trading industrial arrangements with the EU such as those from the African, Caribbean and Pacific countries (ACP) and those covered by the Generalized System of Preferences (GSP).

2. In the rush to 1993, for example, Jacques Pelkmans observed that there was a peculiar silence in policy-making Brussels about this difficult issue (Pelkmans, 1992).

3. In the MFA discussions, for example, the EP made its views known to the Council and Commission, but its input was limited.

4. The SEA amendment to Article 238 requires EP majority approval for preferential trade and cooperation agreements proposed by the Commission. In one example of the use of this power, the EP held up Association Agreements with Israel and Turkey in 1988. The EP opposed Israeli policy towards the West Bank and Gaza, and it was dissatisfied with Turkey's progress in restoring civil rights (McAleese, 1990).

5. RETEX is a five year programme (1993–97) offering ECU 500 million to regions in decline, rural areas and areas officially known as 'backwards regions'. Roughly 80 per cent of the funding is given to Portugal, due mostly to the crisis in its textile industry. See *Agence Europe* (1992a). The aim of RETEX is to assist people and regions modernize themselves; this may be achieved by developing more efficient textile manufacturing operations but also by conversion to other types of economic activity.

6. For a recent discussion of the cooperation procedure, see Tsebelis (1994).

7. When asked whether the group would live on if the chair failed to be re-elected in the June 1994 elections, a member suggested that since enough momentum had built up for the intergroup and for representation from regions in which textiles are important, the continued functioning of the intergroup would be ensured (interview with European Parliament, 1 June 1994).

8. Full membership is extended to national textiles federations such as Gesamttextil (Germany) and Fenetextiel (Netherlands) as well as European branches such as the Comité International de la Rayone et des Fibres Synthétique (CIRFS), EURO-COTON, and the Comité des Industries Lainières de la CEE (INTERLAIN). Associate membership extends to certain EFTA member national federations such as the Swiss Textilverband Schweiz and the Swedish Textile and Clothing Industries Association, and similar organizations from the Czeck and Slovak Republics.

9. For a more comprehensive treatment of organized labour in Europe, see Visser and Ebbinghaus (1992), especially pp. 209–214.

10. For stylistic purposes, the arrows in *Exhibit 11.2* suggest a bottom-up approach to the lobbying process – from smaller to larger units. This should not be interpreted as neglecting the important interdependent relationships that exist among the various units.

11. Some have suggested that the campaign made Commission and French government officials more open to the plight of textiles, and this may have had an indirect impact on the consideration of an eventual social clause for the textiles dossier (interview with, ETUCTCL, 27 May 1994).

12.   Interview, with the Commission, 7 June 1994. See also Gay (1993).
13.   The elimination on 1 January 1993 of the use of Article 115 prevented states and their firms from acquiring special protection from cheap, third-country imports that arrived indirectly through member states.
14.   This is not to imply that there are no important differences between a nation-state and the European Union.

References

Agence Europe (1992a) 12 April 1992.

Agence Europe (1992b) 30 October 1992.

Barnes, C. (1991) 'The Portuguese textile and clothing industry', *Textiles Outlook International*, Economic Intelligence Unit, May, pp. 44–70.

Colebatch, H. (1991) 'Getting our act together: a case study in regulation and explanation'. Paper presented to the government/business study group at the XVth World Congress of the International Political Science Association, Buenos Aires, 21–25 July 1991.

COMITEXTIL (1993) *Textiles: An Industry for Europe*. Brussels: COMITEXTIL, 28 October 1993.

Commission of the European Communities (1985) *The European Community's Textiles Trade*, DG I, April 1985.

Commission of the European Communities (1993) *Report on the Competitiveness of the European Textile and Clothing Industry*. COM(93) 525 final. Brussels: CEC.

European Report (1994) 9 June 1994.

Galli, A. (1992) 'Iberia: not cheap enough?' *Textile Asia*, March, pp. 131–134.

Gay, P. (1993) 'Dix mille salaries et chefs d'entreprise ont manifeste dans Paris', *Le Monde*, 17 May 1993.

Greenwood, J., Grote, J. and Ronit, K. (1992) 'Introduction: organised interests and the transnational dimension', in Greenwood, J., Grote, J. and Ronit, K. (eds) *Organised Interests and the European Community*. London: Sage, pp. 1–41.

McAleese, D. (1990) 'External trade policy', in El-Agraa, A. M. (ed.) *The Economics of the European Community* (3rd edn). New York: St Martin's Press, pp. 420–442.

Pelkmans, J. (1992) *Applying to Textiles and Clothing: A Working Document* 67, Brussels: Centre for European Policy Studies, May 1992.

Tsebelis, G. (1994) 'The power of the European Parliament as a conditional agenda setter', *American Political Science Review*, vol. 88, pp. 128–142.

Visser, J. and Ebbinghaus, B. (1992) 'Making the most of diversity? European integration and transnational organization of labour', in Greenwood, J., Grote, J. and Ronit, K. (eds) *Organised Interests and the European Community*. London: Sage, pp. 206–237.

CASE 12

Automobiles
Dynamic Organization in Turbulent Times?

Andrew McLaughlin

Introduction

When the launch of the Association of European Automobile Producers (ACEA) took place in March 1991, Europe's car manufacturers breathed a sigh of relief. The announcement ended a two-year period during which ACEA's predecessor organizations had lost credibility with EU institutions and ultimately their own members (see McLaughlin *et al.*, 1993). This case study reviews the impact of ACEA since 1991. It begins by looking at the structure and role of the group before considering the working relationships that have been developed with Commission officials. The study concludes by analysing how ACEA has coped with the sudden turbulence in its political environment caused by leaked Commission proposals to change the regulations governing vehicle distribution.

ACEA: Organization, Role and Structure

On 4 September 1990 a high-level meeting was arranged between DG III commissioner Martin Bangemann and industry leaders from BMW, Fiat, Volkswagen and Renault to discuss the Commission's concerns about the industry's failure to act collectively on the issue of Japanese car imports. The Commission was determined to replace national import quotas with a European policy but had been unable to reach an agreement with the sector. The issue convinced both the Commission and some member companies that the existing forms of collective organization in the sector were ineffective. One company official recalls the outcome of the meeting with Bangemann:

> The Commission were irritated by the practice of individual companies sounding off about the Japanese issue when no collective position was coming

172

from the sector. Bangemann's officials believed that the Committee of Common Market Automobile Constructors (CCMC), a predecessor organization to ACEA, was next to useless. The industry came away with its ears ringing. The message was clear: an understanding would be concluded with Japan in 1991 so get a group together and agree a common line if you want to participate.

(Interview, 25 March 1994)

This meeting was probably the catalyst for the eventual formation of ACEA and set in train a constant dialogue between the industry and the Commission which led to ACEA's compromise position of March 1991 (see McLaughlin, 1994).

ACEA is dominated by its fourteen company members. The creation of the group reflected a:

clear consensus among its members concerning the need for effective representation. This role has expanded with the advent of the Single Market, the growing importance of EU legislation and action for all member companies and the wider European presence of ACEA member companies is needed. The mission of ACEA must therefore be viewed in a European and global context, in which the complex economic, social, political, technical and legal issues surrounding European integration, regulation, harmonization and trade all play a part.

(ACEA, 1993)

A number of features of the group's structure are noteworthy. Firstly, the American and Scandinavian automotive producers were invited into membership. The fact that these companies were not members of CCMC had undermined its claim to be the 'voice' of the industry. Secondly, ACEA's internal voting procedures were altered to prevent any one producer using a veto in group discussion. Under ACEA statutes, only a 75 per cent majority is required for a decision to be passed. Thirdly, ACEA was structured in such a way as to allow its fourteen member companies direct control over collective policy. The executive secretary argues that these structures have:

allowed ACEA to develop a more dynamic stance not only because we are an exclusive club of producers but also through other steps. For example, our board of directors [the heads of each member company] now meet four times a year. This allows us to have more concise agendas, to deal with major issues effectively and it gives the organization better strategic direction.

(Interview, 24 November 1993)

ACEA has eight divisions in its secretariat, seven of which deal with specific policy areas. In addition there are four standing committees staffed by representatives from member companies. In terms of public affairs the administrative committee is the most significant organ. This committee deals with all general policy matters and the political aspects of special issues under discussion in the other standing committees (ACEA, 1993, p. 14).

Assessing the resources that ACEA commits directly to public affairs and lobbying is difficult. The seven policy-active departments in the secretariat have a remit to cultivate their own relations with relevant officials in the European Commission. On strategic policy issues it is likely that a delegation from the administrative committee will also be involved in interest representation. This was the case with the 1991 negotiations over Japanese imports. This activity will be reinforced by the periodic participation of company presidents and the ACEA executive in the policy process. Thus, ACEA maintains regular high-level contacts with policy-makers as well as cultivating more low-key relations between its experts and the Commission's experts on issues of detail. The executive secretary suggested that at any one time 25–30 per cent of the staff were directly involved with interest representation.

Another important feature of ACEA's organization is the extensive use of *ad hoc* working groups to look at specific policy issues. Their number and meetings at any one time are driven by the policy agenda. The case study discussed later provides a good illustration of how such groups evolve. The membership of these working groups reflects the underlying philosophy of the entire organization which aims to synthesize the expertise of individual companies and national trade associations who previously had their own Euro group. For example, the working groups on car recycling and economic forecasting are chaired by staff from two national associations because these groups have a recognized expertise in those areas. The only rule regarding the working groups is that ACEA will not accept 'antenna' participation, by which it means that the individual concerned must actively contribute to the work of the group and not merely absorb the discussion.

It would be a mistake, however, to believe that ACEA is predominantly a lobbying organization. A large part of its function is to stimulate collective action on common industry problems and issues. This means setting the strategic and working agenda in areas such as recycling of car parts, developing proposals on future traffic management systems and encouraging greater cooperation in collaborative research. Most of this activity is managed through working groups, but the group also has responsibility for organizing conferences on key issues and communicating the industry's efforts to policy-makers.

The automobile case is therefore the classic example of the 'European club' species of European organization. It is dominated by its leading company members and there is frequent interaction between the secretariat staff and personnel from those companies. However, until June 1994 the club remained incomplete following a decision by Peugeot-Citreön not to subscribe. Peugeot's decision was not based on broad policy differences. Rather, the French group objected to the decision within ACEA to shift to a majority voting system and deny any one company a veto. After 1990, Peugeot could participate only in ACEA working groups where its investment of time or finance was in projects that had been carried over from the previous organization. The company was denied participation in any new projects or initiatives where participation was contingent upon full membership.

McLaughlin and Jordan have questioned the efficacy of this form of non-participation. We suggested that in oligopolistic industrial sectors which are represented by just one Euro group, non-participation involves unnecessary risks. We argued that:

> It is not safe to allow the Euro-group bureaucratic process to run on uninfluenced; it might decide on outputs which in their particulars do not suit the potential member. Participation in the group is one means to participate in the policy network which will attempt to make policy. It is not sensible to free-ride because the collective benefits might be unacceptable.
>
> *(McLaughlin and Jordan, 1993, p. 156)*

This would appear to shed some light on Peugeot's decision to join ACEA in 1994. The company's decision was based on its desire to participate in the various collective action initiatives organized by ACEA. Peugeot was particularly anxious to participate in the European Council for Automotive Research and Development (EUCAR) established by ACEA in May 1994 to launch a new era of collaborative research between European companies. EUCAR has a potentially vital role to play in the industry's attempts to secure funds from the EU's horizontal research programmes. Since the Commission is willing to fund only R&D into generic technologies with general application, cooperation between the manufacturers is needed to maximize the industry's efforts to gain funding for key projects. By remaining a non-member of ACEA, Peugeot may well have been able to 'free-ride' any eventual technological breakthroughs which stemmed from the EUCAR initiative. However, the risk that its competitors would gain a competitive advantage in the meantime was too great. Moreover, Peugeot (PSA) was keen to influence the dialogue between ACEA and DG III over EU R&D policy and funding.

Working Relationships with the Commission

More than most sectors, the automobile industry illustrates the shift in decision-making authority from nation-state to regional level. The

Commission's policy-making remit for the sector falls into four broad areas. These have been set out in detail by DG III (COM(94) 49 final, pp. 4–10):

1. *Internal market*. This includes all aspects of competition policy relating to state aids and vehicle distribution, the harmonization of vehicle taxes, improvement of vehicle safety, and promotion of environmental standards.

2. *EC policy in the field of structural interventions and human resources*. This includes all EU policy programmes used to facilitate economic adjustments in the sector, such as regional policies and support for training and infrastructure.

3. *Research and technological development*. This includes all horizontally organized funding programmes incorporated in the EU's framework programmes.

4. *External trade policy*. This includes monitoring the gradual opening of the EU market to Japanese car imports and improving market access to third markets for European automobile companies.

Clearly, because the development, production and sale of a vehicle depends on key components and technologies from a range of generic sources, the economic significance of automotive trade and the impact of the car on society, the sector comes into contact with various parts of the Commission. The industry in fact has working relationships with twelve of the directorates-general and issues often transcend departmental boundaries. Indeed, it is important to remember that the Commission is itself political and there is evidence of departmentalism between DGs.

One DG III official commented:

> [T]here is no general scheme for talking to people representing different interests in the Community. As a result, the development of dialogue had been on an *ad hoc*, pragmatic basis and many different patterns of dialogue now exist depending on the people involved both inside and outside the Commission . . . Forms of informal dialogue exist with the motor, pharmaceutical and food industries.
>
> *(Interview, 24 July 1994)*

This shortcoming is a source of great frustration to the automobile industry which has frequently complained about a lack of dialogue and coordination between parts of the Commission when automotive-related issues are being debated. One industry official spoke of being 'exasperated by the inefficiency which resulted from the fragmented organization of the Commission. Sometimes it is clear that they have quite different ideas on an issue and are not even talking to each other about it' (interview, 17 January 1994).

Commission officials readily accept that the political nature of the Commission is a problem in this area. For example, it is evident that while DG III supports the industry's case for renewal of the existing car distribution system for a further ten years after 1995, DG IV wishes to see wholesale changes to the system. A senior DG III official responsible for the industry commented: 'DG III takes the view that you should not change a stable regulatory framework during a period of restructuring. Irrespective of arguments about the principle of selectivity versus multifranchising we believe this point to be paramount. However, the issue has become very emotional in DG IV and they are very resistant to outside arguments' (interview, 20 June 1994). Similarly, when one official was asked to describe the relationship between DG III and DG XI on the issues of engine emissions he commented: 'Quite simply, it's war.'

By 1993 ACEA was convinced that the only way to make progress on issues which transcend DGs was to establish *ad hoc* structures which brought all parts of the Commission and industry together. During discussions with the Commission over proposals to assist the industry with its restructuring efforts in 1992–93, ACEA proposed that 'interservice' working groups be established to overcome the problems of communication and coordination on automotive issues. An ACEA official commented: 'We can accept the fact that DGs have a different view on some issues. We cannot accept the fact that they won't sit down and talk about those differences. The interservice groups will break down those barriers' (interview, 17 January 1994). By the summer of 1994 two interservice groups had been established to discuss the issues of EU R&D policy and training policy. The latter group met three times during 1994 before being disbanded and the R&D group was still operating at the time of writing (August 1994).

The other side of the coin is that because the sector is the subject of so much legislative activity ACEA finds itself a central player in many of the policy networks that have evolved in Brussels to deal with specific questions or areas. Peterson (1994, p. 2) describes the EU policy process as a 'hothouse of different types of sectoral policy networks'. He argues that these networks proliferate because the EU lacks the institutions which can facilitate bargaining between interested actors (1994, p. 27). A good example of such a network structure is the Motor Vehicle Emissions Group (MVEG) which has enjoyed substantial influence over the development of emissions policy in recent years by virtue of the technical expertise of its members. Not surprisingly, ACEA is a key participant in this grouping.

From ACEA's standpoint, the essential task of interest representation is to ensure that once sectoral priorities have been defined in working groups, that all parties stick to that line in any separate dealings with the Commission and, importantly, in their consultations with national governments. The whole essence of the ACEA structure which involves companies and national trade associations in working parties is designed to reflect the decision-making structures of the EU as a whole. The industry realizes the importance of nation-state influence on issues such as environmental and safety standards and effective interest representation means communicating a strong industry line to the twelve member states as well as to the EU institutions. As one ACEA official put it: 'Lobbying at the Commission level is twice as effective if you already have national support' (interview, 21 June 1994). Thus, the use of national and European lobbying strategies need not be alternative options. Rather, in a comprehensive approach to corporate representation, one can reinforce the other.

Case Study of the Selective Distribution Issue

As Mazey and Richardson (1993) have pointed out, the unpredictability of the EU policy agenda is something that all groups have to contend with. In the automobile case, this point was illustrated well in 1994 when DG IV's plans to alter the existing regulations on vehicle distribution were leaked to a French journal. While ACEA was aware that the Commission was reviewing its policy in this area it did not know that a draft policy had been completed. The case provides an opportunity to look at how a trade group responds to an unexpected source of turbulence in its political environment.

The history of the selective distribution (SD) issue and its importance to the industry can be stated briefly. All the major automobile companies sell and service their vehicles through a network of authorized dealers. The existing distribution system has some basic features which in theory breach the competition laws of the EU. Firstly, every authorized dealer is granted a clearly defined geographical territory within which he has the sole right to establish premises for the distribution of the manufacturer's vehicles. In return for his exclusive territory the dealer undertakes a contract with the manufacturer to provide a full range of after-sales services. The manufacturer supplies spare parts for its vehicles through this exclusive network. Moreover, the dealer is not allowed to sell other brands unless in exceptional circumstances it can be shown that the dealership would not otherwise be viable. Finally, resellers outside of the official dealer network are not allowed to buy or sell new motor vehicles.

The system sits uncomfortably with EU competition laws since it denies consumers the choice to compare a range of brands at any one dealership and restricts competition in the after-sales and servicing markets. Most cars come with a three-year warranty which requires all servicing to be undertaken at an authorized dealership. Thereafter the consumer can shop around, but often many spare parts can only be obtained from authorized dealers and there are risks attached if replica parts are installed.

The manufacturers put forward a number of arguments to support the SD system. They argue that cars are the most complex consumer goods on the market and because they are in constant use there are significant safety and environmental implications from their use. Manufacturers also argue that they invest large sums in their distribution systems and that these sums continue to rise as cars become more complex and more sophisticated diagnostics and repair equipment is needed. This is long-term investment which can have a payback period of more than ten years. The companies further argue that their distribution systems provide highly skilled and quality employment to over one million people in the EU. Finally they argue that the system is geographically comprehensive with all the main producers having a representative in each territory. In theory, the consumer can rely on a guaranteed level of service wherever the car may be when the need for service and repair arises.

Consumer groups dispute these arguments, maintaining that non-franchised dealers with access to manufacturers' parts can provide a comparable service. Consumer groups have also claimed that the system allows manufacturers to segment national markets in Europe and maintain high prices for vehicles in some markets. Such claims encouraged both the Monopolies and Mergers Commission in Britain and DG IV to investigate car prices and the SD system in 1992/93. The results of these investigations in 1992 were inconclusive, but the Commission did remind the manufacturers of their obligations under the 1985 block exemption and requested that they produce comprehensive lists of the prices for each model in different EU national markets.

When the Commission reviewed the situation in 1985 it was persuaded by the manufacturers' arguments and decided that the benefits of the system in terms of quality of after-sales service to the consumer outweighed the disadvantages of reduced competition. As a result, the SD system was granted a block exemption from EU competition law for a period of ten years whereupon the situation would be reviewed. The current controversy over the leaked draft relates to this review process and it is clear that DG IV wants to make major changes to the system before renewing the exemption.

The leaked draft in essence takes a copy of the existing rules attached to the block exemption and deletes those with which the Commission is unhappy while adding paragraphs where changes are sought. This rather simple drafting process has produced dramatic changes to the draft's interpretation. The Commission prefaced its new draft with the following comment:

> [E]xperience over the past ten years has shown that the present Regulation has significantly contributed neither to the opening of national markets nor to the development of effective and flexible channels for the distribution of vehicles and spare parts.

Some of the proposed changes and their implications are outlined below. In essence they are designed to open the market and to shift some of the power in the distribution relationship away from the manufacturer and towards the dealer:

1. At present, manufacturers can prevent their dealers taking on a second franchise and selling other brands. Multifranchises are therefore quite exceptional. The Commission proposes to allow dealerships to become multifranchises, making this the rule rather than the exception.

2. Under the existing system dealers may not seek customers outside of their territory. The Commission proposes to scrap this clause and in effect end territorial exclusivity.

3. At present, disputes between manufacturer and dealer over sales objectives are settled by the manufacturer. In future it is proposed that all of these will go to binding arbitration.

4. Dealers are at present forbidden from appointing subdealers within their exclusive territory unless the manufacturer has consented. It is proposed to allow the dealer more freedom to appoint subdealers. Again, any disputes would go to binding arbitration.

5. The new proposals oblige manufacturers to provide all technical information distributed to authorized dealers to any repair shop that has the appropriate equipment and professionally trained staff. This is designed to open the market to high street operators such as Halfords.

6. At present, dealers are allowed to sell only the manufacturer's spare parts or those of matching quality. The new draft gives dealers more freedom to supply other spare parts unless the manufacturers can prove through an independent test that they are below the quality of its own part. Again the power in the relationship is being shifted to the dealer.

7. The Commission proposes a renewal on these terms for a further ten years but makes it clear that a thorough review will be conducted mid-way through this period.

For the present purposes, the important point to note is that these were dramatic changes introduced into a redrafted document without any formal consultation with the industry. Moreover, the changes were made public before the industry had a chance to shape the policy details in private. As one industry official has pointed out: 'the ideal time to make representations is at the drafting stage because changes can be made and no-one has to lose face' (interview, 17 January 1994). It is much more difficult for policy-makers to change their minds in public and the issue has presented a serious challenge to the public affairs skills of ACEA.

ACEA's Response

On 20 June 1994, three weeks after the draft was leaked, an *ad hoc* ACEA working group on automobile distribution (attached to the permanent working group on legal and taxation issues) met in Brussels to discuss the industry's response. The group's membership was composed on the basis of members' expertise on the issue. Thus, five of the national trade association were represented, eleven of the fifteen member companies and five members of the ACEA secretariat. In addition to sending a company official from HQ who dealt with distribution issues, nine of the companies were also represented by their government relations representative based in Brussels.

The working group took three decisions which have formed the backbone of ACEA's initial rearguard strategy. Firstly, the group produced a position paper which identified ten areas where the new proposals as drafted could have legal or practical drawbacks. This document was also used to communicate the industry's surprise that the Commission should propose radical change without bringing forward detailed evidence of the deficiencies in the existing system. This was a predictable industry response which the ACEA members could easily agree upon. However, the working group had rather more difficulty in agreeing whether or not the industry should make concessions on issues of detail at this early stage and, if they were to give ground, on what areas this should happen. Thus the second part of the strategy was to resolve to work on an agreed collective line on this strategic issue over the summer months. The third and final leg of the strategy was perhaps the most important from a government relations standpoint. It was agreed in the working group that certain companies would have responsibility for communicating the industry's views to selected policy-makers and politicians at a European and national level. For example, if a company had an established relationship with a key politician then it was allocated the task of approaching this individual. Thus, the various national and multinational members of ACEA are being used to make contacts with key policy-makers in a bid to gather support at a higher level.

It is clear at the time of writing that the ACEA strategy has a credibility problem and is being undermined by direct contacts between some companies and the Commission. Some companies are more willing than others to make concessions, and this has been communicated to DG IV officials. While some companies insist that the best way forward is a resolute defence which involves no concessions at the first draft stage, others have indicated to the Commission those areas where they would be prepared to give ground. This type of 'own-account' interest representation by large companies makes the task of the Euro group that much harder, but it has, in this sector at least, become an ingrained feature of the policy process. Seventeen automotive companies have their own public affairs facilities in Brussels and these are used to make company representations to policy-makers. One DG IV official dealing with the distribution issue underlined why Commission staff themselves welcome contacts with the large companies. He argued: 'The need [for company contacts] is becoming greater because on many key issues it is clear that we are getting filtered views from ACEA. Like all bureaucracies, its secretariat has become a gatekeeper' (interview, 24 July 1994). Thus, it is important to stress that large companies have various 'voice' strategies when approaching the Commission and are likely to use several of these simultaneously.

Despite this tension between ACEA's efforts to lead on the issue and the direct efforts of large company members, the industry's strong reaction to the first draft appeared to be having some effect by late summer and DG IV was already backtracking. On some issues it became clear that while the Commission's intentions to open the market were well meant, the actual proposals have major practical problems. However, even though some issues of substance may be changed between the first and second draft, the major loss for the industry is likely to come after 1999. One of the industry's strongest arguments at present is that the SD system is vital to the implementation of the 1991 EU/Japan car understanding which monitors imports. This monitoring exercise is simplified by the precise nature of the existing distribution system. The understanding runs out in 1999 and thereafter the industry will probably face greater pressure for changes from the Commission. The Commission proposal to have an interim review of the system after just five years was probably designed with this point in mind.

Concluding Remarks

The automobile case has thrown up a number of general lessons for business alliances and interest representation. Firstly, perhaps the major strength of ACEA is the amount of work it is able to cover through its extensive system of *ad hoc* working groups. Secondly, that any collective organization derives its authority from its members. If the members break ranks from the common line then the business alliance is undermined in the eyes of policy-makers. There is a danger of this happening on the selective distribution issue. Thirdly, and following this, it is important to recognize that in every sector companies have multiple voice strategies available when communicating with policy-makers. The Euro group is an important option but it is by no means the only or even the best option on some occasions. Fourthly, because the European policy agenda is so unpredictable and issues can arise suddenly, groups need structures which allow them to respond to changing circumstances. Fifthly, for large companies in oligopolistic sectors, there is little to be gained and much to be lost by not participating in a Euro group. If Commission officials are regularly in discussion with representative Euro groups, companies will want to have access to this dialogue.

References

ACEA (1993) *Aims and Objectives*. Brussels: ACEA.

Mazey, S. and Richardson, J. J. (1993) *Lobbying in the European Community*. Oxford: Oxford University Press.

McLaughlin, A. M. (1994) 'The EU-Japan understanding on cars: engineering elements of a consensus', in Pedlar, R. and van Schendelen, R. (eds) *Lobbying the European Union*. Aldershot: Dartmouth.

McLaughlin, A. M. and Jordan, A. G. (1993) 'The rationality of lobbying in Europe: why are euro-groups so numerous and so weak?', in Mazey, S. and Richardson, J. J. *Lobbying in the European Community*. Oxford: Oxford University Press.

McLaughlin, A. M., Jordan, A. G. and Maloney, W. (1993) 'Corporate lobbying in the European Community', *Journal of Common Market Studies*, vol. 31, pp. 191–212.

Peterson, J. (1994) 'Policy networks in the European Union'. Typescript, University of York.

CASE 13

European Actions of Organized Shipping

Global and National Constraints

Karsten Ronit

Introduction

Shipping is older than recorded history and so is its global character. Although a part of shipping is confined to short sea trade within single nation-states, shipping is transboundary in the sense that it connects states and continents. Moreover, as markets become global, tonnage tends not to be lifted so much in trade to and from the paternal nation in which shipowners are registered. Under these circumstances many shipowners operate in different countries just like any other transnational corporation.

Given this industrial pattern, the drive towards global associability and regulation is logical. Associations with a global membership and outlook were formed early this century to handle different sets of relations, namely the International Shipping Federation (ISF) founded in 1909 and the International Chamber of Shipping (ICS) established in 1921 (Farthing, 1993). In these fora national associations from Europe have always played an important role.

That associations influence both market behaviour and public policy and can perform governance functions of some kind has been stressed in national sectors (Streeck and Schmitter, 1985; Lindberg et al., 1991) but has been less elaborated theoretically, and less empirically investigated at global levels (Hollingsworth et al., 1994). This is evident in shipping. In this sector – and corresponding with the trend towards global associability which helps govern shipping as a sector – a more advanced system of international organizations designed to regulate shipping on a global scale was created after the Second World War, although a number of international conventions had already been adopted. Today, organizations such as the ILO

184

(International Labour Organization, founded 1919), UNCTAD (United Nations Conference on Trade and Development, founded 1964), OECD (Organization for Economic Cooperation and Development, founded 1961) all have specialized bodies to cover shipping, but of particular importance is the IMO (International Maritime Organization, founded 1956) which is exclusively committed to shipping. Each of these has played a leading role in the regulation of this sector (Farthing, 1993).

In shipping there is a strong tradition for organized action at the global level, and an equally strong desire to find global solutions to regulate the industry. Specific national or regional arrangements which do not comply with already established global standards are discouraged, although sustained in many areas. Accordingly, the European process of organization and integration is constrained by the different sets of global traditions. This is not to suggest that there is no specific European process; indeed, specialized associations have been created to represent shipping in various European contexts, and public policies have gradually been developed, but this process is still to a large extent embedded in a larger and global framework. This is often deliberately addressed to emphasize the limits of European arrangements.

The greater role attributed to shipping by the Commission in recent years has, however, challenged the unity of shipowners' interest representation and thereby produced and activated existing cleavages. On this background the 'Brussels' perspective has become more salient.

European Interest Organizations in Shipping: CENSA and ECSA

The global scenery described above is of extreme importance to shipping and the European process, and is reflected in the structure of shipping's associations. On the European scene there are two main associations – CENSA and ECSA – based upon almost the same membership, but each committed to its own particular geography of shipping.

CENSA (Council of European and Japanese National Shipowners' Associations) was formed in 1974 by its predecessor organization, also with the name CENSA. This had its origins in an *ad hoc* arrangement dating from 1958 between the associations in Europe (in the form of the previous Committee of European National Shipowners' Associations), the Japanese association and CES (Committee of European Shipowners, representing individual liner companies and international container consortia). The merger in 1974 was invoked by a number of factors which included the unsatisfactory forms of industry representation in European shipping, but also the 'increase in governmental involvement in shipping at both the national level and international levels . . . [and] . . . the close interrelationship between shipping policy developments in whatever parts of the world' (CENSA, 1974, p. 1) were important arguments behind the organizational restructuring.

Today CENSA consists of national associations from Belgium, Denmark, Finland, France, Germany, Greece, Italy, Netherlands, Norway, Sweden and the UK plus Japan. The Japanese liaise with the other associations from their office in London. This is also where the secretariat of CENSA is based.

From the very beginning of the European/Japanese cooperation, attempts were made to monitor closely US shipping policy and global developments in shipping. This task was shared with the Consultative Shipping Group, consisting of governments from the same group of countries as CENSA, and resulted in a number of exchanges with Washington on shipping. Under these circumstances CENSA's exchanges with EU institutions have been pushed to the periphery and delegated to ECSA (European Community Shipowners' Associations).

A number of attempts have been made to amalgamate CENSA and ECSA in order to reduce costs and avoid any duplication. A major reservation from within CENSA circles was that a new association would have a regional profile, causing it to lose its image as a globally active association. A further concern is that Japanese interests could hardly be hosted in a proper European association continuously involved in a dialogue with the Commission.

Founded in 1962, in the very formative years of the community, ECSA members are national associations from all EU countries bar two: Luxembourg and Portugal. Observer status has recently been granted to Sweden, Norway and Finland. Whilst it has enjoyed an unchallenged position as the sole Community-based association of shipowners, in the 1960s ECSA could build upon only a small fraction of those national associations affiliated to the more encompassing CENSA. Consequently, the shipping interests represented in a narrow Community context were relatively weak. Major European shipping nations were still missing. ECSA was endowed with few resources, and for many years it had more the appearance of a letterhead association to hold in readiness than that of an active spokesperson for shipping interests. Little was done to seek the interest of the Commission in the sector's affairs.

The advent of Denmark and the UK into the Community and the establishment of a secretariat in Brussels in 1973 was the catalyst for ECSA to become more representative of European shipping. The later inclusion of

Greece, by far the biggest shipping nation in the EU, added significantly to the voice of ECSA, which, together with simultaneous promptings exerted by member states, provided an influence upon the development of European shipping policies.

Although the potential for political action by organized shipping has improved, and a growing political understanding is also evident, there is an outspoken preference among the larger and more globally orientated parts of organized shipping for free enterprise, self-regulation and limited public regulation of the sector. The industry itself retains a preference for making arrangements in a global rather than in a regional setting. This is recognized in the Commission, but disagreements as to the degree to which this global framework should be observed do prevail across national shipowners' associations and the member states.

ECSA and National Shipowner's Associations

ECSA is the only transnational shipping association based in Brussels. However, a few national associations of shipowners retain a small infrastructure in Brussels. In this way not only do they partly support the ECSA secretariat, but they are also in a better position to control it, and in some cases even offer the national shipowners' associations an alternative voice. For instance, apart from the Belgian association based within reach in Antwerp, the Swedish and Norwegian associations use a consultancy agency in Brussels, and the Italians use a partial envoy. The Danish Shipowners' Association has an independent office which plans to devote more resources to the office in the future because of a perceived need for monitoring the Commission, to commit ECSA to the 'global line', and to avoid protectionist inputs from other national associations. Indeed, there are a number of cleavages in ECSA which are most manifest in the areas of shipping policy, and less pronounced or non-existent in labour relations. These are very much based on the different conditions of shipping in the individual countries and show that, despite belonging to the same sector, national patterns are of great importance (Wilks and Wright, 1987).

The basic dividing line goes between those who have a global orientation, and those whose interests are confined to domestic waters and whose national industries are rather small in terms of tonnage in global and European shipping. With the exception of Greece, this dividing line generally runs between shipowners in northern and southern Europe, although this is somewhat modified by the fact that Greek shipowners are not involved in those trades of shipping based on more advanced technologies such as cool carriers.

The distinct global orientation of some member associations in ECSA is articulated differently. Greece has a reputation as 'fundamentalist' and unwilling to compromise. In many ways the national associations of the UK, Germany, the Netherlands and Denmark share the views of the not very amenable Greeks, but make a greater effort to convince the other members of ECSA in serious dialogue. Compromises, where they occur, have the function of providing a platform for unified action via ECSA and in assisting the uniformity of dialogue between national associations and their respective governments. This may increase the likelihood of a compromise in the Council of Ministers.

Together with the Greeks, northern European associations have been most successful in influencing ECSA, partly because they pay active attention to the associational dimension in Brussels, and partly because those more inclined towards protectionism are satisfied with the status quo of doing business within their own domestic or Mediterranean markets. However, the lack of cohesion, sometimes leading to paralysis, is taken by national associations as an opportunity to address the Commission directly. Although ECSA is involved in an ongoing dialogue with the Commission, exchanges with national associations are only *ad hoc*. Thus, after a compromise has failed, national associations resort mainly to separate action where vital interests are affected. In addition to approaching the Commission directly, it is likely that in such cases alliances are already formed at national levels between governments and national associations of shipowners.

The priority given to shipping in the twelve member states is far from similar, and only a few national associations can be considered strong within their national political environment. In France the importance attributed to the shipping industry is relatively limited, whereas in Greece it is more-or-less a national interest, and access to government is unlimited. On the other hand, in countries where shipping cannot be classified as marginal and there are strong domestic alliances with individual governments, the very different positions of the member states in the Council of Ministers may modify the otherwise significant influence of national shipping communities. Here countries like Greece and Denmark, hosting strong shipping interests, count relatively little. Certainly, this is not an argument against using the national route wherever possible, but the route is not always sufficient. These processes must be carefully considered by each national shipowners' association in applying its strategy of interest representation to the European level.

Representations by single shipowners are rare in general questions of shipping policy. However, it is often seen in specific and uncontroversial cases where interests are affected outside the EU, provided they do not interfere with other EU shipowners. In these circumstances the role of ECSA is in no way challenged by such actions by shipowners.

Regulation and Representation

The first major steps in the Community's shipping policy were taken as late as December 1986 in the form of four regulations concerning:

1. The freedom to provide services between member states, and between member states and third countries (Council Regulation No. 4055).
2. The application of the competition rules of the Treaty of Rome on shipping industry (Council Regulation No. 4056).
3. The unfair pricing practices of non-EU liners (Council Regulation No. 4057).
4. The restrictive practices of third countries in not granting free access to cargoes (Council Regulation No. 4058).

Progress in implementing and interpreting the four regulations has been slow, and ECSA has invested much effort in negotiating with the Commission, for example regarding the competition articles. The practices of liner conferences and consortia have here been seen as restrictive to competition, but ECSA has stressed that rules should not be rigidly applied and that existing traditions of this particular trade should be accepted in the form of self-regulation in order not to reduce the global competitiveness of European shipowners.

The importance of the global dimension is reiterated in terms of improving the competitive environment in which European shipping is operating. The safety issue which has traditionally occupied governments, the EU and shipowners is also a matter for the International Maritime Organization. Thus, after the Commissions' communication on safe seas in February 1993, ECSA, with some inputs from INTERTANKO (International Association of Independent Tanker Owners), emphasized the leading role of IMO without in any way seeking to belittle the potential contribution of the EU (European Community Shipowners Associations, 1993).

On some other issues ECSA has had difficulties in adopting a common platform. One case has been the Europe/West Africa trades, where notably French shipping interests have benefited from such arrangements. In response, the Danish Shipowners' Association and the Danish government jointly approached the Commission and pointed to the violation of European regulations on maritime transport. After several years of investigations, shipowners involved in such practices were fined (Commission Decision, 93/47/EEC). This is just one example of the dissenting views sometimes found within ECSA, emphasizing the importance of taking the national route via one's own governments or by developing issue alliances.

The Single European Act also gave rise to internal conflicts. Increased attention was focused on the role of intra-EU seaborne transport in the overall discussion of transport policy, where the interests of short sea trade interests have reached the agenda. Within ECSA an internal committee was set up and some smaller national associations representing this interest category joined as associated members. However, it has been difficult to reach a balanced decision and there has been serious disagreement between Mediterranean shipowners seeking protection from international competition via European regulations and (in particular) north European shipowners in favour of open markets.

In 1989 the fundamental problem of disagreement within ECSA's ranks was discussed in more general terms, and it was agreed formally to include references to dissenting views in ECSA statements, and surrender to each member a formal right to make its position public outside the framework of ECSA (CAACE, 1989). To that end an entirely new article was incorporated into the statutes. This practice may satisfy a divided membership on the one hand, but on the other it questions cohesion and weakens representation.

The first major EU initiatives in shipping were in part prompted by ECSA. The spirit of ECSA's ambitions can be seen in communications such as *For a Common Maritime Transport Policy* from the summer of 1986 (CAACE, 1986a) and *Strengthening the Competitive Standing of EEC Fleets*, issued on the eve of the 1986 regulations (CAACE, 1986b). These initiatives were later accompanied by other ECSA statements and responses to studies carried out by the Commission. These include *Measures to Improve the Operating Conditions of Community Shipping* in May 1989 (Commission, 1989a), in which the idea of creating a common register (Euros-register) was presented to avoid further 'flagging out', i.e. registrations in countries outside western Europe. At the same time the *Guidelines for Financial and Fiscal Measures Concerning Shipping Operations with Ships Registered in Member States* (Commission, 1989b) were issued to further specify the idea of a European register, and to seek to reduce costs. Together they marked the beginning of a new phase in EU regulation to which ECSA could not remain silent, but needed instead to adopt an active line.

A solution to all problems addressed in these communications has not been achieved yet, and the Euros-register, for example, has been exposed to severe criticism in that it is seen as an attempt to harmonize the conditions of registration. The shipping community has seen this initiative as mostly an ill-conceived idea in a sector which is not European but global in character, and where it makes little sense to establish fair competition between European shipowners alone. Some national shipowners' associations have, however, welcomed parts of the proposal not least because of the future prospects for indirect subsidizing which could emerge if political measures were adopted to reduce the costs of less competitive shipowners in the EU.

Today, these and other initiatives are subject to not just an occasional dialogue between the Commission and ECSA: a larger machinery has been established to formalize exchanges. Thus, a previous *ad hoc* group was, in July 1987, replaced by the Joint Committee for Maritime Transport, which is basically a tripartite body involving the Commission as host, and relevant shipowners and unions in the field. Participation in this committee is interpreted in the industry as a step towards greater recognition and an extension of the right to be consulted automatically where interests are affected.

A new encompassing body involving a broad spectre of maritime industries was created in 1992 as the Maritime Industries Forum in order to coordinate interests and elaborate policies which could eventually materialize into EU measures (Annual Report, 1992–93). Member states are involved in the forum as observers. Only transnational interest groups are full members, with ECSA participating and coordinating interest in membership. In the subgroup on short sea trade, ECSA even provides the secretariat.

When proposals in the forum to formalize the dialogue among the maritime industries (in order to establish further a maritime transport policy by setting up a high-level panel of industrial representatives and Commission officials) were launched, the maritime industries were reluctant to enlarge and further formalize coordination. Behind this reservation stood not only the usual scepticism against bureaucratic structures and the fear that issues might be buried in committee work, but also the long-standing preference of organized shipping not to indulge in relatively narrow European work, but to seek global solutions. In retrospect this fear was unfounded. The panel, involving the ECSA president, has not exaggerated its directive role.

Having welcomed several of the Commission's initiatives, it is nevertheless felt within ECSA that the proposed measures to improve the conditions of shipping are insufficient and that too little has been achieved. In relation to the Social Charter and the Single European Act, organized shipping has seen the EU as trying to harmonize the different national conditions of European shipping, which it regards as inappropriate in a global industry. In a similar vein, ECSA would like to see EU regulation conform with existing global standards adopted in international organizations like IMO and ILO. The aim is to ensure that the EU should work actively and press for global solutions in its foreign diplomacy and be an ardent spokesperson against protective national measures adopted by any government throughout the world. For its part, the Commission has previously used its diplomatic muscle to good effect with countries of the former Eastern Bloc.

Encouraged by organized shipowners, EU diplomacy in the field of shipping has also been successfully used *vis-à-vis* Third World countries. However, different interests have complicated matters, and there is certainly no guarantee of unified action. This was illustrated during and after the UNCTAD negotiations which sought to establish a code of conduct for liner conferences concerning cargo-sharing arrangements with Third World countries. The UNCTAD code finally went into force in 1983 after a compromise between the member states (the Brussels Package) on the conditions to accede to the code had been reached. Germany and the Netherlands were the first to accede, while other countries, backed by their national shipping communities, hesitated and acceded only with some reluctance. Thus a cleavage across member states and to a certain degree also among national shipowners' associations was again evident.

Given the different interests attributed to shipping and the ambitions of the Commission to include shipping in the integration process more generally, these cleavages are likely to occur in future and to influence the strategies of national associations of shipowners and the degree to which a common platform can be found within ECSA.

Concluding remarks

The transboundary activities and commercial interests attached to the overwhelming majority of tonnage in European shipping provide it with a global profile which is also reflected in the patterns of associability and regulation. Compared with other sectors, shipping is relatively globalized, but it is not an exceptional case from which little can be learnt about business associability. Indeed, the importance attached to global organization in this sector makes it worth studying at the European level.

The case of shipping also emphasizes the importance of an historical perspective. Global associations like the International Shipping Federation (ISF) and International Chamber of Shipping (ICS) predate European associations by several decades, and have become established and recognised political players. A large machinery has been established to regulate different aspects of shipping, and an impressive number of international conventions have been adopted emerging from authoritative international organizations. These global arrangements frame the European system of regulation. Organized shipping has needed to learn to adapt to new environments and to meet new challenges. Exchanges with European authority has brought a degree of unpredictability.

Given these circumstances, it is perhaps suprising that shipowners have experienced no major problems in finding an appropriate outlet for representing interests in Brussels, and the duplication which is evident in some other sectors has not arisen in shipping. Indeed, the tradition of associability in the sector discourages large-firm single representation, a tradition which has survived reorganization to accommodate the European level. Rather, the resources of the large players can be drawn upon for collective needs where necessary.

The issue for shipping interests at the European level is not one of merging competing outlets into a single representational format, but rather to divide attention between global and European outlets and to manage conflicts within ECSA. Where consensus is not possible in this forum, affiliated national associations can build alliances with domestic governments in an attempt to influence the Council of Ministers. Although this route is frequently activated, interest representation along this channel is not equally accessible to all national associations; national variations between industrial interests should not be ignored. In shipping, the larger member states do not always host large shipping industries, and, as is evident from the case of Greece, the contrary is sometimes true. The greatest emphasis put upon the European level comes from north-west Europe and Greece, and in these cases there also exists excellent contact with the respective national governments. However, in an emerging policy field it has been necessary for this group to monitor closely via ECSA every step of the Commission in order to ensure that EU regulation observes the global interests of organized shipping in Europe, which the group is particularly keen to emphasize.

References

Comité des Associations d'Armateurs des Communautes Européennes (CAACE) (1986a) *For a Common Maritime Transport Policy*. Brussels: CAACE.
Comité des Associations d'Armateurs des Communautes Européennes (CAACE) (1986b) *Strengthening the Competitive Standing of EEC Fleets*. Brussels: CAACE.

Comité des Associations D'Armateurs des Communautes Européennes (CAACE) (1989) *Brussels (1989) Statutes*. vol. 1, September 1989.

Commission of the European Communities (1989a) *Measures to Improve the Operating Conditions of Community Shipping*. COM(89)266 final. Brussels.

Commission of the European Communities (1989b) *Guidelines for Financial and Fiscal Measures Concerning Shipping Operations with Ships Registered in Member States*. SEC(89) 921 final. Brussels: Secretariat of the European Commission.

Commission of the European Communities (1993) Commission Decision of 17 December 1992 imposing a fine pursuant to Article 19 of Council Regulation (EEC) No. 4056/86 (IV/32.447). 93/47/EEC, 393 D 0047.

Council of the European Communities (1986) Council Regulation (EEC) No. 4055/86 of 22 December 1986 applying the principle of freedom to provide services to maritime transport between member states and between member states and third countries. 386 R 4055.

Council of the European Communities (1986a) Council Regulation (EEC) No. 4056 of 22 December 1986 laying down detailed rules for the application of Articles 85 and 86 of the Treaty to Maritime Transport. 386 R 4056.

Council of the European Communities (1986b) Council Regulation (EEC) No. 4057/86 of 22 December 1986 on unfair pricing practices in maritime transport. 386 R 4057.

Council of the European Communities (1986c) Council Regulation (EEC) No. 4058/86 of 22 December 1986 concerning coordinated action to safeguard free access to cargoes in open trades. 386 R 4058.

Council of European and Japanese National Shipowners' Associations (CENSA) (1974) *Terms of Reference*. London: CENSA.

European Community Shipowners' Associations (1993) Annual Report 1992–93. Brussels: ECSA.

European Community Shipowners' Associations (1993) *Safety and Pollution Prevention*. *Brussels:* ECSA.

Farthing, B. (1993) *International Shipping* (2nd edn). London: Lloyd's of London Press Ltd.

Hollingsworth, J. R., Schmitter, P. C. and Streeck, W. (eds) (1994) *Comparing Capitalist Economies: Variations in the Governance of Sectors*. New York: Oxford University Press.

Lindberg, L. N., Campbell J. L. and Hollingsworth, J. R. (1991) 'Economic governance and the analysis of structural change in the American economy', in Campbell, J. L., Hollingsworth, J. R. and Lindberg, L. N. (eds) *Governance of the American Economy*. Cambridge: Cambridge University Press, pp. 3–34.

Streeck, W. and Schmitter, P. C. (1985) *Private Interest Government: Beyond Market and State*. London: Sage.

Wilks, S. and Wright, M. (eds) (1987) *Comparative Government: Industry Relations, Western Europe, the United States and Japan*. Oxford: Clarendon Press.

PART 6

National (Non-EU) Cultures

The American Organization of Firms

Henry Jacek

Collective action by American business is an interesting topic because American firms have a strong tendency to be freebooters, that is, they believe they have sufficient market power and political resources to act alone in the political arena. As Graham Wilson has observed, 'American corporations seem skeptical of organizations created to protect their collective interests' (Wilson, 1990, p. 287). Yet at the same time they have created one of the most effective collective action networks to complement their individual efforts.

The organization of American business interests in Europe is part of the worldwide network of the American Chamber of Commerce system. Sitting at the top of this American network is the United States Council for International Business in New York. It had previously been known as the United States Association of the International Chamber of Commerce and then later as the United States Council of the International Chamber of Commerce. One of its constituent units is the United States Industry Coordinating Group on European Community Affairs (USICG). This unit in turn is composed of the National Association of Manufacturers, the US Chamber of Commerce itself, the National Foreign Trade Council and the EC Committee of the American Chamber of Commerce in Brussels.

The USICG, first of all, is a communicator of information through its *EC Update* and its newsletter summarising economic developments in the EU. The USICG sees itself as an informal and loose confederation of business associations on both sides of the Atlantic. Its purpose is to ensure that American business speaks with one voice to the European Commission on matters affecting operations in Europe. It does so primarily through promoting the exchange of information among its members, and where necessary facilitating coordination of positions. Each of its constituent units maintains its own channels of communication to the Commission (personal communication, 1994).

The presence of organized American business in the European Community began with the founding of the European Council of American Chambers of Commerce (ECACC) in Paris in 1963. It was formerly known as the Council of American Chambers of Commerce in Europe and later as the Council of American Chambers of Commerce–Europe and Mediterranean. It has fifteen national American chambers as members: Austria, Belgium, France, Germany, Greece, Hungary, Israel, Italy, Netherlands, Portugal, Republic of Ireland, Spain, Switzerland, Turkey and the UK, representing more than eighteen thousand firms and businesspersons. The ECACC has a number of goals:

1. It seeks to further a solidarity of interests among the American chambers in Europe and the Chamber of Commerce of the United States (US Chamber).

2. It assists in improving trade and investment opportunities, activities and programmes.

3. It informs members of recent business developments in the USA and Europe.

4. It promotes relations between member countries and intergovernmental organizations based in Europe and the USA.

5. It represents and gives effect to the aims and views of US business interests in Europe and to reciprocal European interests.

6. It monitors and represents positions on US, European and international issues of relevance to US business in Europe.

7. It conducts occasional fora on international trade investment and other issues (Daniels and Schwartz, 1994).

The ECACC in turn has designated the EC Committee of the American Chamber of Commerce in Brussels as its lead policy organization on EU affairs. This committee, which calls itself AMCHAM-ECC, was originally just a committee of the American Chamber of Commerce in Belgium, and AMCHAM-ECC still has its offices in AMCHAM-Belgium. However, AMCHAM-ECC has taken on an institutional life of its own, is headed by an EC affairs manager and is now one of the key elements of the worldwide American Chamber of Commerce system found in most countries of the world. AMCHAM is the basic generic designation given to the many American chamber organizations.

AMCHAM-ECC has a full-time staff of seventeen and besides representing AMCHAM's in eleven EU member states, it also represents six hundred American corporations. It was founded in 1965, just two years after ECACC was founded in Paris. AMCHAM-ECC sees as its basic goal representing the views of the six hundred European companies of American parentage to the EU and its working groups and taskforces (Eldrige, 1994). Especially impressive are the research and policy publications which are sometimes used by EU officials in drafting their own documents and programmes (Bindi, 1994). Among the more important annual AMCHAM-ECC publications are the *EC Information Handbook,* the *EC Environmental Guide* and the *EC Financial Services Guide*. In addition it produces a bi-weekly newsheet and the semi-annual *Business Guide to EC Initiatives*. In the past, noted documents have been 'Countdown 1992' and the 'Countdown Directory of the Status of EC Proposals'.

Buttressing the efforts of ECACC and AMCHAM-ECC are the specific offices and activities of the large American firms in Europe. The European operations of American firms, their office staff and the American consultants who work for them are given considerable autonomy from head office control. Although these firms do carry on activities in EU member countries, their main focus has been on EU policies. They were early in setting up offices in Brussels for the task of influencing Community policies. In turn they became the model for Japanese multinationals. For the American firms, the politics of Brussels is easy to understand since it has more features in common with freewheeling Washington politics than with the more orderly European national patterns (Andersen and Eliassen, 1991).

In an important sense, the politics of Brussels has encouraged the emergence of a new set of policy actors of which the big American companies are among the most conspicuous (Kohler-Koch, 1994). Yet although they are conspicuous by their presence, their lobbying style is one of quiet discreteness bolstered by high quality technical research. When making their case to EU officials, a connection is drawn between the interests of the firm and the interests of the entire Community.

Another way in which American firms extend the possibilities for collective action is through their commercial action. The logic of the single market moves an American firm along a continuum of European involvement. Firstly, there is an interest in exports to Europe. This is followed by a pattern of direct investment particularly in high growth, high tech industries (Jacquemin and Wright, 1993). The third stage involves deals linking American and European firms, a form of European business alliance that is just as common as European firm mergers (Sandholtz and Zysman, 1989).

A fourth structure utilized by American corporations are the various Euro groups in different business sectors. The large American corporations are willing to become highly involved in these business interest associations (BIAs) because they are a natural extension of producer-based groups so familiar to them in the USA. In one well known example, the car industry, the American automobile manufacturers as part of the liaison committee of the Automobile Industry of the Countries of the European Communities (CLCA) 'became the federation's most active members' as well as of its successor, the Association of European Automobile Constructors (ACEA) (McLaughlin and Jordan, 1993, p. 146).

Amplifying the multiple structure strategy of the American firms is a fifth strategy: active participation in national BIAs. This strategy is not overlooked 'because of the enduring importance of the Council of Ministers (CM) in the EC decision-making process' (McLaughlin et al., 1993, p. 196). Again, with examples drawn from the car industry, it is clear that American firms recognize that when the goal is to block policy initiatives, it makes sense to lobby at the national level (McLaughlin et al., 1993).

Complementing the perspective of the subsidiary of the American corporation is the identity of the national interest with the activities of large business plants in the nation. Thus, returning to the car industry, an employer of many well-paid industrial jobs, the EC was debating new automotive emission standards in 1985, in particular the adoption of a mandatory catalytic converter for each car. Ford UK had invested substantial sums in the technology of lean-burn engines. This technology, which was 'designed to decrease engine pollutants by changing the engine design' (Vogel, 1993, p. 58), would go for naught if catalytic converters were made mandatory. The threat to Ford UK was substantial: The catalytic converter technology would make the lean-burn engine design obsolete and Ford UK would have to invest new large sums in converter design and production from an inexperienced position. The British government became a vocal opponent to EC regulations requiring the catalytic converter technology. Instead it argued that lean-burn engines were the wave of the future and the add-on catalytic converter technology was old technology. The political positions of the British government and Ford UK became identical (Vogel, 1993).

The multiple structures and strategies of American firms can be basically understood as a rough congruence between the political conditions of the USA where American firms initially developed their structures, strategies and techniques and the current complex political atmosphere of the European Union. In both cases the complexity of state institutions produces a fluidity and complexity that results in political uncertainty about future public policy decisions. Thus, the safest approach is to follow a multiple lobbying strategy and not to put all your eggs in one basket.

European nation-state policies have been far more predictable. This may be due to a strong state tradition, corporatist policy-making traditions or norms of strong party political discipline. In this type of political atmosphere it may be clear that there is only one basic political strategy for the firm.

The movement to Euro policy-making has changed this cosy picture. Theoretically, this is not too surprising. Some time ago, Olson argued that jurisdictional integration beyond traditional market borders affects policy-making. When market borders expand, he argued, the previously stable, predictable relationships between organized interests and public officials break down. Decisions are now made by market calculations or by officials at a higher supranational level in an unpredictable manner (Olson, 1982).

Streeck and Schmitter (1991) believe they now observe what Olson predicted. The close, relatively simple and predictable relationships between organized economic interests and the national state, particularly of the corporatist model, has given way to:

> an American-style pattern of 'disjointed pluralism' or 'competitive federalism' . . . [and as] in the United States, and perhaps more so, this system would be characterized by a profound absence of hierarchy and monopoly and a wide variety of players of different but uncertain status.
>
> *(Streeck and Schmitter, 1991, p. 159)*

To the extent that they are correct, American firms should feel very much at home in a political sense.

Streeck and Schmitter are not alone in recognizing the instability of the interest representation system in Europe today. Mazey and Richardson see three elements in a state of development: state institutions, Euro policies and interest representation organizations. In such a state of adolescence, producer interests have the edge. Early organization goes to the best resourced (Mazey and Richardson, 1992). Large American corporations are among the most heavily endowed of potential political actors.

While many would agree that Washington patterns of lobbying seem to be replicated to a significant degree today and that those patterns favour American corporations, a question is, how long will these pluralistic conditions last? If more stable, predictable, simple and orderly processes of interest intermediation become institutionalized, how will this affect the perceived political advantage of American firms? If and when these changes occur, at least two possible answers exist. American firms with their substantial resources and habits of multi lateral lobbying thrusts might lose their edge in the policy process. On the other hand, they may adjust to a more traditional European pattern of policy-making better than many observers now think possible.

If anything, American firms have shown themselves to be highly resilient and also adaptable to changing circumstances. They have entered into the European political arena with two key orientations. Firstly, they assumed from the beginning that European officials and American corporations share the same goal: the Europeanizing of all business. Thus, in recent years many American firms looked forward to 1992 by simplifying their operations by organizing their plants and operations into a single European Economic Interest Grouping (EEIG). This has led to consolidation and specialization of production and services on a Europe-wide basis rather than continuing a national branch/plant strategy. The result has been higher productivity and profitability (Hufbauer, 1990).

Secondly, the desire to form a European Economic Interest Grouping led most American companies to form 'internal 1992 strategy groups'. These groups drew on many different corporate skills and professions. The purpose of these teams was to recommend basic policy to the Euro firms' managers. A key component of these teams was the firm's Brussels coordinator (Bates, 1990).

Ironically, the influence exerted by American firms was aided by attempts to exclude these very same corporations from having a decisive role in the determination of the public policy outputs of European institutions. After the Second World War and through the 1970s and 1980s, American corporations were excluded from many Euro BIAs. The response of the excluded companies was to build up the organizational infrastructure and policy capability of AMCHAM-ECC as well as the governmental affairs departments of the major American corporations in Brussels. The latter development was a natural extension of corporate behaviour in the USA. As a result of these developments it became clear to many of these sectoral Euro BIAs that it was better to have these American firms integrated into the sectoral Euro groups rather than leaving them outside pursuing their own narrow interests. However, the most powerful Euro BIA, the European Round Table of Industrialists (ERT), still excludes American firms.[1]

The lobbying techniques of American firms work best on issues surrounding European policy harmonization, and this is for at least five reasons. Firstly, American firms have the ability to organize themselves into a well integrated, cohesive position. They find it natural to present themselves as the enthusiastic proponents of a pan-European approach to policy problems. In contrast, they implicitly paint European firms as promoting the nationalistic concerns of their home countries. Not only is this pan-European perspective deeply imbued in the organs of American big business in Europe but it is also buttressed by American BIAs in the USA itself: 'Not surprisingly, the principal organizations that speak for US business – the Business Roundtable, the US Council for International Business, the National Association of Manufacturers, and the US Chamber of Commerce – are enthusiastic about Europe 1992' (Hufbauer, 1990, p. 25).

Secondly, American firms never put all their eggs in one basket. For them, the only safe strategy is a multitrack strategy. At the European level this means cultivating all the institutional complexity of the EU. This includes the Commission, the European Parliament and the Council of Ministers. American lobby groups such as the Chamber of Commerce recommend heavy business lobbying, especially at the early stages of policy formulation such as Commission legislative proposals, the first reading of the European Parliament and the common position by a qualified majority of the Council of Ministers (Hufbauer, 1990). In addition, American firms are careful to exploit ambiguities between national and EU policies.

A good example of how American corporations deal with political problems involves an American winemaker and an American lawyer, Frank Fine, based in Brussels. The problem for the American winemaker was that its wine shipments were being stopped at the borders of individual EU countries. The argument given for the interference was that the labels were not in conformity with national specifications. However, these specifications were vague and capable of being used with a great deal of discretion and consequent protection of national wine industries. The American lawyer took the wine labels to Brussels and the relevant directorate. The winemaker was told how to word the labels so as to meet EU standards. Once this was done, the company was able to use EU approval when confronting national customs officials. The principle employed was to use EU approval to override national impediments (Hunter, 1989).

Thirdly, American lobbyists present policy harmonization as an exercise in technical standards-setting. The issues involved are presented as merely technical ones, and not political. By depoliticizing policy issues the American lobbyists aim to reduce national emotions and political symbolism and to remove the issue from public attention. At the same time the argument is made to EU officials that the quick resolution of policy harmonization will aid job creation. American lobbyists are quick to point out that the US experience of harmonization, especially in tax rules, was seen as a mechanism for successful job creation in the US during the 1980s (Bates, 1990).

Fourthly, American firms and BIAs quickly learned the utility of having their interests represented by Europeans or Americans with a substantial

European education. In the 1980s AMCHAM-ECC benefited from having an Irish-born director, Eamonn Bates, who recognized that to be effective he had 'to get in early and affect the drafting' of directives, legislation and policy. In the case of the American lawyer Frank Fine, Fine studied for a postgraduate degree in England and speaks fluent French. Fine believes that anyone who speaks only one European language 'has little future as a lobbyist in Brussels' for American business interests (Hunter, 1989, p. 43). Even Fine admits, however, that American firms are more successful in general when represented by Europeans (Hunter, 1989).

Not only do American firms try to look European in their representation, they also restructure their operations so as to have these look European. In one typical case, the Republic National Bank of New York consolidated all its European subsidiaries into one company, Safra Republic Holdings. The bank then sold stock to European shareholders and at the same time installed local management. The result was a European-looking company with local management, shareholders, and with an infusion of new capital for expansion (Quickel, 1989).

Finally, American business interests provide useful information, systematic facts and legal help, the latter for drafting purposes. Americans recognize that the directorates-general are understaffed. Most EU directives and regulations begin as the work of a single official and thus needs help in drafting. American lobbyists are only too happy to provide that help in the form of 'credible outside information' (Hunter, 1989, p. 43). In providing this information, American groups and firms are aided by the many management, political and public relations consultants and law firms that have set up offices in Brussels. Many of these are American firms[2] or employ American nationals.

The European telecommunications industry provides an excellent example of how American firms can use arguments about technical harmonization to increase their policy influence. The European Telecommunications Standards Institute (ETSI) is the major policy-maker on telecommunication standards in Europe. However, ETSI depends on the European committee for standardisation (CEN) and the European Committee for Electrotechnical Standardization (CENELEC) for standards of terminal equipment. Since the telecommunications standards produced by these various bodies affect the ability of telecommunications equipment manufacturers to sell their products, having European standards harmonized with American ones is crucial for American manufacturers. In order to achieve this end, American firms use American standards bodies. The American manufacturers have been able to get the American National Standards Institute (ANSI) a voice in CEN and CENELEC. At the same time, US firms, AMCHAM-ECC and ANSI participate as observers in ETSI. Particularly important is the ability of American organizations to comment on drafts of European standards. Even more directly, American firms like IBM and Digital Equipment Corporation are active in ETSI. American firms leverage their influence still further by having membership in national standards associations which are the eighteen members of CENELEC and CEN (Cowhey, 1990).

American firms sometimes bring their own industry associations for lobbying at the highest levels. In the spring of 1989, the French government pushed aggressively for a directive that would have required at least half of all television time to be occupied by shows made in Europe. The Motion Picture Association of America (MPAA) lobbied the Council of Ministers and was able to persuade the Dutch, Danes and Germans to vote against the directive. A Dutch-speaking lobbyist headed the MPAA team (Hunter, 1989).

In contrast, when American firms take positions that seem purely American and are on symbolic, non-technical issues, the success of American business lobbying is less likely. American business has a managerial supremacist approach to employee relations and thus finds employee participation in firm decision-making strange and unacceptable. In 1980, American firms were able to stop an extension of German laws on employee participation to all EC countries. The American firms, although successful at that point, created an image of themselves as anti-labour, anti-social democratic and insensitive to Continental European traditions. However, by 1994 the Americans could no longer stop the establishment of EU works councils even though the new policy would affect about two hundred and fifty US firms operating in Europe (Gardner, 1994).

The structure of the organization of American firms in Europe and the firms' strong influence upon the public policy outputs of the EU institutions is a paradox. The unexpected impact of these firms has occurred despite the fact that, or perhaps because, European firms and some European state officials desired to keep American influence out of the important evolving policies of the EC in the 1960s and 1970s. Because of this initial attempt to shut out American firms, these companies drew on their domestic political experience and developed their own political infrastructure. They, of course, developed their governmental affairs departments but their real strength was and is the American Chamber of Commerce system. The American Chamber parent is well-resourced and provides a great deal of help to American firms looking for success in Europe. From the parent association, American chambers were created in most countries, and a small unit of the Belgian branch was established to deal with Community political issues. That unit has grown into a formidable organization of its own. AMCHAM-ECC is well supported, as are American firms generally, by the large numbers of American consultants and lawyers in Brussels.

Also surprising at first glance is how American firms worked successfully at the national level, in some cases mobilizing an EU member state as its ardent defender. This is understood for at least two reasons. Firstly, even by the early 1970s the branch plants of American firms were contributing up to 15 per cent of the manufacturing production of some European countries. Secondly, these manufacturing plants were usually high value-added, high wage fabricating and processing plants (Dunning, 1994). This is exactly the type of business investment that countries desire.

Faced with the economic power and the independent political infrastructure of American firms, European sectoral business groups and organizations dedicated to setting Europe-wide standards allowed American firms into these organizations or at least gave them an important role as associates and active observers. However, the older, stand-off approach lingers on in some organizations, most notably the European Round Table of Industrialists. Nonetheless, this continued exclusion is more than made up by all of the other organizational resources of American firms including the intervention of American state officials themselves.

The most serious limitation on the political influence of American firms is cultural, not organizational or structural. These companies do not understand well or feel comfortable with European industrial relations, especially Continental ones. Rather than adjusting to European traditions in this area, they have tried to get the EU to adopt the American tradition of employer supremacist, a chronic battle they have clearly lost.

Notes

1. For a good description of the influence of the ERT see Green Cowles (1993a), and for deeper analysis, see Green Cowles (1993b).
2. This is especially true of management consultants (see Philip, 1991).

References

Andersen, S. and Eliassen, K. (1991) 'European Community Lobbying', *European Journal of Political Research*, vol. 20, pp. 281–288.
Bates, E. (1990) 'Outsiders inside', *European Management Journal*, vol. 8, pp. 526–527.
Bindi, F. (1994) 'Economic Eurogroups and the EU decision-making process'. Paper presented to the IXth International Conference of Europeanists, Council for European Studies, Chicago, 31 March–2 April 1994.

Cowhey, P. (1990) 'Telecommunications', in Hufbauer, G. *Europe 1992: An American Perspective*. Washington, DC: Brookings Institute.

Daniels, P. and Schwartz (eds) (1994) *Encyclopaedia of Associations: National Organizations of the United States*, vol. 1, no. 2 (28th edn). Detroit: Gale Research.

Dunning, J. (1994) 'The strategy of Japanese and US manufacturing investment in Europe', in Mason, M. and Encarnation, D. (eds) *Does Ownership Matter?* Oxford: Clarendon.

Eldrige, G. (1994) *Encyclopaedia of Associations: International Organizations* (28th edn). Detroit: Gale Research.

Gardner, D. (1994) 'EU states agree law to set up works councils', *Financial Times*, 23 June 1994, p. 18.

Green Cowles, M. (1993a) 'The rise of the European multinational', *International Economic Insights*. vol. 4, July/August, pp. 15–18.

Green Cowles, M. (1993b) 'The politics of big business in the single market program'. Paper presented to the European Community Studies Association, Washington, DC, 27–29 May 1993.

Hufbauer, G. (1990) 'An overview', in Hufbauer, G. (ed) *Europe 1992: An American Perspective*. Washington, DC: Brookings Institute.

Hunter, M. (1989) 'How to get your way with the EC: lobbying Brussels', *Business Month*, August, p. 43.

Jacquemin, A. and Wright, D. (1993) 'Corporate strategies and European challenges', *Journal of Common Market Studies*, vol. 31, pp. 525–537.

Kohler-Koch, B. (1994) 'Changing patterns of interest intermediation in the European Union', *Government and Opposition*, vol. 29, pp. 166–180.

Mazey, S. and Richardson, J. J. (1992) 'British pressure groups in the European Community: the challenge of Brussels', *Parliamentary Affairs*, vol. 45, pp. 92–107.

McLaughlin, A. and Jordan, G. (1993) 'The rationality of lobbying in Europe: why are Euro-groups so numerous and so weak? Some evidence from the car industry', in Mazey, S. and Richardson, J. J. (eds) *Lobbying in the European Community*. Oxford: Oxford University Press.

McLaughlin, A., Jordan, G. and Maloney, W. (1993) 'Corporate lobbying in the European Community', *Journal of Common Market Studies*, vol. 31, pp. 191–212.

Olson, M. (1982) *The Rise and Decline of Nations*. New Haven: Yale University Press.

Philip, A. (1991) *Directory of Pressure Groups in the European Community*. Harlow: Longman.

Quickel, S. (1989) 'Entry via Europeanisation', *Business Month*. August, p. 44.

Sandholtz, W. and Zysman, J. (1989) '1992: Recasting the European bargain', *World Politics*, vol. 42, pp. 95–128.

Streeck, W. and Schmitter, P. (1991) 'From national corporatism to transnational pluralism: organized interests in the single European market', *Politics and Society*. vol. 19, pp. 133–165.

Vogel, D. (1993) 'Environmental protection and the creation of a single European market', *Business and the Contemporary World*, vol. 5, pp. 48–66.

Wilson, G. (1990) 'Corporate political strategies', *British Journal of Political Science*. vol. 20, pp. 281–288.

Mastering the System
How Disparities within the European Union Contribute to Japan's Lobbying Success

Dan Morrison

Japanese lobbying has received considerable attention in the USA, but it has not been well documented in the European Union. While there has arisen in the USA a growing tendency either to knock or to apologise for Japan, the study of Japanese lobbying in the European Union is best approached with a degree of agnosticism.

It should be clear that although Japan is tackling the European market much in the same way that it successfully penetrated America in the 1980s, fears on both sides of the Atlantic that Japanese lobbying will 'cripple' the European political system are unfounded. Reasons for this include:

- The differences between the political institutions in the Community and those in the USA.

- The stark contrast between the 'revolving door' administrations of Washington and the more static EU governmental bodies.

- The inherent differences between Europe's socially-minded market economies and America's abbreviated efforts towards *laissez-faire*.

- The cost of entering a market of fifteen countries with eleven official languages.

- The bursting of Japan's economic 'bubble' in the 1980s.

- The current political and economic woes in Japan's domestic market.

- The increasing attention that Japan is paying towards the south-east Asian economies.

In a nutshell, Japanese lobbying activity in the EU will remain small compared with that in the USA. Nevertheless, it is important to look at methods by which the Japanese lobby effectively in Europe.

Japan spends an average of $400 million annually on lobbyists and lawyers to conduct federal and 'grass roots' campaigns in the USA. Some observers suggest that such hefty sums are a 'bargain' for Japanese corporations, which save several million dollars annually in potential tariffs and anti-dumping duties (Choate, 1990). Indeed, Japanese lobbying of such intensity is a natural response towards protecting Japan's foreign direct investments (FDI). As Japanese FDI has developed in the European Union, so has the Japanese lobbying industry; and as the Japanese lobbying industry has grown, so have European concerns that Japan is somehow 'invading' the European Union:

> Brussels is not a federal government, like Washington. The [EU] is a reactive institution, mainly due to sovereignty issues between Member States, and between Member States and the Commission. This seriously limits the [EU's] negotiating strength *vis-à-vis* Japan, and has fuelled such fears of Japanese invasion. America has a negotiating problem, as well, but this is mainly due to the debt issue. Europe's vulnerability is a combination of the lack of a common commercial policy towards Japan, sovereignty issues, and relative economic weakness in the US/EU/Japan economic triad.
>
> *(Interview with a senior European Commission official,*
> *Brussels, December 1992)*

Perhaps the best expression of such paranoia has come from Jacques Calvet, chairman of Peugeot, who in the late 1980s personified Britain's high level of Japanese investment as an 'aircraft carrier' for Japan's entry into Europe.[1] Equally, former French prime minister, Edith Cresson, characterized Japan as 'the enemy which is not playing the game'.

Like the Americans, the Japanese prefer to lobby at the level of the nation-state capital before raising issues in Brussels (interview with Christopher Norall of Forrester, Norall, Sutton, Brussels, December 1992). Indeed, as one representative of a Japanese trade association comments: 'My organization normally does not try to change [EU] legislation single-handedly. If a directive is created which could affect us, we can always ask the UK government to lobby on our behalf' (interview with representative of Japan Machinery Exporters' Association, Brussels, December 1992).

It is in Paris or London or Berlin that the Japanese attempt to persuade policy-makers to lobby for Japan. The amount of Japanese FDI in a particular country is the most significant factor for determining how earnestly national policy-makers lobby on behalf of Japanese interests. As with any group that lobbies, the Japanese must work within the established political framework in which policy-makers are housed. In this sense, there is but one strategy: to master the loopholes in the system. Japanese groups, therefore, do not appear to be much different from any other party that attempts to protect its economic holdings in the EU, but the fact remains that, in the eyes of European policy-makers, the Japanese do seem different. They differ in their level of foreign direct investment in the EC compared with other countries; they differ in that they represent one of the world's three main trading blocs; they differ in their ability to target markets; they differ in that their home market is understood to be closed to European products; and they differ in that they are perceived to be more threatening to European industry than most other third countries.

> What scares the [EU] most about Japan? In the main it is a combination of Japan's closed market in relation to the [EU], Japanese long-term strategies as opposed to Europe's short-termism, and Japan's export economy as opposed to the more domestically-oriented [EU] economies.
> *(Interview with Commission official, Brussels, May 1993)*

It must be said that, for better or for worse, it is Europe which has differentiated itself from Japan, and not the other way around. European trade associations and policy-makers have in effect closed the Japanese out of their information loops, barring them from privy information about the EU political system. In light of this, the Japanese have been forced to develop their own channels of lobbying. Though this may have short-term benefits for European companies, it may put the Japanese in a competitively advantageous position in the long run.

For the sake of this discussion, 'routine' lobbying refers to channels already present in the EU political system, that is those methods normally used to influence EU policy-makers (e.g. consensus-building, private meetings with EU officials). 'Grass roots' lobbying refers to the channels which are outside of the political framework (e.g. public relations efforts to promote Japanese companies and trade associations as 'good European citizens' within local communities.[2]

In his book, *Agents of Influence*, Pat Choate (1990) suggests that Japanese companies in the USA are crippling the American political system through the influence of Japanese FDI and, additionally, through subtle propaganda.[3] He cites the following methods used in grass roots campaigns:

At the national level:
(1) Japanese firms buying US colleges to produce Japanese-oriented studies;
(2) hiring ex-government officials to lobby for Japanese corporations;
(3) financing the Republican and Democratic parties; and,
(4) giving large amounts of money to Politcial Action Committees (PACs)[4] for congressional races.

At the state and local level:
(1) pressuring US employees of Japanese companies to vote for a particular candidate; (2) developing Japanese chambers of commerce and five regional associations of US governors and Japanese business leaders; (3) strategically placing sixteen consulates and trade offices throughout the states; and, (4) donating massive amounts of money to local civic and social projects as a means of influencing the US Congress through constituencies.

Japanese corporations and trade associations in Europe are using these grass roots tactics. Japan's Brother Computer, for example, sponsors the UK football team, Manchester City, and spent £500,000 in 1990 to sponsor the Manchester Hallé Orchestra (Cooke, 1990). Toyota and Honda regularly donate large sums of money to local civic clubs and community projects in Derbyshire and Wiltshire in the UK. Further, a look at a 1990 report entitled 'Public Relations Strategy for the Japan Automobile Manufacturers' Association (JAMA) in Germany',[5] gives us a glimpse at some of the lobbying methods that the Japanese are currently using in Europe:

Public Relations Projects – In order to establish and emphasize that JAMA is also concerned with German topics and linked to social and environmental subjects, [we] recommend that JAMA finance and support studies about subjects which altogether or in parts are related to the automobile industry in Germany. The results of these studies will be used for media and lobby work. Respective press releases/features could be placed with suitable newspapers and magazines.

Sponsorships – There is no doubt that sponsoring has many advantages and encourages goodwill and understanding for a company. With regard to JAMA, the prime reason for sponsorship is to show a sense of social responsibility in Germany and close linkage to Germany . . . [We] recommend sponsorship in the following spheres:
   A. *Education*. JAMA will support students who study mechanical engineering, design, automotive technology or other subjects which are linked to the automotive industry.

Cultural Events and Interests – [We] propose supporting cultural events such as concerts, art exhibitions, etc. in Germany . . . An ideal constellation would be if a famous Japanese musician or orchestra were to tour Germany. A concert could be supported by JAMA for a selected audience. The concert should be recorded and copied on CDs. These would be used as incentives for further PR activities.

Speaking Platforms – [We] will . . . identify possibilities for background talks, roundtable discussions, expert workshops, etc. at which JAMA-representatives will be given opportunities to talk about suitable automotive issues . . .

In addition to cultural events and speaking platforms, large amounts of Japanese funding are given to scholarly research. Notably, the Japanese are not the only non-EU country engaging in such activity. Saudi Arabia, for instance, donates a considerable amount of money to research in the UK. For Japan's part, however, the Kobe Institute at St Catherine's College, Oxford, and the Asia section of the Royal Institute of International Affairs at Chatham House regularly receive Japanese funding. In Belgium, the Europe–Japan Economic Research Centre at Louvain is under the joint patronage of the European Commission, the Japanese Mission to the EU and the Japan External Trade Organization (JETRO).

As for routine lobbying, the Japanese have established consulates and trade offices throughout the EU. The Japanese External Trade Organization, for example, has seventy-six offices world-wide (eleven in the EU). The Ministry of International Trade and Industry (MITI) sets JETRO's ¥20 billion annual budget, 30 per cent of which goes towards administration, 30 per cent towards relations with Third World countries, and 30 per cent for the import promotion of products from industrialized countries into Japan (interview with representative of JETRO, Brussels, January 1993).

The Japan Centre for International Finance (JCIF) has offices in London and Brussels, which also handle eastern Europe (interview with a representative of JCIF, Brussels, December 1992). The director in Brussels is a representative of the Japanese Ministry of Finance. The organization is a half private (composed of trading companies, insurance companies and banks) half government-run research facility dealing with financial markets. It coordinates with Japan's twenty-six bank branches throughout Europe.

Japan's European cobweb of grass roots and routine lobbying appears to be paying off. In what was deemed by practitioners to be one of the single most successful Japanese lobbying campaigns in the EU (the Vreideling directive (1980–81) on worker participation in the UK based on the German industrial relations model) the Japanese sent a full *Keidanran* (Japanese big business organization) delegation to the Department of Trade and Industry in the UK. They also persuaded the American Chamber of Commerce to lobby on its behalf in London. The directive went against the grain of Thatcherism, as the British government was sympathetic to the potential problems that could have faced Japanese manufacturers in Britain. The UK, therefore, rallied against the directive in Brussels (interview with Bob Taylor, Brussels correspondent of *The Economist*, December 1992). In the end, this particular lobbying effort was most notable for the amount of money spent and the level of Japanese officials involved.

What clearly has not paid off for the Japanese in Brussels is the practice of hiring former government officials – a Washitonian tactic. Geoffrey

Tucker, a former deputy-chairman of the British Conservative Party, was a one-time liaison between Nissan and the European Commission. A high-ranking bureaucrat from DG XIII (telecommunications) was hired in the late 1980s by Sony Corporation to advise it on potentially harmful European telecommunications legislation, and former EU commissioner Etienne Davignon is on the board of directors of Fujitsu. With the exception of Commissioner Davignon, the relationships were not long-lasting.

Hill and Knowlton, a British consultancy, hired former US ambassador to the EU, Alfred Kingon, and later former EU environment commissioner, Lord (Stanley) Clinton Davis. Again, there were disappointing results, and it became clear that, in Brussels, a public official is only as good as when he or she is in office. This is in stark contrast to the practice in Washington, where former administration officials are keenly sought by Japanese firms for their expertise and for their political clout. What accounts for the difference? Japanologists such as Karel Van Wolferen attribute it to the fact that Americans can be 'bought' more easily than Europeans. Perhaps a more plausible explanation is that public service at the EU level is better paid and more highly regarded than in the USA (interview with Bob Taylor of *The Economist*). In this sense, there is less of a 'revolving door' culture in the EU upon which the Japanese can capitalize.

Critics of Japan often claim that such relationships with former officials are examples of unfair disadvantages conferred upon the Japanese solely due to the amount of money that Japanese firms are willing to pay for former policy-makers. To be fair, this can hardly be the case, for just as the Japanese can use such officials as forms of industrial espionage and political leverage, so European policy-makers can use them as windows onto Japan's corporate culture.

Arriving at unanimous decisions has been a chronic problem for EU bureaucrats in Brussels, and will continue to be a source of frustration. Meanwhile, Japanese multinationals are in a prime position to capitalize on Europe's disparities. Interviews with Brussels-based Japanese executives have revealed that most Japanese multinationals approach the EU as if they were part of a 'sixteenth nation'. Just as member-state governments use the 'sovereignty conflict' as a weapon with which to bargain with the Commission, the increasing level of Japanese FDI (primarily in Britain, Germany and the Netherlands), and the consequent political clout that goes along with job creation and the refurbishing of local industry, has allowed Japanese corporations to bargain as a 'thirteenth country', without its needing to deal with the day-to-day frustrations of being an actual member of the EU.[6] This is not unique to Japanese corporations, however. American multinationals experienced the same phenomenon in the 1960s, and continue to balance conflicts among the twelve member states to suit their investment goals.

The notion of acting like a sixteenth country has instilled a certain boldness in Japanese executives as they approach the EU institutions – again in contrast to the way the Japanese lobby in Washington. As one trade representative in Brussels has noted:

> So far, lobbying does not seem to be that necessary in Europe, because Europe is predictable; the US is not. We [the Japanese] feel more on par with Europe politically. We feel that we can argue more vigorously here. This is not the case in the United States. America is still a powerful country, much more powerful than the [EU]. When Washington decides on something, Japan must deal with it; when the [EU] reacts on a particular issue, we [the Japanese] feel more inclined to debate.
>
> *(Interview with a representative of the Japan Machine Manufacturer's Association, Brussels, December 1992)*

Ironically, while Japanese industrialists view themselves as sixteenth countries, Japanese financial institutions in the Community often refer to the Commission itself as a sixteenth member state. Understandably, Japanese banks in London and Luxembourg do not share the current enthusiasm about creating a single European market;

> Japanese banks in Europe normally speak directly to each country's central bank. This is still a sound policy, as Japanese banks are concerned about transparency laws at the end of the day. What we [Japanese banks] are worried about is a supranational power (i.e. the Commission) governing as a 'thirteenth nation'. A European Central Bank is not that interesting for us at the moment. It is still more important to deal with the individual member states.
>
> *(Interview with a representative from the Bank of Japan, London, December 1992)*

Perhaps the most glaring difference between Japanese lobbying tactics in Brussels and those of their American/European counterparts is collective versus direct lobbying. The literature on business federations in Europe is vast. Analysis upon analysis has shown that Euro groups, that is collections of interest groups with similar concerns, are effective in putting coalition pressure on EU decision-makers. As directives are being developed, EU officials, who are pressed for time and eager to bring about a consensus among Euro groups rather than to interview individual companies, are 'prepared to offer groups preferential access at the early stages of policy development in return for detailed information they would otherwise struggle to get' (McLaughlin, 1993, p. 53). One Eurocrat has characterized this process as follows:

> [The Commission official] is a very lonely official with a blank piece of paper in front of him, wondering what to put on it. Lobbying at this very early stage therefore offers the greatest opportunity to shape thinking and ultimately to shape policy. The drafter is usually in need of ideas and information and a lobbyist who is recognized as being trustworthy and a provider of good information can have an important impact at this stage.
>
> *(Hull, 1993, p. 83)*

Aside from formal Euro groups, there are the chambers of commerce; the American Chamber of Commerce (AMCHAM) and the Brussels-based British Chamber are the most influential. The Commission regularly seeks their opinions on proposed legislation, and normally deals with their interests quickly. AMCHAM, for example, has intricate levels of communication with the Commission based on colour-coded 'papers', which are intended to correspond with the Commission's often confusing system of 'Green Papers' and 'White Papers'.[7] The two chambers are more of an insurance policy for American and British multinationals to keep in the EU information loop than centres of invaluable information.

For corporate members, the chambers are fora to conduct low-level corporate espionage, and to lead drafting coalitions when his/her company has a vested interest in a piece of Commission legislation. For consultants and lawyers, the chambers can be a place to pick up new business. Lobbyists in both forms are allowed to join the chambers with the understanding that they will often be called upon to lead discussions, provide contacts and to act as icebreakers when corporate members are hesitant to reveal privy information about their operations.

While Euro groups and chambers of commerce have their advantages, they also have a number of flaws which are of direct benefit to Japanese lobbying efforts in Brussels. Firstly, Euro group papers have a tendency to be watered down. Corporate public affairs representatives always take more than they give in this type of communal environment. Secondly, it can be extremely difficult to dislodge a powerful corporate member from his/her 'king of the mountain' position when coalitions are being drawn up. If a piece of Commission legislation is potentially detrimental to a member company, the public affairs officer of that firm will do everything in his/her power to guarantee that his/her company takes the lead in drawing up that particular Euro group proposal. If more than one company feels strongly about a proposed directive, they may reach a compromise, but as is often the case, companies temporarily abandon the Euro group in favour of direct lobbying of the relevant EU institution. Obviously, this can have drastic implications for the effectiveness of the group as a whole.

Thirdly, Euro groups and chambers of commerce normally act with 'bounded rationality'; that is, they do not necessarily adopt the best solution, but the first best solution that comes across their desks (Simon, 1961). They adopt 'satisficing behaviour', rather than maximizing behaviour (McLaughlin and Jordan, 1993).[8] This is due mainly to the fact that time constraints limit the depths which companies can enter when formulating solutions to corporate predicaments. There is little evidence that the Japanese, having been ostracized from Euro groups and European-based chambers, suffer either from time constraints, or from pressure to minimize their problems for the sake of the larger group:

> We [the Japanese] don't feel a sense of urgency when we raise our problems with the Commission. It is part of our long-term strategy. If there is an industry-specific problem among Japanese companies, it is normally worked out between the companies and the relevant ministries in Japan.
> *(Interview with Japanese company representative, Brussels, December 1992)*

Japanese multinationals in Brussels, therefore, engage in 'maximizing' behaviour. They do not have to contend with satisficing, bland position papers, or 'king of the mountain' situations.

Fourthly, organizations such as the American and British Chambers are in a 'Catch 22' position when it comes to allowing consultants and lawyers to join their ranks. Lobbyists are useful to have on hand when meeting rooms fall silent, as corporate members refrain from discussing certain topics or are not completely candid about their companies' concerns. On the other hand, lobbyists are not required to disclose the names of their clients. In this sense, Japanese companies can engage in low-level corporate espionage by hiring consultants and lawyers to sit on either of the two chambers. Although there is little evidence to suggest that Japanese firms hire lobbyists solely for this purpose, the process is a type of 'icing on the cake' for the Japanese. Regardless of whether or not Japanese corporations actually ask their consultants to monitor the corporate members of the chambers, such information no doubt makes its way into monthly and *ad hoc* monitoring reports. Conversely, there is no 'Japanese' chamber of commerce in Brussels. In this sense, there is little reciprocity in American/European efforts to monitor the activities of Japanese multinationals.

The above lobbying channels were not devised by the Japanese. They are the result of European (and recently American) efforts to exclude Japanese firms from the Euro group forum. What has been the result? Commission officials (who are pressed for time, and who often do not have the staff to process input from the dozens of corporations feeding them information) prefer to ask Euro groups to consolidate their data. Again, those data are often watered down, and the voices of individual companies can be lost in the clamour. Japanese companies (because they are excluded from Euro groups), however, must speak to Eurocrats directly. In such a scenario, Japanese multinationals which provide timely, accurate information to Eurocrats often speak with a louder voice than their American or European counterparts, which can find themselves stifled by the cacophony of the Euro group.

Finally, Japanese lobbying efforts in Brussels benefit by the strong government/corporate connection inherent in the post-war Japanese culture. Although it is true that certain members of the EU (e.g. France and Germany) have long traditions of government and business cooperation, this amounts to less than a handful of the fifteen EU member states. The Japanese have the link down to a science. For example, many Japanese trade association officials in Brussels wear two hats. They act as the prime liaison between the association and the Community institutions, but they also work for one of the various ministries in Japan. The representative from the Japan Machinery Exporters' Association (JMEA) in Brussels, for example, is employed by MITI. The same is true of JETRO's Brussels director. The three main officers in the Japan Centre for International Finance hail from the Ministry of Finance, the Bank of Japan and a Japanese commercial bank, respectively. The head of the Livestock Industry Promotion Corporation is linked to the Ministry of Agriculture, and the director of 'Posts and Telecommunications International' works for the Ministry of Posts and Telecommunications in Japan.

Not all Japanese trade association representatives in Brussels have direct access to the Japanese ministries. The director-general of one of the most powerful associations – the Japanese Automobile Manufacturer's Association (JAMA) – for example, deals strictly in the private sector: 'It is difficult for him [the JAMA director] to talk to the ministries since he is in the private sector, whereas I have a much easier time going between the business and governmental spheres' (interview with the director of a Japanese trade association in Brussels, December 1992).

Whereas trade association officials maintain formal links with the Japanese mandarins in Tokyo, senior executives in Japanese companies enjoy informal bonds. Many who are in their late 59s or early 60s are living out their *amakudarai*, or descent from heaven – the process whereby long-standing officials in the mandarins are rewarded for their lifetime civil service by being placed in a high-ranking position in a Japanese corporation. The same term can be applied to civil servants who were given comfortable posts within the Liberal Democratic Party prior to Japan's recent political reform. The combination of formal and informal links between business as a whole and government is unrivalled in Europe, and offers the Japanese a distinct advantage when they lobby a comparatively disorganized European Commission or member-state national government.

What scares Europeans about Japanese grass roots and routine lobbying tactics is that such channels are becoming uncomfortably similar to those which European companies and trade associations pursue themselves. The Europeans, like the Americans in the 1980s, are frustrated that the Japanese have begun to master Western lobbying techniques. What is more, the Japanese are out-lobbying them. Established American and European firms do not necessarily feel the need to prove that they are good European citizens. They tend to assume that their concerns vicariously find their way to policy-makers' desks. Choate (1990), for example, notes that only 30 per cent of all company presidents in the USA bother to lobby in Washington. While it can be argued that corporate presidents may prefer to hire lobbyists rather than to lobby themselves, this does not disqualify the notion that corporate leaders often assume – falsely – that policy-makers are aware of their concerns.

The distinction between Japanese and European lobbying tactics has, therefore, become blurred. Grass roots lobbying is beneficial to Japanese corporations in the long term, in the sense that it lessens the need for extensive routine lobbying. Routine tactics serve both long- and short-term needs. In twenty years' time, however, established Japanese companies in Europe will find it less necessary to engage in grass roots lobbying. The next newcomer will have taken their place.

In summary, Japanese corporations and trade associations in Europe have mastered the labyrinth of the EU political structure. They capitalize on the 'system', but more accurately, the system plays into their hands. In this sense, Japanese lobbying is neither good nor bad; it is simply a reality. What distinguishes Japanese lobbying channels from those of other groups is:

1. The financial resources availabe to Japanese forms to conduct grass roots lobbying, often to a greater extent than indigenous EU multinationals.

2. Exclusion from Euro groups, and the consequent need to develop new lobbying channels.

3. An unrivalled link between government and business which is not present even in the most organized trade oriented member states of the Community.

However, keeping in mind the inherent differences between the American and EU political systems, the costliness of entering a Community market of fifteen countries and eleven official languages, the lack of cheap capital at home, and the basic fact that Europe is not as much of an investment priority for the Japanese as is Asia or America, it is unlikely that Japan will have the means or the desire to muster the kind of lobbying strength in Europe that it has achieved in the USA.

As for future predictions, interviews conducted with Brussels-based Japanese and European representatives between December 1992 and May 1993 give us an idea of how Japanese lobbying will evolve in the EU in the 1990s.

New Japanese FDI in Europe will be in suspense for the next four to five years as the Japanese adopt a 'wait and see' attitude towards 'post-1992' unification and enlargement. As a consequence, Japanese lobbying activity will temporarily taper off. Consultancies and law firms in Brussels have already noticed a dip in work sanctioned by Japanese clients. Following this 'wait and see' period, however, Japanese lobbying in the high-technology, automobile, banking and financial sectors will increase dramatically as the Japanese partially abandon their renowned sense of patience in investment decisions. This will be due to the shift from concerns about market share to those about profit margins. Equally, Japanese FDI and lobbying activity will increase in Germany and EFTA countries as Japan capitalizes on east European markets.

Japanese lobbying campaigns against all forms of European protectionism will become bolder as the Japanese become more familiar with the Community institutions. On the issue of local content, they will continue to pose difficult questions to the EU, such as, 'who is the more European company – Philips, which produces two-thirds of its products outside of Europe, or Sony which is under pressure to have local content in Europe?'

Economic and political doldrums at home will have little effect on Japanese multinationals operating in Europe. This is largely because: (1) it would be politically embarrassing for Japanese multinationals to reduce their presence in Europe. They are more likely to shrink their domestic operations before lessening their activity in Europe; (2) Japanese multinationals are less dependent on their *keiretsu*[9] banks than at any other previous time. Most have insulated themselves from domestic shock by taking advantage of international financing mechanisms.

Although the Commission is running out of legal mechanisms to restrict Japanese companies in the European market, there will be an increase in the level of protectionist measures taken against Japan. This will be due mainly to the fact that Europe will fail to develop a common commercial policy towards Japan, and Japan's recovery from its current economic and political crisis will be complete. Anti-dumping duties are already giving way to local content requirements as a form of European protection against Japan. This will continue as the main EU protectionist measure, though the Japanese will certainly challenge it.

Japan's Ministry of Foreign Affairs will continue to be pushed out of lobbying campaigns in the EU as the other ministries take the lead on specific trade issues.

The Japanese will target EU countries which have high English-speaking skills (i.e. the Benelux countries). Where to invest is always an economically complex issue, but the Hechscher/Olin model of chasing cheap labour does not appear to be as applicable to Japanese firms as it is to their American and European counterparts. Although economists often shun 'language' as a legitimate investment concern, interviews with Brussels-based Japanese representatives confirm that language is indeed a major factor in investment decisions in Europe. Indeed, the cost of linguistically re-training an entire generation of Japanese businessmen who are already competent in English outweighs the advantages of conducting business in nine official EU languages.

Finally, the Japanese will continue to lobby Europe as fifteen seperate markets, despite the single market programme and regardless of efforts by the Commission to create a perception of the EU as a single entity. The reason for this is, simply, that notwithstanding the rhetoric about an integrated Europe, nationalism is still healthy and localization by Japanese companies continues to be profitable.

Notes

1. Speech at the OECD conference on 'Globalisation of the Automobile Association', Paris, 19 March 1992.
2. It is important to note that effective grass roots lobbying often diffuses local situations which can evolve into larger EU issues, thereby limiting the need for extensive 'routine' lobbying.
3. This is one of the general themes of Choate's book.
4. Political Action Committees (PACs) are organizations established by private groups to support candidates for public office. Created by the Federal Campaign Act of 1971, they essentially introduced corporations to the political financing scene (corporations were previously barred from forming PACs, unlike labour unions). About one-third of all campaign financing in the US comes from PACs. That has spurred public criticism of corporate involvement in campaigns to the point where Clinton in 1992 said he would not accept PAC money during the Presidential campaign.
5. Prepared on behalf of JAMA by Kommunication & Marketing, Bonn, 9 July 1990.
6. This was the general feedback from the author's December 1992 interviews with Japanese representatives in Brussels.
7. A Commission Green Paper refers to a preliminary proposal for a directive which has

not yet been approved by the twenty Commissioners. A White Paper is a more formal drafting than a Green Paper, but which also has not been approved by the Commissioners. AMCHAM uses a system of yellow, green and pink papers to differentiate between initial comments, and more formal ones.

8. McLaughlin and Jordan point out that Simon (1961) argues that companies act with 'bounded rationality' as opposed to pure rationality of the nature that Olson assumes in *The Logic of Collective Action* (1965).

9. *Keiretsu* is the Japanese system of corporate families traditionally linked to banks and trading houses, the three largest of which are Mitsubishi, Mitsui, and Sumitomo. The banks distribute the money and in return companies confine their businesses to a rigid web of suppliers, distributers, etc. *Keiretsu* has been widely criticized by Europe and the United States as one of the main reasons for Japan's so-called 'closed markets'.

References

Choate, P. (1990) *The Agents of Influence: How Japanese Lobbyists are Manipulating Western Political and Economic Systems*. London: Business Books.

Cooke, K. (1990) 'Japanese investment in Europe', in Watanabe, S. (ed.) *Japan's Presence in Europe*. The Europe–Japan Economic Research Centre, The Catholic University of Louvain.

Hull, R. (1993) Lobbying Brussels: a view from within', in Mazey, S. and Richardson, J.J. (eds) *Lobbying in the European Community*. Oxford: Oxford University Press.

McLaughlin, A. (1993) 'Weak groups or strong members? The politics of European business federations', *Journal of Common Market Studies*, vol. 31, pp. 191–212.

McLaughlin, A. and Jordan, G. (1993) 'The rationality of lobbying in Europe: why are Euro groups so numerous and so weak? Some evidence from the car industry', in Mazey, S. and Richardson, J. J. (eds) *Lobbying in the European Community*. Oxford: Oxford University Press.

Olson, M. (1965) *The Logic of Collective Action*. Cambridge, MA: Harvard University Press.

Simon, H. (1961) *Administrative Behaviour: A Study of Decision-making Processes and Administrative Organizations*. New York: Macmillan.

PART 7

Size, Partnership and Associability

The European Round Table of Industrialists

The Strategic Player in European Affairs

Maria Green Cowles

The European Round Table of Industrialists (ERT) represents a novel form of business alliance at the European level. Historically, European business groups have comprised business associations as opposed to individual firms. The national business associations of the member states, for example, are the primary members of the Union of Industrial and Employers' Confederation of Europe (UNICE). In turn (with the exception of the Confederation of British Industry), each national association is made up of various sectoral associations. The ERT, however, comprises some forty chairpersons or chief executive officers (CEOs) of major European multinational companies. Consequently, ERT members – most of whom carry significant political clout within their home countries – meet and lobby directly European Community (EC) and member state policy-makers. Indeed, the ERT was one of the first groups of CEOs to participate actively in the EC policy-making process (Cowles, 1994).

The ERT also differs from traditional European business alliances in that its members view the group as a 'strategic' organization. The ERT does not seek to duplicate the work of UNICE, for example, which reviews and provides position papers on most horizontal (cross-industry) legislation of the European Community. Rather, the ERT serves as an idea generator and agenda-setter for specific issues of importance to its membership, such as trans-European infrastructure, information highways, employment and competitiveness.

The strategic outlook of the group, coupled with the fact that ERT members are CEOs of leading firms, have enabled the ERT to be an important player in European policy-making. As discussed below, the ERT has proved to be successful in promoting its agenda and raising the profile of business in EC affairs.

A Brief History

The ERT was created in April 1983 by Pehr Gyllenhammar, CEO of the Swedish automaker, Volvo. Gyllenhammar was alarmed by the failure of member state and EC officials to address Europe's economic situation. In the aftermath of the recession and oil crises of the 1970s, European economic growth had virtually stopped by the early 1980s. For the first time since the post-war recovery, the European standard of living began to fall. Calling for a 'Marshall Plan for Europe' to 'spur growth, and to build industry and infrastructure', Gyllenhammar gathered together a group of seventeen CEOs to lead the way to address the economic situation by formulating industrial strategies in cooperation with EC institutions (Cowles, 1993).

With a small secretariat in Paris, the newly created ERT was composed of individuals such as Umberto Agnelli (Fiat), Carlo de Benedetti (Olivetti), Wisse Dekker (Philips), Roger Fauroux (St Gobain), John Harvey-Jones (ICI), Olivier Lecerf (Lafarge Coppée), and Hans Merkle (Bosch). In public statements and policy memoranda, the group began to promote actively the creation of a unified European market. The ERT argued that a single market would enable European firms to exploit economies of scale and to compete more effectively with Japanese and American companies. The ERT also forwarded its agenda to national governments through highly visible pan-European projects, funded by the companies, that would demonstrate the firms' commitment to a united Europe. One of the most famous projects was the *Missing Links* study in which the ERT advocated the development of trans-European networks such as a route between the UK and Continental Europe (that later influenced the European Channel Tunnel scheme), and a European high-speed train system.

In January 1985, ERT member Wisse Dekker delivered his 'Europe 1990' plan to member state and Community officials. In many respects, the CEO played an important role in setting the agenda for the single market programme. Dekker's plan outlined the precise steps needed to create a unified European market in four key areas by the year 1990: trade facilitation (elimination of border formalities), open public procurement markets, harmonized technical standards and fiscal harmonization. ERT members strongly supported 'Europe 1990'. The document is viewed by many today as the precursor to the Cockfield White Paper in June 1985 that ultimately served as the blueprint for the 1992 programme (Cowles, 1995).

Once the White Paper was adopted, ERT members continued to play an active role in promoting the single market programme, often appearing in public fora with European Commission officials to lend their support to the 1992 project. When member states wavered in implementing the single market programme, the ERT lobbied European heads of state and government directly with a simple message: support the single market programme or European industry will move its investments out of Europe. Today, the ERT is recognized as one of the key forces behind the success of the 1992 programme.

The Collective Action of the ERT

In 1988, Dekker took over as chair of the ERT, moved the secretariat to Brussels, and hired an ERT secretary-general. That same year, the ERT increased its membership to some forty members. A few members contested the change in size because they thought a larger organization would become unmanageable. Others lobbied to open up the ERT to all major European companies (excluding American multinationals). The larger organizational size would be more in line with the US Business Roundtable (BRT), comprising some two hundred CEOs from diverse companies. Some members believed that a larger ERT would make the organization more representative of European industry.

The ERT's decision to restrict the membership to four dozen or so individuals relates to issues of collective action. As Olson predicted in his work on collective action theory (Olson, 1965; 1971), the ERT's smaller size allows for easier maintenance (the undisclosed membership dues cover the secretariat expenses) and promotes personal contacts among members in a 'club-like atmosphere'. The ERT's cohesiveness also can be explained in part by the material (economic) rewards accrued by members, for example, in the form of future participation in ERT-inspired trans-European network projects.

Material rewards alone, however, cannot account for the ERT's viability. As Clark and Wilson pointed out in their seminal piece, individuals also will join groups for purposive (political/goal-oriented) or solidarity (sense of belonging) reasons (Clark and Wilson, 1961). In the case of ERT membership, the CEOs also are motivated by their purposive, political commitment to the organization. Ensuring that national and EC policymakers hear and act upon the opinions of leading European businesspeople is a primary goal of the organization. The CEOs view the ERT as an important vehicle by which they can speak out publicly and set an agenda for Community and member state officials to improve the overall business environment in Europe. In this respect, ERT members recognize what Polanyi pointed out earlier: that a market is not merely an economic arena that occurs naturally. Rather, the rules of the market are shaped by a socio

Exhibit 16.1 *ERT membership, 9 June 1994*

Jérôme Monod (Chair)	Lyonnaise des Eaux-Dumez (F)
André Leysen (Vice-Chair)	Gevaert (B)
Helmut Maucher (Vice-Chair)	Nestlé (Swi)
Giovanni Agnelli	Fiat (I)
Américo Amorim	Amorim Group (P)
Jean-Louis Beffa	Saint-Gobain (F)
Marcus Bierich	Robert Bosch (G)
Yves Böel	Sofina (B)
Bertrand Collomb	Lafarge Coppeé (F)
François Cornélis	Petrofina (B)
Gerhard Cromme	Fried. Krupp (G)
Etienne Davignon	Société Générale de Belgique (B)
Carlo De Benedetti	Olivetti (I)
Casimir Ehrnrooth	Kymmene (Nokia) (F)
José Antonio Garrido	Iberdrola (Sp)
Fritz Gerber	Hoffmann-La Roche (Swi)
Denys Henderson	ICI (UK)
Daniel Janssen	Solvay (B)
Jak Kamhi	Profilo Holding (T)
Heinz Kriwet	Thyssen (G)
Luis Magaña	CEPSA (Sp)
Brian Moffat	British Steel (UK)
Harald Norvik	Statoil (Nor)
Theodore Papalexopoulos	Titan Cement (Gre)
Heinrich Von Pierer	Siemens (G)
Antony Pilkington	Pilkington (UK)
Lars Ramqvist	Ericsson (Swe)
Edzard Reuter	Daimler-Benz (G)
Antoine Riboud	Danon (BSN) (F)
Manfred Schneider	Bayer (G)
Patrick Sheehy	B.A.T Industries (UK)
David Simon	British Petroleum (UK)
Poul Svanholm	Carlsberg (Den)
Morris Tabaksblat	Unilever (UK/N)
Serge Tchuruk	Total (F)
Jan Timmer	Philips (N)
Marco Tronchetti Provera	Pirelli (I)
Candido Velàzquez	Telefónica (Sp)

Key: (B) Belgium, (Den) Denmark, (F) France, (G) Germany, (Gre) Greece, (I) Italy, (N) Netherlands, (Nor) Norway, (P) Portugal, (Sp) Spain, (Swe) Sweden, (Swi) Switzerland, (T) Turkey, (UK) United Kingdom.

political framework (Polanyi, 1944). Through the ERT, business leaders have a direct voice in issues relating to the European marketplace. Consequently, in the parlance of collective action theory, the membership of the ERT is maintained as much by purposive, political reasons as it is for material, economic ones (see Plotke, 1992; Sabatier, 1992).

The members' political commitment to the organization is supported by the fact that ERT membership remains by invitation only. Membership guidelines require that CEOs be selected according to their political involvement and influence, and not merely according to the size or name of the company. Nevertheless, efforts have been made to recruit members from the top one hundred European companies and to ensure that all EC member states are represented in the ERT membership roster. Members who retire or resign from their companies (more than a couple of members have been lost through corporate take-overs) must withdraw from the ERT. Also members may be removed for failing to participate actively in the ERT plenary sessions and activities.

In 1994, ERT membership represented a wide range of industry sectors (although service sectors continue to be under-represented in the group), produced a combined turnover of some ECU 500 billion and employed more than 3 million people worldwide. A list of the ERT membership in June 1994 appears in *Exhibit 16.1*.

General Organization

ERT members formally meet twice a year in the member state hosting the current EC presidency. These ERT plenary sessions serve as the primary decision- and policy-making bodies of the organization. The ERT steering committee, comprising five to seven members, meets more often to coordinate activities between the plenaries. In addition, ERT members may participate in eight policy groups chaired by ERT members. Often, these policy groups hire outside consultants to undertake more specific studies or to assist in writing up policy group reports. In addition, the ERT has devised expert watchdog groups composed of company experts in particular fields to monitor subject areas, produce policy papers and to alert the ERT to particular developments (*Exhibit 16.2*). The expert watchdog groups are a

Exhibit 16.2 *ERT policy groups and expert watchdog groups* (Source: *ERT Brochure,* April 1994)

Policy groups	Expert watchdog groups
Competition policy	Environment
Competitiveness/industrial policy	Europe–US relations
East–West infrastructure	Export controls
Education/Euromanagement	Industrial Relations and Social Policy Committee
Employment/labour markets	Young Managers' Development Programme
Information highways	
North/South	

new addition to the ERT and reflect the growing need for particular expertise in EC policy areas. ERT associates – designated company officials, usually the EC affairs representatives – support the members' activities and play an important, behind-the-scenes role in the organization.

The ERT's Political Access

Over the years, the ERT has developed close relations with the European Commission. This relationship was solidified under the Delors Commission, and especially by President Jacques Delors himself. Indeed, the ERT enjoys a form of political access unknown by any other business group in Europe. The fact that the ERT is represented by CEOs of leading European companies – and not by administrators of business associations – facilitates the organization's access.

During the early years of the single market programme, the Commission recognized the importance of having the support of leading industrialists. With no political constituency of their own, the Commissioners have looked to the ERT to strengthen their powers *vis-à-vis* the member states. Commission officials often call on ERT members to appear at Commission press conferences or to serve on high-level groups, such as the 1994 Bangemann group on information highways.

Moreover, the Commission consults the ERT in order to improve its own policy-making, particularly regarding the single market programme. ERT policy and expert groups often work closely with Commission officials to ensure that EC policies address the concerns of industrialists. Because ERT members face numerous obstacles when operating in the pan-European marketplace, they can provide practical advice on and solutions to various pieces of legislation. On several occasions, Commission President Delors met alone with ERT members during lengthy ERT plenary sessions to discuss the feasibility and cohesiveness of Commission policies. Delors also met ERT chairpersons on a personal and more regular basis to discuss ERT initiatives.

In many respects, the relationship between the Commission and the ERT is similar to that found between government and big business in the member states. While it is too early to assess, it is likely that the close ties between the ERT and the Commission will continue in the post-Delors era given the industrialists' European orientation and political clout.

The ERT has also established strong ties with the member states. During the plenary sessions, ERT members meet a high-level official (often the head of state or government) from the current Council presidency at the beginning of each six-month term. At these meetings, the ERT members present what they view as the priorities for the new presidency (for example, deregulating the telecommunications industry by 1995, providing additional funding for trans-European networks, etc.).

On occasion, an *ad hoc* group of ERT members meets an EC head of state or government or other high-level official to promote other matters. In September 1993, for example, fourteen ERT members held a two-hour luncheon meeting with Prime Minister Edouard Balladur in Paris to impress upon the French government the need to follow through on the General Agreement on Tarrifs and Trade (GATT) negotiations in the Uruguay Round.

ERT members also meet government officials on an individual basis. Indeed, individual ERT members usually serve as the primary interlocutors between the ERT and the national leaders in their home countries. ERT members, for example, may use the occasion of a new ERT report or policy group study to reinforce the group's message to member state leaders. Given that most ERT members enjoy a modicum of political clout, the role of individual members *vis-à-vis* the member states is important. Of course, ERT members also meet with senior government officials to discuss matters relating solely to the business of their companies, and not in an ERT capacity. An aim of the ERT, however, is to encourage the membership to promote the ideas and language of the ERT in their everyday conversations with the member states.

Often, government officials approach the ERT – and not vice versa – to ascertain the group's position on particular issues. Similarly, ministers from the member states, for example, have met ERT members to discuss the findings and strategies of ERT reports in education, infrastructure and competitiveness.

Today, the ERT liaises with numerous groups both inside and outside Europe. Members of the ERT secretariat meet European Parliament leaders to discuss legislation. The ERT secretary-general works with the secretary-general of UNICE and the EC affairs manager of the EC Committee of the American Chamber of Commerce to coordinate policy positions on key issues such as social legislation. Moreover, ERT members meet their counterparts in the US Business Roundtable, the *Keidanran* (the Japanese big business organization), and the relatively new organization, the African Business Roundtable.

Today, the question of ERT access has, in certain respects, been turned on its head. In the early years, the ERT sought institutionalized contacts with the Commission, the member states and others. In the 1990s, it is often these same groups that seek the ERT for its input into the policy-making process. In the 1990s, the channels of access have become two-way.

Strategic Programmes

The ERT views itself as a 'strategic' organization. The group's purpose is not to provide position papers on EC legislation but to serve as an idea generator and a developer of 'practical policies' in key areas such as education, employment and infrastructure. Again, the ERT's approach is unlike that of other European business alliances.

In the area of education, the ERT has undertaken a number of novel projects. In 1986, concerned that European education systems were not preparing students for the twenty-first century, ERT members agreed to fund one of their largest project budgets to examine the competence of European education systems. Recently, the ERT undertook a project to encourage European universities to address the educational needs of industry and to provide improved education to older, working adults. The ERT established the European University-Industry Forum in 1988 together with the Standing Conference of Rectors, Presidents and Vice-Chancellors of the European Universities. Their goal is to prepare adults for what ERT officials call 'lifelong learning': the ability to adapt to different jobs and, indeed, careers as the European labour market changes.

The ERT has also developed its own 'in-house' education programmes including Conferences for Young Managers which are held in their companies. The organization also established 'Eurojobs', a system of three-to-six month rotations for these managers to work in other ERT companies headquartered outside their member states. Recently, the ERT Conferences for Young Managers have invited participation from professionals from Poland, Hungary and the Czech and Slovak Republics. Since 1991, the ERT has also run a series of high-level seminars for senior managers from these countries.

One of the most recent ERT education projects was to sponsor a study of the 'European Management Model'. Conducted by the ESC Lyon Business School, the purpose of the study was to examine the difference between European management styles and American and Japanese styles, and to assess the advantages and disadvantages associated with each model. An underlying aim was to promote the notion of a European management model in European business schools whose teaching materials on management are based primarily on American business styles.

In the area of employment, the ERT policy groups have produced publications that focus on unemployment and its purported causes, examine efforts by private industry to promote job creation, and suggest alternative job creation programmes for national and European governments. Their aim is to shift the European employment strategy from one of artificially supporting employment through the subsidizing of ailing industries to one of promoting job creation by alternative methods. More recently, the ERT has emphasized the need to increase labour market flexibility as an important step in revitalizing the European economy.

Of all ERT projects, the promotion of trans-European infrastructure remains a cornerstone of the group's activity. Since the 1984 *Missing Links* study, the ERT has published five major reports covering everything from telecommunications networks, to road/rail transport systems, to air traffic control systems. It is in the area of infrastructure that the impact of the ERT's work is most readily apparent. The incorporation of Trans-European Networks under Title XII of the Maastricht Treaty on European Union, for example, is cited as a direct result of the ERT's actions over the years. In March 1994, the ERT created the European Centre for Infrastructure Studies (ECIS) in Rotterdam. ECIS is charged with improving the flow of information among specialist groups, private and public decision-makers as well as users, suppliers and the financial community in Europe. The Centre is viewed as the think-tank and clearing-house for future EC infrastructure studies. While set up as an ERT project, ECIS today operates as a non-profit association supported entirely by membership subscriptions and research contracts.

In recent years, the ERT has adopted a new agenda-setting strategy to improve European industrial competitiveness. With rising unemployment, the disputes over the Maastricht Treaty and, once again, the perceived inability or unwillingness of member states to take positive coordinated action, a crisis of leadership emerged in the Community in the early 1990s. This lack of progress, however, spurred the ERT into action. As a senior ERT secretariat official explains:

> Industrialists observed in the Maastricht crisis . . . [that] governments are saying: 'We don't want to give up our sovereignty', 'We don't want this or that interference from Brussels'.
>
> But on the whole, governments are not saying 'What's the best way of running the system? How do we make European industry efficient?' Governments don't really care about that. And so we have to make our views heard, in the same way as we did in the '80s, and say 'industry needs the development of Europe'.
>
> . . . You see, crisis produces response. And the more the industrialists feel that the politicians are making a complete mess of things, the more strongly they will feel to intervene. There's no percentage in being silent.
>
> *(Cowles, 1994)*

The ERT has responded with a series of what it calls 'mega-reports' formally issued to the European Council and disseminated to a wide audience, including members of the media. The purpose of these public reports is to spell out in clear language an agenda for Europe, the problems that must be addressed, and the strategies for facing these challenges. The reports are designed to promote action on the part of member states as well as to influence the ideological debate surrounding the future direction of the Community.

In September 1991, the ERT published its first mega-report, *Reshaping Europe*, designed to highlight an agenda for the 1990s. The sixty-four-page document was prompted by the numerous changes occurring in Europe – the unification of Germany, the emergence of free nations in central and eastern Europe, new trading patterns and ever-globalizing financial markets, the crisis in the Gulf states, as well as the decision to move towards monetary and political union in Europe. With governments in disarray, the ERT wanted to outline clearly the challenges facing European business and the necessary strategies for Europe's political leaders.

In December 1992, the ERT presented another report, *Rebuilding Confidence*, to the heads of state and government at the Edinburgh summit. The report outlined a straightforward four-point action plan to attack the economic recession and to end the political crisis surrounding the Maastricht Treaty. Members of the ERT reminded governments of the need for concerted action despite the state of crisis, and aggressively promoted increased infrastructure funding as a first step in alleviating the economic malaise. While no decisive action resulted from the Edinburgh summit, the European Council did agree to spend $200 billion on infrastructure projects.

The ERT initiated policy ideas again with another mega-report, *Beating the Crisis*, unveiled at a press conference with Delors in December 1993. The report was timed to coincide with the European Commission president's White Paper on growth, competitiveness and employment. In the report, the ERT called for 'a radical shift in Europe's approach to industrial development and economic growth'. *Beating the Crisis* focused on the competitiveness of European industry, arguing that high labour costs were the primary reason for falling competitiveness and rising unemployment. The ERT called for the creation of a Charter for Industry, that member states might commit themselves to a strategic approach to industry. Not surprisingly, the charter embodied the critical issues highlighted by the ERT over the years, including education and trans-European infrastructure as well as an open world economy. To ensure proper monitoring and advice regarding the charter, the ERT also proposed the establishment of a European Competitiveness Council representing industry, government and science.

With each mega-report, the ERT has launched an accompanying media campaign. The report *Beating the Crisis*, for example, received considerable coverage by the European press, radio and television. Over twenty-two thousand copies of the report were printed in French, German and English. Two ERT members also issued Dutch and Italian versions.

ERT Influence

'There is no doubt that the ERT influences the views of the Commission', according to a senior Delors cabinet official who liaised with the ERT (Cowles, 1994). Officials credit the ERT for introducing new policy ideas and for prompting the Commission to re-evaluate policy directions. President Delors himself publicly states that the industrialists were critical to the success of the single market programme. Perhaps the most important contribution of the ERT, however, has been its promotion of what one Commission official terms a new 'culture' within the Community regarding Europe and the global economy. This culture combines deregulation and industrial policy; it embraces both economic openness and trans-European projects. Consequently, Commissioners from the political left will listen to the ERT's position on competitiveness, for example, because they know ERT policies also support research, training, education and infrastructure. It would appear highly unlikely that the ERT would enjoy such close relations with the Commission, and indeed, the member states, if the organization merely promoted deregulation in the Thatcherite or, indeed, American sense.

The ERT also influences the member states. One can point to various examples where member-state governments met ERT members to discuss an ERT position, and/or later picked up key ERT ideas in member state position papers or documents. Michael Heseltine, head of the Department of Trade and Industry (DTI) in the UK, for example, returned a draft copy of the DTI's paper on competitiveness to the authors and asked that they incorporate the ideas of the ERT report, *Beating the Crisis*. Nonetheless, it is difficult to gauge the power or influence of the ERT *vis-à-vis* the member states on any one issue or report. The purpose of the ERT/member state meetings is not to sell a singular policy stance to national officials. Rather, the intent of the ERT is to sensitize member state leaders to the ERT's perspective, and to offer alternative EC policy directions.

Conclusion

It can be argued that, more than any other business alliance, the ERT has played an important role in setting the agenda for larger economic and industrial policies of the EC throughout the 1980s and 1990s. Today, the organization also looks beyond the traditional economic arena to the political/military issues of the future. Many ERT members, for example, are important investors in eastern Europe and Russia as well as key contractors in military defence systems.

The future of the ERT will see a number of changes. The arrival of a new Commission president in 1995 signals a new era of Commission/ERT relations. National elections promise to usher in new political leadership and different political coalitions in the member states. Based on its history, the ERT will adapt to these political changes. In the end, the viability of the ERT will depend largely on the members' continued political commitment to the organization – and to the larger European goals that the ERT espouses.

References

Clark, P. B. and Wilson, J. Q. (1961) 'Incentive systems: a theory of organization', *Administrative Science Quarterly*, vol. 6, pp. 129–166.

Cowles, M. G. (1993) 'The rise of the European multinational', *International Economic Insights*, vol. 4, pp. 15–18.

Cowles, M. G. (1994) 'The politics of big business in the European Community: setting the agenda for a new Europe'. PhD thesis, The American University.

Cowles, M. G. (1995) *Setting the Agenda for a New Europe: The ERT and EC 1992*, forthcoming.

Olson, M. (1965) *The Logic of Collective Action*. Cambridge, MA: Harvard University Press.

Olson, M. (1971) *The Logic of Collective Action* (2nd edn). Cambridge, MA: Harvard University Press.

Plotke, D. (1992) 'The political mobilization of business', in Petracca, M.P. (ed.) *The Politics of Interests: Interest Groups Transformed*. Boulder, CO: Westview Press, pp. 175–198.

Polanyi, K. (1944) *The Great Transformation: The Political and Economic Origins of Our Time*. Boston: Beacon Press.

Sabatier, P. A. (1992) 'Interest Group Membership and Organization: Multiple Theories', in Petracca, M. P. (ed.) *The Politics of Interests: Interest Groups Transformed*. Boulder, CO: Westview Press, pp. 99–129.

Relevance of Size and Territory for the Organization of Business Interests in Europe

Jürgen R. Grote

Introduction

The concept of small and medium-sized enterprises (SMEs) is an elusive one (Loveman and Sengenberger, 1990): it hides a large heterogeneity of all types of firm. An enormous variety of different regulatory frameworks and support measures across the twelve member states of the EU dealing with SMEs complements that heterogeneity. Moreover, policies aimed at improving competitive conditions for small firms are not only being elaborated at the national level but, at least in cases where such structures exist, at subnational, regional or district levels as well. Since about the time when the European Parliament declared 1983 the 'European Year of Small and Medium-Sized Enterprises and the Artisanat', the Commission has constantly increased the attention it pays to small firms, not least as a result of the debates on post-Fordism and the claimed superiority of flexible forms of specialization in industrial districts and in other geographically-bound agglomerations of small enterprises. Meanwhile, a supranational strategy for the support of SMEs is available, most of which have been designed and hammered out by DG XXIII, the Commission's most recently established (1989) directorate-general (enterprise policy, tourism, and the social economy). In general, however, the supply of policies for small firms is still largely fragmented. Because of their short track record, it is difficult to judge the success of these initiatives with the necessary degree of accuracy.

The elusiveness of the definition of SMEs has repercussions in the organizational format adopted by these firms' interest associations. The fragmented supply just mentioned largely corresponds to a fragmented demand on the part of the groups concerned. Contrary to most of what is resulting from the sectoral chapters of this book, there is no all-encompassing logic of membership pertaining to size. A couple of national exceptions apart,[1] most (industrial) SMEs are organized in their national sectoral or in their peak associations of industry which, eventually, run special sections for these firms' specific concerns.

Size alone does not lend itself easily as a criterion for collective action. It is insufficient as an organizing principle and, hence, unlikely to supply the ingredients necessary for the definition of something like organizational identity. Firms simply do not organize themselves according to statistical yardsticks applied by national or supranational authorities. There are great differences, therefore, among both structural (sector) and territorial (region) principles of organization. Even where firms are eventually being organized in SME associations, organizational loyalty is more likely to lie with the firm's sector or with its territorial location. Size may then become an important factor where these two latter organizing principles coincide. Although often negatively perceived,[2] small/medium size may, in some cases, furnish an additional rationale for collective action, especially in situations where national authorities fail to deliver specific support frameworks for minor firms, or where leading peak associations of industry tend to be dominated to such an extent by large enterprises that SMEs have a hard time making their voice heard and codetermining 'their' associations' policies (as, for example, in Italy's Confindustria).

Where large SMEs are concerned, the situation appears to be much the same, except that factions are more clearly defined. This is especially true of craft enterprises and the like, where it is possible to identify quite distinct features of public or, for that matter, private (interest) governance (Grote, 1992; 1993a). Craft, indeed, is organized neither according to size alone nor because of the reluctance of the state to deliver specific policies for the category. On the contrary, craft is heavily regulated, not least by way of associational self-regulation in some of the EU member states. It is the most cohesive subgroup of SMEs. It is also quite important in terms both of the number of firms as a percentage of all units operating in non-primary sectors and of its employment share within the category of SMEs. The associational history of craft enterprises is well established and reaches far back into the past in most national cases. The category is subject to substantial regulation, professional standards are high and well-defined, and entry is most often restricted and contingent on master certificates or the like. Interestingly, it has been underlined by the Commission,[3] that the performance of small firms and as the relative success of newly established SMEs seem to be far better in countries such as Germany and the Netherlands which possess a strict system of professional qualification regulating entry into the category, than in countries lacking such devices.

This chapter is organized into four parts. Firstly, some light is shed on the definition of SMEs using the most recent statistical information supplied by EU authorities. This is followed by a brief history of the EU's policy initiatives in that area before the current structure of EU-level interest associations is described. A final section tries to add evidence to the relevance of 'space' in combination with size: the so-called regional dimension of SME policies.

What is an SME?

Because of its relatively short track record, a European enterprise policy for small and medium-sized enterprises is first of all a question of appropriate statistics. There have been many problems as regards a Europe-wide definition of factors determining whether a firm would formally qualify to be treated as an SME. Until recently, national statistical offices and official measurement tools used by public authorities have largely diverged across European countries. For example, the OECD operates a definition according to which small firms would not employ more than 99 employees, while medium firms would fall into the size class of 100–499. Everything going beyond would qualify as being large. Alternatively, in countries such as Belgium and the Netherlands, a company with 201 employees would already be large since the upper ceiling for SMEs is defined to lie at 199. This is also the case for Italy, whose law for SMEs (Law 317 of 5 October 1991) has set the same margin. Germany's Small Business Research Institute (Institut für Mittelstandsforschung) establishes 49 employees as the margin for small and 499 as that for medium-sized enterprises. Contrary to this, the country's peak association of industry, the BDI, which also runs a special section for SMEs, defines small firms to have fewer than 500, medium firms between 500 and 1,000, and large ones more than 1,000 employees. Comparison is further complicated by variation in what is being taken as the basic unit for structural statistics. Although most statistics refer to the 'enterprise', in some cases national data refer to the 'establishment' (Ireland, Norway), the 'legal unit' (Denmark), or to the 'employer' (Belgium).

The European Commission tends to use the OECD definition. Yet, in its first 'SME action programme' of 1986,[4] the pure criterion of size is complemented in the following way: a small and medium-sized enterprise is 'any firm with a workforce not exceeding 500, with net fixed assets of less than ECU 75 million and with not more than one-third of its capital held by a larger firm'. Small and medium-size firms, especially in manufacturing, are generally defined for policy delivery purposes, i.e. to determine which firms are eligible for special treatment in industrial, R&D, and in competition policies. As can easily be grasped from *Exhibit 17.1* the above definition does not lend itself to singling out a specific category of enterprises that could reasonably become the target of future policy interventions by the EU: 99.9 per cent of firms would qualify for SME treatment.

Accordingly, much of the Commision's effort in the early 1990s has been aimed at establishing more sophisticated statistical tools in order to be able to 'define SMEs so as to be aware when size becomes an important discriminating variable' (CEC, 1992a, p. xviii). Backed by a number of Council decisions,[5] which substantially increased that fraction of the Community budget dedicated to the SME issue (especially after the institutionalization of DG XXIII), the Commission concentrated on the development of a 'European Observatory for Small and Medium-sized Enterprises'.[6] Such an observatory was finally established in December 1992. The network of associated research institutes responsible for the collection and elaboration of data consists of twelve member organizations[7] coordinated by the Dutch Economisch Instituut voor het Midden en Kleinbedrijf. The first annual report of the observatory was published only a couple of months after the network's establishment (ENSR, 1993)[8] – too soon to have enabled it to generate its own encompassing data set and, accordingly, heavily based on previously published statistical material such as Eurostat's *Enterprises in Europe* (CEC, 1992a).[9] Data presented in this chapter are based exclusively on Eurostat material.[10]

In order to reduce the number of firms eligible for special treatment, the Community now operates a *restricted* notion of SMEs. Firms genuinely belonging to this category do not include the 92 per cent of so-called micro firms. That reduces the number of enterprises to be dealt with in the first place to 7.9 per cent of all firms active in the NACE 1-8 sectoral divisions (manufacturing, construction, and services, non-market services being excluded). (NACE is the Nomenclature Générale des Activités

Exhibit 17.1 *Distribution of enterprises, employment and turnover by employment size class* (Source: *Derived from CEC (Eurostat), 1992a, p. 3)*

	Enterprises		Employment		Turnover	
	%	Cum. %	%	Cum. %	%	Cum. %
Micro (1–9)	92.0		29.4		21.8	
Small (10–99)	7.4	99.4	25.4	54.8	25.9	47.4
Medium (100–499)	0.5	99.9	15.4	70.2	22.6	70.5
Large (500+)	0.1	100.0	29.8	100.0	29.7	100.0

Economiques dans le Communauté Europééne: the official sectoral categorization of economic activities used by EUROSTAT.) These firms account for roughly 911,000 enterprises in the EU and employ about 33 million people. Using this definition, the picture changes substantially. In terms of numbers of firms, small enterprises (10–99 employees) now represent 94 per cent (55 per cent in size class 10–19 and 39 per cent in size class 20–99) of all SMEs, and medium-sized enterprises represent 4 per cent (2 per cent in size class 100–199 and 2 per cent in size class 200–499).

With regard to the domination of sectors, SMEs (in the restricted sense) clearly dominate the consumer goods industry (NACE division 4) where they employ about 62 per cent of all workers in that sector, all sizes (i.e. micro and large enterprises) included. Their employment share is 64.5 per cent in footwear and clothing, 59 per cent in miscellaneous articles (jewellery, musical instruments, toys and sports goods), 59 per cent in wooden furniture, 56 per cent in paper, printing and editing, and 53.5 per cent in the food industry. Apart from that, the restricted version of SMEs also dominates parts of the equipment goods industry (manufacturing of metal articles, precision instruments, mechanical engineering and the manufacturing of machinery) and parts of the service sector (wholesale trade, travel agencies, recovery services and business services).

Certain size classes of enterprise are dominant in specific sectors, and sectoral class boundaries can be drawn around them. This procedure leads to four types of cluster:

1. *Large business sectors*, where enterprises employing 500 people and over account for 5 per cent and more of enterprises in the sector (energy and water, metal processing and chemical industry, machinery and electrical engineering).

2. *Small and medium-sized business sectors*, where enterprises employing fewer than 500 people account for 95 per cent or more of all enterprises. Within this are defined the third and fourth clusters:

   (a) *Micro business sectors* where enterprises employing from 1 to 9 people account for 80 per cent or more of the total number of enterprises in the sector (retail, construction, repair of consumer goods and vehicles, hotels and catering);

   (b) The rest, i.e. '*SME sectors in the restricted sense* (see previous paragraph).

This latter is the class of enterprises to which the Commission seems inclined to pay most of its attention in the future. This may cause some problems with regard both to the number of enterprises operating within this size class across the countries of the EU, and to the relative employment shares of these firms. These problems become apparent when looking at *Exhibit 17.2* and, basically, are of two kinds.

Firstly, with regard to the large countries of the EU, there is a high divergence in terms of both the number of firms belonging to the (restricted) SME class and their relative employment share as a percentage of all size classes together. German SMEs account for 12.5 per cent (266,053) of the overall population of enterprises active in the old Federal Republic but for 46.7 per cent of employment. The opposite cases, both in relative and in absolute terms, are represented by the UK and Italy, where SMEs account for 6.7 per cent (175,991) and 7.9 per cent (134,318) of all enterprises, respectively, while their employment shares are 30.9 per cent in the UK and 33.7 per cent in Italy. France occupies an intermediate position with 6.7 per cent (133,989) of firms and 38.9 per cent of employment. Particularly interesting are the extremely low (9.9 per cent) and extremely high (47.6 per cent) employment shares of Italian medium-size and micro enterprises. Given that Italian micro firms possess an average employment per firm of between 2 and 3.6 times higher than, for example, the corresponding firm in Germany or Spain, this size class in Italy may have to be treated in a completely different fashion from the same class in most other EU member states (the Netherlands excluded).

Secondly, neither the *typical* small firm (between 10 and 30 employees) nor the *typical* medium-size enterprise (between 100 and 300 employees) are likely to be organized in those business interest associations that have combined to form one of the sixteen European-level associations presented later in this chapter. Most of these firms, but especially the medium-sized ones, can be expected to form part of their national branch or peak associations which, in turn, will be affiliated to UNICE, the EU's powerful employers' association. Hence the Commission is facing a paradoxical situation: either it includes micro firms in the SME class and ends up with 11,588,650 potential canditates for special treatment, i.e. 99.9 per cent of all European enterprises, or it excludes them which would mean that its main interlocutor for SME policies would become UNICE and its national member associations, themselves most often being dominated by the interests of large enterprises.

Of particular importance is the relevance of craft enterprises[11] in the EU, not least because their interest associations possess the highest degree of organizational cohesion among national and European organizations representing the interests of small firms. According to the most recent figures

Exhibit 17.2 *Distribution of employment shares (es) and average number of employees (ae) by employment size class and by country (NACE divisions 1–8) (Source: derived from CEC (Eurostat), 1922a)*

	Micro		Small		Medium		Large		Total Employment
	es	ae	es	ae	es	ae	es	ae	
Belgium	17.2	1.0[a]	24.1	25.4	16.6	203	30.9	1,728	2.570,217
Denmark	19.7	3.3	38.4	23.4	17.5	193	24.4	1,395	1,640,331
Germany	17.2	1.7	28.7	21.6	18.0	199	36.1	2,085	18,731,643
Spain	24.5	1.0[a]	36.3	23.9	19.8	196	19.5	1,342	6,996,416
France	28.2	2.0	24.6	26.7	14.3	200	32.9	2.176	13,731,643
Italy	47.6	3.6	23.8	21.7	9.9	195	18.7	2,312	11,638,815
Luxembourg	22.0	2.4	28.8	25.7	22.8	213	26.4	1,530	139,091
Netherlands	24.7	5.0	38.7	37.6	14.6	1,580[b]	22.0	1,580[b]	2,588,859
Portugal	24.4	1.0[a]	32.4	24.6	19.8	197	23.4	1,479	2,204,166
UK[c]	26.2	2.2	13.2	16.8	17.7	241	35.2	2,362	20,425,250
Mean	25.2	2.3	28.9	24.7	17.1	204	27.0	1,823	

[a] Due to inconsistencies in the EC data, micro firms in Belgium, Spain and Portugal appear to have slightly less than 1 employee. In all these cases, the figures have been rounded up to 1.
[b] There are no separate data for the average number of employees in Dutch medium-size and large enterprises. The two size classes together have an average employment of 1,580 people per firm.
[c] Due to inconsistencies in the EC data, the percentage figures (es) do not add up to 100.

available (ENSR, 1994, pp. 25–26), craft enterprises account for 38 per cent of all economic units operating in the EU. Their Europe-wide employment share has continuously increased in the early 1990s and now stands at around 30.4 per cent. There are enormous differences across countries, though, ranging from 42 per cent in Greece to less than 1 per cent in the UK. Craft's share in the total number of enterprises varies between almost zero in the UK and more than two-thirds in Greece.

In terms of the status accredited to craft enterprises in individual countries, three national clusters can be distinguished. Firstly, France, Italy, Germany and Luxembourg, where this type of firm is legally sanctioned and where, accordingly, entry into the category is contingent on some measure of formal certification. Secondly, countries such as Denmark and the Netherlands which lack a legal definition, although the category is being run according to principles similar to those in the first group. Finally, Portugal, Spain, Greece and the UK where craft is exclusively defined by size (Ireland operates a kind of working definition of craft).

A European Enterprise Policy for Small Firms

Although the Community has never actually run a comprehensive enterprise or industrial policy proper, initiatives in individual sectors and domains have come quite close to such a definition. Most of these have benefited the interests of large enterprises, especially those dealing with high-technology industries and R&D. Hardly astonishing, then, is the concern brought forward by a number of authors (Grote, 1993a; Peterson, 1991) and most often advanced with regard to the Community's large-scale research networks such as ESPRIT and Eureka, that SMEs, 'despite apparent European Commission provisions to the contrary, are gradually squeezed out of the market' (Shearman, 1989, p. 6) of high-technology products and those with a strong R&D component. This is confirmed by the Commission itself. In a recent communication on SMEs and on Community activities in the field of R&D, it is said that:

> because of the limitation of joint R&D activities to precompetitive research, most EU initiatives have remained the domain of research centres and of large enterprises. Most programmes concern high-level research projects to which access by SMEs is relatively low. At EU level, there are not more than a couple of thousand SMEs which, because of their technological composition and managerial assets, would fulfil the preconditions for participating in one of the Community programmes.
>
> *(COM(93) 356 final, 30 September 1993; translation by author)*

Meanwhile, there are indications supporting the likelihood of an increase in SME's share in R&D activities, not least in the context of the Fourth Framework Programme for Research and Technology. Indeed, SMEs account for twice as many innovations per employee and develop three-and-a-half times as many new products per dollar invested into research activities than do large firms (based on US data). Overall, however, the supply of specific policies for this category still appears to be largely fragmented and uncoordinated although the importance being accorded the issue has constantly grown since the late 1980s. The, albeit slow, emergence of a European enterprise policy for SMEs may be said to be a result of the drastic differences in employment creation between micro and small firms on the one hand and medium and large ones on the other. While three million jobs have been created by the first group in the period 1988–93, the second group has lost more jobs than could be created, with a particularly bad performance in the medium-sized category (ENSR, 1994). Job generation apart, SMEs consistently out-perform the rest in terms of organizational and productive flexibility as well as with respect to their adaptability to a changing environment (CEC, 1992a, p. xix).

At the same time, EU authorities have taken account of the fact that most SMEs are actually badly equipped to take advantage of the benefits expected to result from the single market. According to the Commission's *Whitebook on Growth, Competitiveness, and Employment*, the main factors impeding this are:

1. Lack of capacity to cope with administrative procedures.
2. Value added tax formalities.
3. The payment of social insurance;
4. New environmental and social standards.
5. Entry barriers to some specific markets (and to public procurement).
6. Problems of financing.
7. Too much paperwork and lack of credit facilities.
8. Problems with management qualifications and the development of strategic guidelines. (CEC, 1993, p. 78)

Accordingly, most of the EU's initiatives in favour of SMEs try to help overcome these difficulties. A number of Council decisions assigning to the Commision the task of becoming active in the field of SMEs[12] and the Declaration of the Edinburgh Council Meeting of 11–12 December 1992 (where the Commission was asked to develop appropriate policies to alleviate the burden put on SMEs as a result of the coming into force of the internal market), finally resulted in the adoption of an action programme for SMEs[13] (June 1993), endowed with ECU 112.2 million and covering the period July 1993 until December 1996. Most policy deliberations of the action programme coincide with the suggestions already made in the *Whitebook* and in essence concern the improvement of activities and pilot programmes, most of which have been in progress since the early 1990s. The most important of these are:

- Euromanagement – advice given to the management of SMEs to increase their participation rate in European high-technology programmes.
- MINT – Managing the Integration of New Technology.
- EURO-INFO-CENTRES.
- CRAFT – Cooperative Research Action for Technology.
- BC-NET – Business Cooperation Network.
- SPRINT – Strategic Programme for Innovation and Technology Transfer.
- VALUE-SME – Distribution and use of research results by European SMEs.
- Europartnership – Establishment of joint ventures, alliances and other forms of international cooperation between SMEs.
- Interprise – Interregional agreements aiming at an increase of contacts and alliances among SMEs from at least three different regions of three different countries.

These programmes are complemented by a series of conferences coorganized by the interests associations of SMEs togther with the Commission's DG XXIII.[14] Yet, little is known about the impact of these initiatives on the competitive environment of their target groups. Most likely, the bulk of the programmes continues to have little effect, which is also corroborated by the insistence with which some try to push the issue on the policy agenda of the EU. UEAPME's (European Association of Craft, Small and Medium-sized Enterprises) general secretary, for instance, has recently criticized the EU's small enterprise policy as 'terminological juggling'.[15] The Commission's most recent proposals in favour of SMEs would miss their target and would hardly benefit any of these firms.

Also, following the main essentials of the *Whitebook* and calling for a more integrated approach to the problem in question, the Belgian Council presidency presented a memorandum on 30 September 1993 suggesting the nurturing of 'a systematic and concerted action between the Commission and the SME interest associations' which is intended to 'become the rule in all phases of the EU's decision-making process. The SME associations should become direct partners to the Social Dialogue'.[16] The latter, indeed, is still limited to the representations of large enterprises (UNICE and CEEP). According to UEAPME's president, the exclusion of UEAPME (and other associations) from this exercise would result in a policy 'where all problems of concern to small firms would be looked at from the viewpoint of large enterprises'.[17] The 'Integrated Programme for SMEs' which also foresees a more systematic incorporation of the responsible business interest associations into Europe's policy deliberations, is now standing for approval by the Council.

In general, and contrary to the claim that DG XXIII would belong to the most corporatist divisions of the Commission,[18] this part of Europe's bureaucracy does not suffer from the problem of many of its fellow directorates – demand overload. Overload often results in the search for alternative devices of governance such as corporatist-like exercises. DG XXIII cannot be said to have embarked on such a strategy yet. That it is 'underloaded' with demands and that this is due to the vast fragmentation among interest associations representing small firm interests are demonstrated in the following section.

Organizational Format of SME Representation at EU Level

While more integration is needed in the supply of SME policies, the same can be said with regard to the demand-side, i.e. essentially, the organizational outlet for SME representation at European level. The *Directory of EC Trade and Professional Associations* (CEC, 1992b) mentions nine proper SME organizations (*Exhibit 17.3* and below) and seven craft associations (*Exhibit 17.4*) representing small firms in Brussels – a perfect example of pluralist fragmentation. The definitions used by the directory are somewhat misleading, however. Europe's most powerful national craft associations are organized within the group of organizations represented in *Exhibit 17.3* (namely by UEAPME), and not in the group of associations coming under craft (*Exhibit 17.4*). This is the case, for instance, for the German ZdH (Zentralvernband des deutschen Handwerks) and for Italy's Confartigianato. Italy's even better resourced and more representative CNA (Confederazione Nazionale dell'Artigianato) maintains affiliations both to EUROPMI (European Committee for Small and Medium-sized Independent Companies) and to EMSU (European Medium and Small Business Union),[19] the latter of which organizes politically, rather conservative,

Exhibit 17.3 *EU-level associations of small and medium-sized enterprises predominantly representing (A) proper craft and some SMEs, (B) proper SMEs and some craft, (C) commerce and self-employed, (D) middle classes, (E) building companies, (F) middle classes (Source: CEC, 1992b, pp. 238–244)*

	A UEAPME[20]	B EUROPME	C CEDI	D EMSU	E EBC	F UEM
Austria	1[e]			1		1
Belgium	1	3	1			
Denmark	1			1		
Germany	2[a]	1	1	8[f]		1
Greece	1			1		
Spain	1	2[c]		3[c]	2	
France	3[b]	1	1	2	1	
Ireland	1					1
Italy	2[a]	2[d]	1	2[g]	5	1
Luxembourg	1			1	1	
Netherlands	2	1	1[e]	2		1
Portugal	1		1[e]	1		
UK	1	2		1	1	1
Total EU members	18	12	6 (+2)[e]	23	10	6
Switzerland					1	
Czechoslovakia	1[e]			1		
Poland	1[e]					1
Hungary	((1[e]))			1		
Turkey	((1[e]))			1		1
Ukraine						1
Total	20 (+2)	12	6 (+2)	26	11	9

[a] 1 full member, 1 associated
[b] 2 national, 1 permanent assembly of professional chambers
[c] All regional
[d] 1 craft, 1 SMEs
[e] Only associate member
[f] Political and branch associations
[g] 1 national, 1 regional

UEAPME = European Association of Craft, Small and Medium-sized Enterprises
EUROPME = European Committee for Small and Medium-sized Independent Companies
CEDI = Confédération européenne des indépendants
EMSU = European Medium and Small Business Union
EBC = European Builders Confederation
UEM = European Union of Small and Medium-sized Companies

Figures in double brackets are supplied by an UEAPME documentation of 1994 and, hence, are more up-to-date.

middle-class associations such as Germany's Mittelstandsvereiningung der CDU and others. Three further associations have to be added to the groups listed in *Exhibit 17.3*. They do not report any national affiliation by interest groups and seem to be direct membership associations. These are:

   G. Comité des petites et moyennes entreprises commerciales des pays de la CEE.

Exhibit 17.4 EU-level associations of craft and the artisanat (Source: CEC, 1992b, pp. 229–235)

	A COBCCEE	B ANOBCCEE	C UIPCG	D EUROPECHE	E EAPO	F AEGRAFLEX	G UIEP
Belgium	1	1	1	1	1	1	1
Denmark	1	1	1	2	3[b]	1	
Germany	1	1	1	2	2	2	1
Greece		1		2			
Spain	1	2	1	3	7[c]		
France	2	2	1	1	2	1	1
Ireland	1			1		2[b]	
Italy	1	2	1[a]	1	1		1
Luxembourg	1	1	1				
Netherlands	1	1	1	1	2[b]	2	
Portugal	1	1	1	1	2[d]		
UK	1	1		2[b]	6[b]	1	1
Austria	1		1			1	1
Norway		1	1			1	
Sweden		1	1			2	
Finland			1			1	
Switzerland	1		1				1
Total	13	16	14	17	28	13	7

[a] Regional
[b] 1 national, rest regional
[c] 7 sectoral (different types of fish)
[d] 2 regional

COBCCEE = Comité des organisations de boucherie et charcuterie de la CEE
ANOBCCEE = Association of National Organisations in the Bakery and Confectionery in the EEC
UIPCG = International Union of Confectioners, Pastrycooks, and Ice-Cream-Makers
EUROPECHE = Association of National Organisations of Fishing Enterprises in the EEC
EAPO = European Association of Fish Producers Organisations
AEGRAFLEX = Association Européenne des Graveurs et des Flexographes
UIEP = Union Internationale des Entreprises de Platrerie, Staff, Stuc et Activités Annexes

H. European Independent Business Confederation (AECM).

I.   Young Entrepreneurs for Europe (YES).

The latter is a grouping of young entrepreneurs from different national peak associations of industry such as the German BDI, Italy's Confindustria and the British CBI, most of which do seem to be in a minority position within their home organizations – a fact that has led them to set up their own European structure better able to represent their interests than their EC peak association, UNICE. A 'fifth column' of UNICE, namely its Committee for Small and Medium-sized Enterprises has been listed on a lobbying list of DG XXIII for the consultation of small firms in 1990 (Grote, 1992). Another section of one of the large national peak associations of industry, Confindustria's National Committee for Small Firms, is organized in UEAPME.

Of the nine associations mentioned, UEAPME and EUROPMI are the most representative. In a 1994 speech, UEAPME's president proudly announced the accession of the twenty-ninth member, one of which is an important branch association, IMU (International Metal Union). With 3.5 million enterprises associated that represent 13 million employees, UEAPME clearly dominates the associational landscape among SME organizations. Note, however, that its core members are craft associations, a fact that may explain the relative clout of the grouping. Craft, indeed, has something to defend in Europe, namely a number of well established national regulatory regimes – something which other SMEs cannot lay claim to. Not surprisingly, UEAPME was run from West Germany's capital, Bonn, until 1990 when it moved its headquarters to Brussels. With the competition of the internal market, there was a great deal at stake for Europe's most powerful national craft association, the German ZdH which has been the main net contributor to UEAPME's organizational costs since the creation of the the the latter's forerunner, UACEE (Union de l'Artisanat de la CEE), in 1959. Outright enthusiasm for deregulation and other assaults of the Thatcherite type threatened to undermine the very existence of the firmly established system of craft in Germany and a few other countries operating comparable devices for the maintenance of high levels of professional qualification. Since a strategy of social dumping was out of the question for UEAPME, the only feasible alternative would have consisted of helping to upgrade regulatory standards in competing member states by generalizing the most far-reaching ones to the level of the EU. The ENSR's recommendation, advanced in the executive summary of its second annual report (1994) of an 'international exchange of experiences of best practice in professional qualification for the stimulation of employment creation by

SMEs' may be an indicator of the success of UEAPME's activities in Brussels. The association is fully backed in its policy by the Federal government which mentions only this one and no other European-level association of SMEs to be formally admitted to the European Social Dialogue.[21]

A Scottish fisherman, a Belgian pastry cook or an Italian *gelatiere* is not usually what one has in mind when one thinks of the typical artisan. Yet, in the EC directory's section on craft associations, five out of seven represent the food and the food-processing industry (*Exhibit 17.4*, columns A–E) while the rest organize plasterers and rubber stamp manufacturers. These collective formats represent an extremely small fraction of typical SME sectors – four of the seven associations even have to cope with competing membership, namely the ones organizing fishermen and fish producers (D and E) and those collecting the interests of confectioners (B and C). The fact that the suppliers of EU-gourmets are represented so numerously at EC level cannot be explained other than by the inflation of EC directives in the food sector. In any case, the very names of the associations mentioned underline the lack of a more comprehensive system of interest representation at the branch level.

By way of conclusion, the interests of small enterprises in the EU are represented by a total of at least sixteen associations. That is far too many to be credible as a competent interlocutor with EU authorities. At the same time, one should not forget that something like a European SME policy has just started to emerge. Some organizational engineering might therefore be expected in the near future. European authorities would welcome a more streamlined version of associational representation. There is now increasing awareness among them that the relative 'underload' of the administration with demands brought forward by (hardly any encompassing) private interest association might perpetuate existing coordination problems both within DG XXIII as well as between different directorates, for instance, DG XXIII and DG XVI. Indeed, the fragmentation of the interest system appears to be a reflection of the fragmentation of policies, and progress with the latter, for instance towards an integrated programme for SMEs, might be possible only by overcoming the largely incompatible associational structures. The Council has on several occasions pointed to the danger associated with demand underload. Its suggestions are twofold. Firstly, 'small and medium-sized enterprises are called upon to improve their organizational outlets for interest representation at European level'[22] and, secondly, the Commission is asked 'to establish comprehensive devices for concertation and the timely information of the leading associations representing the category'.[23]

Territorial Dimension of Smallness

Space does not figure prominently on the policy agenda of DG XXIII. This is astonishing if you consider that the divergences among enterprises and countries represented in *Exhibit 17.2* would appear to be squared if a regional or otherwise subcentral level were inserted. Small size and regional development are closely related, at least in countries whose employment shares are clearly above average in columns 1 and 3 of *Exhibit 17.2*. Two arguments can be advanced in favour of inserting space into a European SME policy. Firstly, the most relevant initiatives aiming at an upgrading of the economic environment (or, to use Alfred Marshall's famous notion, the 'industrial atmosphere') of small firms are run by DG XVI, the directorate responsible for regional and structural policies. Efforts undertaken by this division may either duplicate or cancel out the effects of policies undertaken by DG XXIII. Secondly, as we know from the debate on flexible specialization and industrial districts in a number of countries, space actually seems to determine the performance of small firms to extents largely unrecognized by most industrial policies of the 1970s and 1980s. This has to do with how embedded economic activity is in social and spatial relations of trust and reciprocity. These relations may assume such an importance in some instances that pure rational choices and strategies suggested and designed by technicians who are far removed from individual realities may, ultimately, become counter-productive. At least, it is not completely clear to what extent programmes such as Internet and Europartneriat may result in the buy-out of local industrial milieux, although some form of cross-border networking is certainly advisable to prevent encapsulation and atrophy.

There are only few indications that account has been taken of the above in official EU documents. The Commission's *Whitebook* is coming quite close to the point where it underlines the relevance that decentralization would assume in any social market economy. Decentralization would mean 'to give more importance to both small and medium-sized enterprises and to local or regional levels of public policy-making' (CEC, 1993, p. 6). Similarly, the second annual report by ENSR observes a 'strong EU-wide trend towards regionalization in policies dealing with craft enterprises and SMEs' (ENSR, 1994, p. 26). Regional political authorities would assume increasing responsibilities for the design and implementation of craft-related policies. Moreover, as mentioned by the Commission, 'small firms especially dominate in Objective 1 regions which are less densely populated and less industrialized than most other parts of the EU'.[24]

With a view to the relevance that SME interest associations may assume for the provision of public goods at the subcentral level, there is hardly anything to be found in EU documents, the only exception to this being COM(93) 527 final. The impression is being advanced that the use made of the EU's structural funds by firms in Objective 1 regions appears to be quite unsatisfactory, mostly because of inefficient administration by national and regional bureaucracies. This would often result in fragmentation and in a 'policy of slicing the cake' and might 'considerably be improved and made more efficient if financial resources were not directly transferred to individual companies but, rather, to *intermediary organizations*' (COM(93) 527 final, p. 36; emphasis added). That these intermediary organizations may be business interest associations or, for that matter, trade unions, is not made explicit, however. Just these, though, would appear to be the main candidates potentially able both to improve the implementation of EU policies on the spot and to upgrade the productive environment of firms operating at that level.

In general, then, it would appear that the Commission perpetuates the lack of attention being given to subcentral interest associations by focusing in its written outputs mostly on flexible specialization and industrial districts. What remains largely unrecognized is the fact that the first, basic format of an interfirm network is actually the business association. Where such a structure does not work properly, despite the rather low degrees of commitment required, it is reasonable to believe that more binding and risky exercises, such as international joint ventures and business alliances, will have little chance to prosper. This is likely to be the case in areas of southern Europe where entrepreneurs are hesitant to embark on collective endeavours with potential competitors with whom they do not maintain frequent face-to-face contact.

The argument being advanced here is that the associations representing craft and small enterprises should explicitly be made part of the management of territorial problems both by the EU and by the regional governments concerned. If there is anything to subsidiarity, then it is here. As mentioned elsewhere (Grote, 1993b), functional and territorial subsidiarity overlap and combine in the form of subcentral interest associations; they are closer to the people in terms of territorial complexity, and they operate closer to the market in terms of the state/market continuum than most alternative devices for social and economic governance. One does not need to go as far as Hirst (1994, p. 177) who envisages:

> a fully-developed associational welfare state [which] would be federal in that the core organisation of provision would be the region, at which level public funds . . . would be collected and distributed, . . . [with] voluntary associations [entering] into public governance in a decentralised state,

to see the immediate benefits of associational self-regulation of the small-firm domain in regional economies. The problems with such suggestions are, firstly, the high divergence of organizational outlets of this kind across European countries and, secondly, the definition of the most appropriate territorial level at which collective action by small entrepreneurs is to reap the highest benefit.

As to the problem of organizational divergence and disparities, Brussels is the place best suited for the exchange of views and experiences in order to smooth existing incompatibilities. The Commission, in concert with an enhanced outlet for SME representation could contribute considerably to the coming about of such a forum. As regards the second problem, one would have to conceive of business associations not only in terms of field offices of national or supranational authorities having to cope with implementation failure of policies, as is being done by the Commission (note 23), but also as providers of more encompassing types of public good benefiting a maximum number of entrepreneurs. An intermediate level would emerge, then, that would be simultaneously subcentral and also more than just local. This is for the following reasons.

Business associations habitually perform three major functions: interest representation, collective bargaining and the provision of services to their members. The extent to which any one of these predominates over others in a specific organization is contingent upon two factors: the *territorial level* at which an association operates, and its relative *degree of 'modernity'*. From the perspective of interest here – an association as service provider, generator of public goods and, so to speak, a quasi-development agency – three hypotheses can be raised.

Firstly, the less an association is operating in peripheral territory, the more likely its activity is to be outward-looking; in other words, the more centralized an association's organizational epicentre, the more likely its function is going to become a politico-representational one. Secondly, the relative share of services offered to the association's members, as a fraction of its overall activities, is inversely proportional to the size of firms being organized. Lastly, the territorial dimension of an association's activity is likely to become more articulated and, hence, more aimed at the provision of services, the higher the reduction of average firm size among its members (Viviani, 1990; and see *Exhibit 17.5*).

In such a scenario, *regional* business associations emerge as the most appropriate ones to be empowered with the task of co-management of subcentral economies. They are sufficiently far removed from the grass roots of the municipal level to avoid the danger of territorial encapsulation, localism and parochialism. At the same time, they are perfectly situated to arrange for a more general supply of infrastructure for a quite vast area.

Exhibit 17.5 *Relative shares of politico-representational and of service contents of associative action at four levels of territorial complexity* (Source: *adapted from Viviani, 1990, p. 181)*

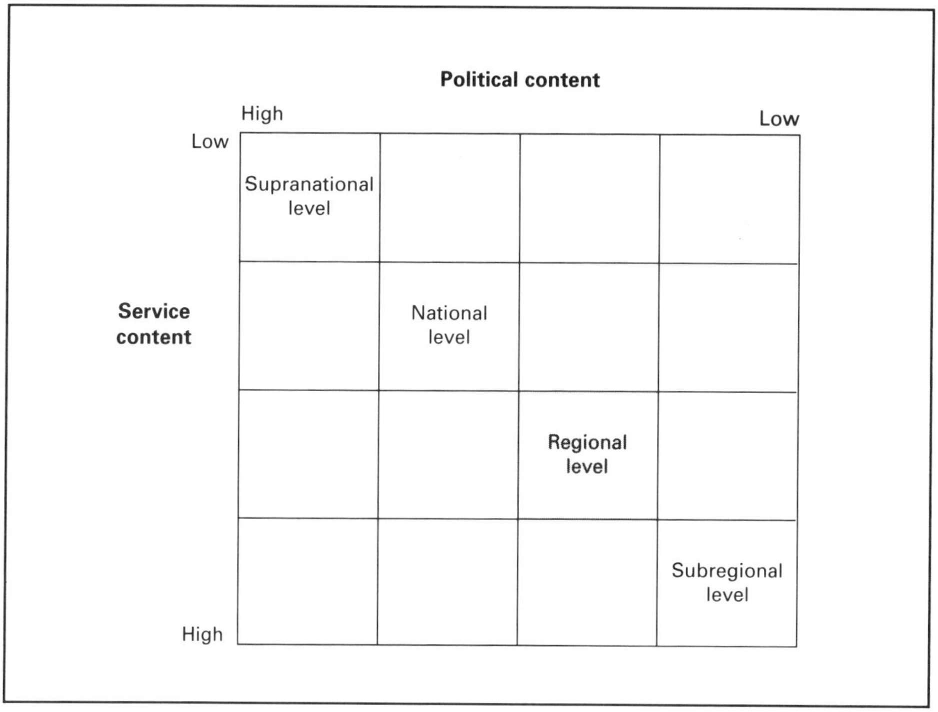

They are not directly engaged in the provision of services but in the supply and management of more far-reaching plans helping to equalize the productive conditions of enterprises everywhere in the region. They do that without completely renouncing political activities aimed at improving their territories' endowment with more modern resources, managerial capacities, know how, and so forth. Representational activities of this kind that try to guarantee a better use of existing resources and of grants paid out to the territory by bodies external to the region may have as their targets regional, national and supranational authorities. With regard to a strategy of subsidiarity of the EU Commission, and with reference to the implementation problems reported by DG XVI in the allocation of structural funds, regional interest associations may represent important actors to improve existing practices.

Yet, the above is not the only rationale which could be used to argue that more attention should be given to forms of collective action by SMEs at the subcentral level. Like any other organization, the history of interest associations of small firms passes through various stages in organizational life cycles. The stages reached by different groups in various countries are hardly compatible with each other, especially if looking at subcentral activities and structures. Action by the most traditional associations merely goes beyond representation and lobbying. Commitment by members is low and mostly limited to the payment of fees. In terms of Preti (1991), these are 'passive associations' representing a form of 'facade-like collaboration' where most functions are delegated to a leadership whose officials are often inexperienced and ideologically biased. To arrive at a proper form of 'group entrepreneurship', thereby becoming a 'catalyst of development', an association has to pass two further stages: a phase where it substitutes for existing market failures in basic service delivery, and a subsequent one where it produces its own and more sophisticated services to enlarge its membership and improve its legitimation. Proper group entrepreneurship in catalytic associations is not concerned any more with the production of its own services but, rather, is aimed at the distribution of advice and consultancy being supplied by third parties, i.e. at the general management of territorial and of structural complexity.

The EU Commission is interested in improving the managerial capacities of small and medium-sized enterprises in order to allow for more of what it calls the international networking of SMEs. As argued above, if basic format and mode of operation of such networks is not improved in the first place, both at supranational and subcentral levels, more far-reaching strategies might easily fail.

Notes

1. For example, Italy's Confederazione Italiana delle Piccole Imprese' (CONFAPI), or the Dutch Kritische Niederlandse Ondernemers (KNO), and a few others, most of which are middle-class associations or organizations of self-employed.
2. Small or medium size is most often perceived in terms of representing a problem rather than a positive asset. Interests of these firms, accordingly, are thought to need defending against negative influences from third countries (USA and Japan), from large multinationals, from the internal market, etc.
3. COM(93) 527 final, p. 13.
4. COM(86) 445 final.
5. For instance, those of 28 July 1989 and of 17 June 1991.
6. See COM(90) final, 18 December 1990.
7. Belgium (KMO Studiecentrum/Katholieke Universiteit Brussel); Denmark (Danish Technological Institute); Germany (Institut für Mittelstandsforschung); Greece (EOMMEX); Spain (Instituto Vasco de Estudios e Investigación); France (Association pour la promotion et le développement industriel); Ireland (Economic and Social

Research Institute); Italy (Centro Studi sull'imprenditorialità Furio Cicogna/Università Bocconi); Luxembourg (Centre de promotion et de recherche, Chambre des Metiers); Portugal (IAPMEI); UK (Centre for Small and Medium-sized Enterprises/University of Warwick).

8. The European Observatory for SMEs–European Network for SME Research, First Annual Report 1993 (Zoetermeer, the Netherlands: EIM). See also Euro-Info 60/93 (June 1993) published in *SME: Craft Industry* by DG XXIII of the EU Commission, pp. 1–3.

9. Although taking account of the short time-frame within which the study had to be produced, the EU Commission (COM(93) 527 final, 5 November 1993) has brought forward serious criticism with respect to the insufficiency of the data. The second (and substantially improved) annual report has now been published by ENSR (1994).

10. Readers interested in more elaborate time series analysis of small firm performance, as well as in more detailed data on individual countries, are advised to consult Sengenberger *et al.* (1990).

11. Craft enterprises are defined by one or more of the following: branch, size, type of product or mode of production. For more detailed information, see Grote (1992).

12. See, in particular, Council Decision 89/490/EEC (*OJ*, L239, 16 August 1989, p. 33); 91/319/EEC (*OJ*, L175, 4 July 1991, p. 32); and, *OJ*, C178, 15 July 1992, p. 8.

13. Council Decision 93/379/EEC of 14 June 1993 (*OJ*, L161, 2 July 1993, p. 68).

14. To the most important of these belongs the European Conference of Craft Enterprises which took place in October 1990 in Avignon. A follow-up meeting, organized in five workshops, was held in Berlin, 26–27 September 1994. The European peak associations responsible are UEAPME and EUROPMI.

15. *Handelsblatt* of 23 July 1993.

16. Euro-Info *SME: Craft Industry*, 63/93, October 1993, pp. 1–2. On Belgian initiatives, there was a special Council meeting on 11 November 1993 dedicated to discuss the SME issue.

17. Mr Ret, president of UEAPME, on the first international conference convened by the association in September 1993 (*Agence Europe*, no. 6068, 20–21 September 1993, p. 1).

18. See Andrews (1991) quoted in Grote (1992, p. 163).

19. This is a curious fact since CNA has its origins in the ex-communist trade union, CGIL, and organizes up to 70 per cent of the entire category in Italy's red North-east and centre regions (Grote, 1992, p. 154). CNA has asked for membership in UEAPME but continues to be excluded because of the veto exerted by its Christian Democratic competitor, Confartigianato. This may soon be subject to change since both organizations are currently discussing problems of a future unification of their associational structures. In general, however, the fragmentation of Italy's interest system, hence, appears to be reproduced at the European level.

20. Figures in double brackets are supplied by an UEAPME documentation of 1994 and, hence, are more up-to-date.

21. Bundestags-Drucksache 12/5682, 16 September 1993, p. 64.

22. Council Decision 93/379 of 14 June 1993 (*OJ*, L161, 2 July 1993, p. 69).

23. *Ibid.*, Article 2, section IE, p. 70 and Council Decision 93/C 326/01 of 22 November 1993 (*OJ*, C326, 3 December 1993, p. 1 (as well as sections 4e, 4f and 5g).

24. COM(93) 527 final, 5 November 1993, p. 20.

References

CEC (Eurostat) (1992a) *Enterprises in Europe. Second Report*. Brussels: Office for Official Publications of the EC.

CEC (1992b) *Directory of EC Trade and Professional Associations*. Brussels: Edition Delta.

CEC (1993) *Whitebook on Growth, Competitiveness, and Employment*. Brussels: Office for Official Publications of the EC.

ENSR (1993) *The European Observatory for Small and Medium-sized Enterprises (SME)*. First Annual Report prepared by ENSR (European Network for SME Research) and coordinated by EIM (Small Business Research and Consultancy), Zoetermeer, the Netherlands.

ENSR (1994) *The European Observatory for Small and Medium-sized Enterprises (SME)*. Second Annual Report. (Summary Report submitted to DG XXIII.)

Grote, J. (1992) 'Small firms in the European Community: modes of production, governance and territorial interest representation in Italy and Germany', in Greenwood, J., Grote, J. and Ronit, K. (eds) *Organised Interests and the European Community*. London: Sage, pp. 119–173.

Grote, J. (1993a) 'Diseconomies in space: traditional sectoral policies of the EC, the European Technology Community and their effects on regional disparities', in Leonardi, R. (ed.) *The Regions and the European Community. The Regional Response to the Single Market in the Underdeveloped Areas*. London: Frank Cass, pp. 14–47.

Grote, J. (1993b) 'On functional and territorial subsidiarity. Between legal discourse and societal needs'. Paper presented at the Fachtagung der Gruppe 'Europäische Integration' der Deutschen Vereinigung für Politische Wissenschaft (DVPW) über 'Legitimation und Handlungsfähigkeit der EG nach Maastricht', Mannheim, 26–27 November 1993.

Hirst, P. (1994) *Associative Democracy: New Forms of Economic and Social Governance*. Cambridge: Polity Press.

Loveman, G. and Sengenberger, W. (1990) 'Economic and social reorganization in the small and medium-sized enterprise sector', in Sengenberger, W., Loveman, G. and Piore, M. J. (eds) *The Re-emergence of Small Enterprises*. Geneva: International Institute for Labour Studies (ILO), pp. 1–62.

Peterson, J. (1991) 'Technology policy in Europe. Explaining the Framework Programme in theory and practice' *Journal of Common Market Studies*, vol. 29, no. 3, pp. 269-91.

Preti, P. (1991) *L' organizzazione della Piccola Impresa. Nascità e Sviluppo delle Imprese Minori*, Milano: EGEA.

Sengenberger, W., Loveman, G. and Piore, M. J. (eds) (1990) *The Re-emergence of Small Enterprises*, Geneva: International Institute for Labour Studies (ILO).

Shearman, C. (1989) *European Technological Collaboration: An Overview of Some of the Issues Arising*, Paper presented at the European Community Studies Association's Inaugural Conference, George Mason University, Fairfax, Virginia, May 24-25, 1989.

Viviani, M. (1990) 'Le funzioni delle associazioni imprenditoriali', in *Sviluppo e Organizzazione*, n.117, Gennaio-Febbraio 1990, pp. 176-196.

Constructing Political Unity by Combining Organizations

UNICE as a European Peak Association

Luca Lanzalaco[1]

One of the main contributions of corporatist theory to collective action has been the emphasis on differences between organizing individuals, and organizations (Schmitter, 1983; van Waarden, 1991). Organizations have different sizes, and size makes a difference in creating collective identities; organizations are endowed with own resources, and this makes collective action less relevant; organizations do not have ethical sensibility, and this makes them less sensitive and responsible towards public concerns; organizations differentiate and integrate individual knowledges, and this makes their rationality less bounded. The collective action of organized collectivities is not a 'reproduction to scale' of the collective action of individuals.

This suggestion throws light on the problems not only that a business interest association has to cope with when it is trying to combine the organization of firms, i.e. large versus small firms, but also that an organization has when it is trying to combine the collective action of various associations, i.e. to constitute *n*-order associations. The latter item is quite relevant since the articulation of a complex architecture of networks of associations, hierarchically ordered and specialized in the representation of small associative domains, is the *main* organizational device for the management of business interests diversity (Schmitter and Streeck, 1981).[2] Hence the problem of 'organizing the collective action of associations' takes on a crucial relevance for business interest representation.

This function is usually accomplished by the *peak associations* (federations or confederations of federations of associations, like the British CBI, the French CNPF, the German BDA and the Italian Confederation of

Industry), namely *n*-order associations[3] representing the *highest* organizational asset of an associative domain on a national scale. In structuring the political action of business interests *vis-à-vis* trade unions and political institutions, peak associations have to face five dilemmas.

1. *Direct versus indirect legitimation.* The organs of an *n*-order association may be directly legitimated and appointed by its membership or, conversely, may be indirectly legitimated, being automatically composed only of the leadership of the member associations. For example, the presidents of all the member associations (as in the British and the German cases) may become *ex officio* members of the council of the peak association, and so this organ enjoys legitimacy only to the extent that its members are separately and autonomously elected by each association which has 'its' representatives (indirect legitimation). On the other hand, the council may be composed of members selected and elected by the assembly of the peak association itself (as in the French case), and so they gain legitimacy not only from their 'original' association but by the whole membership of the peak association (direct legitimation).

2. *Permanent versus temporary composition of organs.* The organs of an *n*-order association may be composed of stable officials or representatives or, conversely, they may be changed by member associations depending on their internal leadership turnover. For example, in the case of UNICE, the peak association of European employers, the post of president can be temporary in that, if he or she loses his/her office of president of a member association, it follows that he or she cannot also continue as president of UNICE. On the other hand, in the case of the Italian Confederation of Industry, as in many other peak associations, this does not occur and the president is in a stable office since he or she, once elected by the assembly, holds this position separately from his or her appointments within member associations. This dilemma is strictly tied to the former one, since the direct legitimation of organs leads to a stable composition. Meanwhile the indirect legitimacy is usually paralleled by a changing composition of organs, depending on the internal politics of each association.

3. *Symmetric versus asymmetric decisional powers.* Each member association may have the same decision-making power, independent of its weight in terms of membership or budget. In this case the 'one man, one vote' principle of democratic representation will prevail, such as in some chambers of commerce and small size and artisan associations or in peak associations in which a non-economic commitment prevails (young entrepreneurs, confessional based associations, etc.). The strongest version of this mechanism is to confer a veto power to each association, such as existed in UNICE until the beginning of the 1990s. Otherwise, decision-making procedures may be adopted that link the decisional power of each member association to its size. For example, each association has a quota of votes proportional to the number of firms it represents, or to the number of the employees of these firms or, more usually, to the financial contribution it devotes (after negotiation) to the peak association. The first mechanism ('one association, one vote') encourages solidarity and a sense of equality among associations, but it reduces the incentive for strong associations to participate in collective action. The second mechanism ('more resources, more votes') penalizes the smallest associations in decision-making processes but provides incentives to the biggest ones to mobilize their resources in collective action.

4.   *Widening legitimacy domain versus deepening policy incisiveness.* The greater the number of member associations, the greater the association legitimacy to representation. However, a large number of member associations creates transaction costs, problems of reduction of complexity and of coexistence of different interests and policy domains. When a peak association represents a high number of products, sectors, regions or nations, it may define itself as the spokesperson' of a huge mass of firms and of their *general* interests, but it also meets obstacles in combining and integrating their different interests, and so both internal consensus-building and policy formulation are quite difficult. On the other hand, when a peak association combines only a limited number of sectors or nations, it may be censured for representing partial and particular interests, but it will be able to provide specific policy proposals and technical advocacy and it will become a crucial interlocutor for policy-makers and public administration. Adopting Schmitter and Streeck's (1981) jargon, the logic of goal formation (calling for a tight coherence between the policy and associative domains) clashes against the 'over-representativeness' of associative domains required to acquire political legitimacy *vis-à-vis* political institutions, state agencies and trade unions. For example, the Italian Confederation of Industry is the peak association in Europe with the smallest membership (110,000 private firms of the industry sector versus more than 1 million firms of almost all the sectors of the economy of the French CNPF, the German BDA and the Spanish CEOE), but it is endowed with a mandate from, and (overall) a capacity of control towards, its members which is wider than that of its homologues.

5. *Political representativeness versus bureaucratic effectiveness.* The organs of peak associations may be composed mainly of *representatives* elected by the membership, namely entrepreneurs and managers, or by paid *officials* appointed by the associations. This makes a difference since, in the first case, the association interests will be defined and perceived on the basis of the direct perceptions of its membership and leadership. Meanwhile, in the second case, they will be defined on the basis of the organizational needs and resources (efficient use of foundings and staff, to make the most of technical competences, seeking political recognition and institutional incorporation, etc.). Not surprisingly, when a peak association has to increase its representativeness, it tends to enlarge and give more relevance to those organs composed of employers (such as the British CBI, the French CNPF and the Italian Confederation of Industry made by means of their reforms in the first half of the 1970s); and when it has to strengthen its lobbying and pressure capacity, it tends to reinforce its administrative staff of paid officials (such as UNICE, the Union of Industrial and Employers' Confederations of Europe, is currently doing). From this point of view it is quite interesting to look at the case of SAF (Svenska Arbetsgivareföreningen), the peak association of Swedish employers. This federation operates in a very 'hard' (not to say hostile) environment (strong trade unions and Social Democratic party) requiring long-term strategies because of the relevance of neo-corporatist arrangements in many policy areas. The main position is that of the director-general who is an official and not an employer.

These strategic choices[4] are hanging over each peak association and different responses are given to them depending on the characteristics of its membership, the mode in which it is born, the institutional constraints it has to face, and the scale on which it operates. Once these strategic choices are made, they become constraints themselves and make collective action more or less attractive for member associations.

The aim of this case study is, from these considerations, to analyse the case of a very peculiar peak association, UNICE, the unit that is the *peak association of the European peak associations* of the industry sector. More specifically, the aim is to try to understand how the above dilemmas are handled in the case of a transnational peak association that has the burden of organizing more than thirty national peak associations operating within more than twenty countries and representing some millions of firms ranging from very small firms to big multinational companies. After having analysed in the next section the organizational properties of UNICE, we seek to understand how these associative arrangements contribute to create the political unity of businesses at the European level.

UNICE: The Peak Associaton of European Employers

UNICE (Union of Industrial and Employers' Confederations of Europe), the most important of the peak associations representing the employers of the industry sector, was created in 1958 by the national employer federations of the six original EC members states (Belgium, Federal Republic of Germany, France, Italy, Luxembourg and the Netherlands). UNICE is not, however, the first form of business interest representation at the European level. The Council of European Industrial Federations (CIFE) was founded in the immediate post-war period (1949) and, after its demise in 1961, some of its functions were accomplished by the Business and Industrial Advisory Committee (BIAC). As Article 5 of its constitution underlines, UNICE was created as a coordinating body among industrial confederations versus the institutions of EC. Thus, even if it operates both in social and economic fields, its main interlocutors have always remained Community institutions and not, as might be expected, European trade unions. Even if its primary objective has been to canvass and influence EC institutions, membership of UNICE goes beyond the borders of the Community. As early as 1962, the Federation of Greek Industry was associated with its work. In 1972/73 the employers organizations of three new member states – the UK, Denmark and Ireland – joined UNICE, while employer associations from western European countries outside the Community also decided to become associated members. The present membership consists of thirty-two central federations of industry and employers from twenty-two countries – the twelve EC members, the six EFTA countries, Turkey, Cyprus, Malta and San Marino (Tyszkiewicz, 1991). Hence, 'UNICE is more than an organization of EEC employers but also an organization of European employers' (Oeschlin, 1980, p. 204). And so, not surprisingly, UNICE is currently strengthening its relationships with the employers of east European countries after the demise of communist regimes.

The structure of UNICE, just as that of any other BIA, is based on the double tier of elected representatives and paid officials – on the one hand, the president, the vice-president, etc., and on the other hand, the secretariat, the directors, etc.[5] According to organization theory, the more relevant the former group, the more the association depends on its membership, and the more relevant the latter group, the more the organization is autonomous and institutionalized.

A further distinction may be added between, on the one hand, the agencies endowed with direct legitimation (either directly elected if representatives or paid by UNICE bodies themselves if officials) and, on the other hand, those bodies possessing only an indirect legitimation since they are formed by representatives and officials chosen separately and sent as spokespersons by each member association. Again, the more relevant that directly legitimated bodies are, the higher the association's autonomy from its membership. The complex chart of UNICE can be analysed in terms of the above two-dimensional typologies in order to assess the association's degree of autonomy. As expected, the degree of autonomy of UNICE is quite low, since many of its bodies are composed of delegates from member associations. Only the top levels of the hierarchy, that is the president and vice-presidents, are directly elected by UNICE agencies themselves. Yet, it appears that many of the committees possessing indirect legitimation are formed by officials and not by representatives. So we may infer that member associations want to guarantee a stable presence in UNICE bodies, with highly technical competences.

Let us now turn to the decision-making process of UNICE. The decision-making structure of UNICE is more complex than that of other peak associations (Lanzalaco, 1992). If we look at the frequency with which the different bodies meet we may identify two different decision-making channels.

The first deals with long-term matters such as the general policies of the association, its budget and its organization. These are considered at the Council of Presidents and the Executive Committee. The low frequency of their meetings, however, and the fact that they are composed of actors (presidents and directors of national federations) that have their main activity in their home countries, render these bodies unable to deal with the current management of association policies. Indeed, the cornerstone of this activity is represented by:

1. The Committee of Permanent Delegates, composed of officials of member federations often living in Brussels and working in the same building of UNICE. These Permanent delegates are the actual 'ambassadors' of national federations.

2. The Policy committees (economic and financial affairs, external relations, social affairs, company affairs, industrial affairs) and the, approximately, fifty-five working groups within them; the members of the committees and the working groups are appointed by UNICE member federations, and the committee chairman and the two vice-chairmen are appointed by the UNICE president and are 'in most cases . . . senior managers from operating companies' (Tyszkiewicz, 1991, p. 91).

3. The secretariat plays a crucial role in supporting the activity of the committees and of the working groups, not only providing them

with information about the legislative outcomes, but also making sure that the final products of their activity, the so called 'position papers', have an impact on EC decision-makers.

UNICE has recently noticed its weakness in front of its member associations (Tyszkiewicz, 1991) and it has perceived the need to strengthen its presence. Recent reforms of UNICE are aimed at the following:

1. Reinforcing the secretariat in order to develop its capacity to translate the proposals of the committees and the working groups into effective political proposals.

2. Creating an Advisory and Support Group (UASG) composed of company representatives; no decision-making powers should pertain to it but it should only have to give advice and cooperate in financing.

Even at this stage of analysis it emerges that the 'decisional core' of UNICE is composed not only of member federation representatives, as we could expect, but also of managers and representatives of *individual firms*, in particular, of large companies. This presence is strengthened and institutionalized by the constitution of the UASG, but it is also assured by the modes of composition of the commission and working groups. Not surprisingly, UNICE has been accused of being the voice of big firms and of fostering EC policies that damage, or at least do not benefit, small firms (Grote, 1992).

Consensus-building Devices within UNICE

The organization properties of an association must be evaluated in conjunction with its policy outcomes (Schmitter and Streeck, 1981). Therefore, to understand how UNICE is able to represent the political unity of so large a membership, we have also to focus on UNICE's activity.

The first point we have to take into consideration is UNICE's policy domain. This peak association is a confederation only of 'horizontal' peak associations, namely of national *intersectoral* confederations. National or local *sector-* or *product-specific* associations are federated into several hundred sectoral *transnational* confederations that are not included in transnational intersectoral federations.[6] This very tight policy domain of UNICE is one important device which allows it to create political unity in spite of heterogeneity. The sectors represented and the functions accomplished by the member associations are very different from one another

(Lanzalaco, 1992) and so political unity can be reached only by identifying a 'lowest common denominator' among the various assciations. UNICE deals mainly with labour relations and general (not sector-specific) political questions, meanwhile questions concerning sectoral assets are dealt with by sectoral federations. In this way, UNICE *externalizes* inter- and intra-sectoral conflicts ('vertical issues'), one of the main obstacles to the political unity of the capitalist class (Streeck, 1988; Lanzalaco and Schmitter, 1992).

Secondly, regarding its activity as an employers' association, we have to take into consideration that it is not a contractual agent, so it can take positions for its members but it cannot stipulate collective agreements.[7] This device also allows UNICE, on the one hand, to avoid being overloaded by consensus-building problems and, on the other hand, to give its members wide margins for manouevre.

Thirdly, UNICE is entrenched with EC bureaucracy so it can be seen as an 'extension' of the Commission itself (Mazey and Richardson, 1993a, p. 194). This institutional incorporation clearly supports the action of UNICE and helps it to overcome, at least partially, the obstacles deriving from the 'individualistic' attitudes of its members (Tyszkiewicz, 1991) and from the survival of a strong national legacy (Greenwood *et al.* 1992; Lanzalaco, 1992).

These three factors jointly considered – restricted policy domain, limited representation mandate and strong institutional incorporation – reduce the possible challenges brought about by international divergencies.[8] In spite of these consensus-building devices, however, divisions emerge. For example, in the debate about the position UNICE has had to take concerning the so-called social dimension, even if UNICE globally has a position contrary to the establishment of a form of collective bargaining at the European level, some associations, for example the Italian, Belgian and Dutch, have been more sensitive than the British to the necessity of strengthening the social and labour market policies of the Community (Rhodes, 1992). These differences lead to cleavages within the federation, and the solution chosen when the differences seem to be too deep is to avoid public positions unless there is agreement among the largest member federations.

Another challenge to the political unity of European employers is the tendency of multinational companies to resort to individual action outside UNICE. In the European system of representation not only is there such a forum – namely the European Round Table (see Case 16) – in which individual large companies may participate directly and elaborate their common political positions, but also, more generally, as Mazey and Richardson (1993b) underline, there is a tendency for these large firms to establish direct relationships with European officials and civil servants. Euro officials, for their part, also foster this channel of communication, since company staff are able to provide them with the information they need. This tendency, which responds both to the needs of EC officials and to the pressure activity of companies – explains the increasing weight that companies have assumed within UNICE.

UNICE, then, follows a double route to strengthen its capacity to act as a political channel. On the one hand, in order to consolidate its position *vis-à-vis* member associations, it is reinforcing its secretariat and administrative staff and is adopting majority (and not unanimity) decision-making procedures. On the other hand, it is devoting more attention to large companies, giving them more weight in its decision-making structure so as to avoid individual action of firms.

Concluding Remarks

UNICE is weak as regards the national federations it combines, and its mandate to negotiate with both trade unions and European institutions is also limited. In the long term, we can can forecast that this situation will not change. This is because of the relative disorganization of trade unions (Case 19), and the tendency of European institutions to fragment representation into more specialized and limited policy domains. In turn, this is likely to reduce the role of UNICE and to foster sector-specific European associations.

The plurality of channels of influence and of strategies of action at the disposal of business (Greenwood and Jordan, 1993) makes the UNICE channel less relevant than we might at one time have imagined. Its relevance is likely to be confined to representing the general political function of European businesses and to create a 'forum' where businesses may define their general strategies in order to reinforce their identity and to define their long-term policies.[9] We may forecast, then, that UNICE will be exposed to the three challenges: (1) the role of specialized trade associations mobilizing their action and resources in specific policy domains giving their contribution to EC agencies; (2) the strong legacy that businesses maintain with their national confederations, given the relevant role that national channels of influence have; and (3) the individual action of big firms that will be able not only to free ride from collective action but also to interact directly with European agencies and institutions. The organizational devices that UNICE is adopting seem to be able to cope with all these challenges, since it is currently reinforcing both its central staffing, institutionalizing its decision making processes and giving space to large companies.

Where UNICE action seems to be weak is in its relationships with the small and medium-sized enterprises (SMEs). Even if UNICE has a section devoted to SMEs, their representation is quite divided on many policy issues and EC institutions seem to give much more space to big firms than to small and medium-sized ones (Grote, 1992). Problems of associability between firms of different sizes that are present at the national level seem to be incumbent also at the transnational level. What is quite striking is that in business interest this divide seems to be more relevant in representation than the allegiances based upon national identity.

To conclude, however, we have to remember that it would be misleading to interpret the relative weakness of UNICE as an indicator of the political weakness of European employers. In fact, as Streeck suggested in his seminal paper (1988, p. 3), in the case of business interest representation:

> political strength seemed to be associated with and protected by organisational weakness, as reflected in the strict limitation of the mandate under which business associations were permitted to take part in tripartite negotiations. Organisational weakness, in that it prevented a spillover of collective political intervention to subjects of 'managerial' or, for that matter, 'proprietorial privilege', thus served, paradoxically, as a source of strength.

Not surprisingly, then, the industry *sector* is unanimously recognized as one of the most powerful (for SME associations *too* powerful) lobbies at the European level and one of the main protagonists of European integration.

Notes

1. The author thanks Justin Greenwood for his comments on the first version of this case study and a careful revision of the English text.
2. Schmitter and Streeck (1981) maintain that management of diversity is the most relevant problem for business associability.
3. A first-order association is an association whose members are *firms*, a second-order association is an association whose members are *associations of firms*, and so on.
4. The choices that a peak association has to cope with are similar to those that an association has to face as regards firms of different sizes (van Waarden, 1991).
5. For a detailed analysis of the organization structure of UNICE see Tyszkiewicz (1991) and Lanzalaco (1992).
6. There is a radical difference, therefore, between the national and the transnational patterns of organizing peak associations: national peak associations include both sector-specific associations and sector-unspecific (horizontal) subnational associations, while transnational peak associations include only the latter.
7. From this perspective, we may conclude that business interest organizations are prone not only to *organizational minimalism* as suggested by van Waarden (1991) (namely the

tendency to limit their organizational structure and resources to as little as possible), but also to *policy minimalism*, namely the tendency to reduce the policy areas with which they deal as much as possible.

8. Another change concerns the gradual substitution of decision-making procedures that require unanimity (and their correlate, namely veto powers) with majoritarian rules (Tyszkiewicz, 1991).

9. This 'symbolic' function is evident if we take into consideration that intersectoral European peak associations such as UNICE emerged at the beginning of the construction of the EC political institutions, namely when their instrumental function was not relevant but their function as reinforcing European institutions was important (Lanzalaco, 1992).

References

Greenwood, J. and Jordan, A. G. (1993) 'The UK: a changing kaleidoscope', in van Schendelen, M. C. P. M. (ed.) *National Public and Private EC Lobbying*. Aldershot: Dartmouth.

Greenwood, J., Grote, J. R. and Ronit, K. (1992) Introduction to Greenwood, J., Grote, J. R. and Ronit, K. (eds) *Organised Interests and the European Community*. London: Sage.

Grote, J. R. (1992) 'Small firms in the European Community: modes of production, governance and territorial interest representation in Italy and Germany', in Greenwood, J., Grote, J. R. and Ronit, K. (eds) *Organised Interests and the European Community*. London: Sage.

Lanzalaco, L. (1992) 'Coping with heterogeneity: peak associations of business within and across western European nations', in Greenwood, J., Grote, J. R. and Ronit, K. (eds) *Organised Interests and the European Community*. London: Sage.

Lanzalaco, L. and Schmitter, P. C. (1992) 'Europe's internal market, business associability and the labour movement', in Regini, M. (ed.) *The Future of Labour Movements*. London: Sage.

Mazey, S. and Richardson, J. (1993a) 'Interest groups in the European Community', in Richardson, J. (ed.) *Pressure Groups*. Oxford: Oxford University Press.

Mazey, S. and Richardson, J. (1993b) 'Policy-making styles in the European Community: consultation of groups and the process of European integration'. Paper presented to the Third Biennial International Conference of the European Community Studies Association, Washington DC, 27–29 May 1993.

Oeschlin, J. (1980) 'Employers' organizations', in Blanpain, R. (ed.) *Comparative Labour Law and Industrial Relations*. Dordrecht: Kluwer.

Rhodes, M. (1992) 'The future of the 'social dimension': labour market regulation in post 1992 Europe', *Journal of Common Market Studies*, vol. 30, pp. 23–51.

Schmitter, P. C. (1983) 'Organizzazione degli interessi e rendimento politico', in Pasquino, G. (ed.) *Le società complesse*. Bologna: il Mulino.

Schmitter, P. C. and Streeck, W. (1981) 'The organisation of business interests'. Discussion Paper of the International Institute of Management Labour Market Policies Division, IIM/LMP 1981/13. Berlin: WZB.

Streeck, W. (1988) 'Interest variety and organising capacity: two class logics of collective action?' Paper presented at the International Conference on Political Institutions and Interest Intermediation, University of Konstanz, Germany, 20–21 April 1988.

Tyszkiewicz, Z. (1991) 'UNICE: the voice of European business and industry in Brussels: a programmatic self-presentation', in Sadowski, D. and Jacobi, O. (eds) *Employers' Associations in Europe: Policy and Organisation*. Baden-Baden: Nomos.

van Waarden, F. (1991) 'Two logics of collective action? Business associations as distinct from trade unions: the problems of associations of organisations', in Sadowski, D. and Jacobi, O. (eds) *Employers' Associations in Europe: Policy and Organisation*. Baden-Baden: Nomos.

ETUC and Trade Unions in Europe

Oliver Roethig[1]

The most striking aspect of the relationship between business and labour at the European level is the absence of significant dialogue or meaningful exchange. Business interests are anxious to keep it this way, but even trade unions in at least some of the member states, such as Germany, feel uneasy, since transnational intervention might challenge present arrangements which suit them. In others, like the UK, the European level represents the opportunity for trade unions to bypass the domestic government; but to what extent do they have the capacity to do so?

In the new Europe, trade unions encounter an environment that has a direct and growing impact on the way they pursue and safeguard their interests. Collective bargaining is affected by the ease with which companies act transnationally and with which regulatory systems are altered by legislation emanating from the European Union (EU). It is no longer sufficient to limit activities to the domestic arena. Trade unions have to enhance their transnational cooperation to be able to fulfil their main role: shaping industrial relations either by influencing legislators or by concluding collective agreements with employers.

The Agreement on Social Policy, which is annexed to the Maastricht Treaty, strengthened the hands of trade unions with regard to both approaches. Firstly, it has given new impetus to progress through legislation. The principal opposition of the British government to EU regulation on social and labour issues has been overcome by the establishment of a parallel policy-making structure allowing the other member states to advance on their own. Secondly, a formal consultation process of the two sides of industry (the social partners) has been institutionalized which precedes the drafting of relevant legislative proposals by the Commission (Article 3). Thirdly, the Agreement on Social Policy provides for a mechanism through which the social partners can conclude collective agreements that are legally binding, if sanctioned by the EU institutions (Article 4). On their request, it can even be used in place of legislating. In such instances, policy formulation (but not decision-making authority) is therefore transferred to them.

Although the Maastricht Treaty enhances the role of the two sides of industry on the European level and, in particular, gives them an incentive to cooperate, it is doubtful if they will use these opportunities. Employers remain opposed to binding EU regulations in this policy area and unions can expect more extensive EU legislation. Each side perseveres in achieving its goals against rather than with the other one by exerting pressure on EU legislators.

This case study, therefore, addresses the strategies employed by national trade union federations to influence EU policy-making, either individually or collectively through the European Trade Union Confederation (ETUC). Firstly, it assesses the impact of the European system of governance on trade union interests and their representation. This is followed by an analysis of the ETUC: how is policy-making conducted and how are interests aggregated? Then, the different channels are examined that can be used by the ETUC and its affiliates to represent their positions to EU decision-makers. The case concludes with an attempt to explain the patterns of trade union participation in EU policy-making.

The European Union and the Social Dimension

The EU forms a system of governance in which transnational, supranational and intergovernmental elements do not replace, but overlie and complicate the relations between the nation states (Taylor, 1993; Sbragia, 1992; Streeck and Schmitter, 1992). The latter remain the loci of main decision-making power as well as of interest identification and organization: national actors continue to be in charge of policy-making. The EU is therefore best described as a structure where domestic politics is extended to the European level and European regulation is incorporated into national systems. Thus, paradoxically, the Union is integrated into the different nation states rather than vice versa. The EU objective is to agree on common policies that address common problems, but that are implemented separately according to different national conditions and interests. It is about managing diversity together.

In contrast to legislative and policy development procedures in the member states, which are normally dominated by the ministries concerned, in the EU the procedures are non-centralized: the Commission is in charge of policy initiatives while the Council, representing national interests, is the ultimate decision-maker. Policy-making means a compromise between national sets of interests has to be found. Governments are confronted with the task of satisfying simultaneously the demands of each other and of their respective domestic clienteles. In the fields of social and labour issues particularly, such a pattern leads to a limitation of the potential for European regulation. Common European rules could challenge the differently evolved and often deeply ingrained symbiosis among capitalist competition, state regulation and the countervailing power of trade unions. Intervention poses a threat to the established balance among government, employers and labour that lies at the foundation of the state and society (Scharpf, 1990; Weidenfeld, 1990).

The consequence for policy-making is reflected in the comment of a government official that 'one century of tradition cannot be outvoted by a qualified majority'. Commission proposals are therefore only taken as a point of reference in the Council. Negotiations there continue until a mutually acceptable solution is found, and often proposals are virtually reinvented. Moreover, the objective is not to equalize national conditions, but to lay down minimum requirements that, on the whole, are below existing domestic standards and to leave implementation to individual countries (Jacobi, 1992). European rules are designed to conform with the regulatory systems of the member states: an aim defined in the Agreement on Social Policy (Article 1).

Nevertheless, principal opposition to a proposal by member states does not lead to a halt in negotiations. Bargaining continues with a view to remove as many obstacles as possible. Therefore, Council discussions on many stalled proposals have not been 'cheap talk' (Lange, 1992, p. 242), but an attempt to progress under adverse institutional and political conditions. When these are overcome, decision-making can proceed rapidly, as was recently demonstrated with the 1994 European works council directive (the formal legislative process took less than a year). Since Maastricht, the fashionable instrument for satisfying both the opponents and supporters of a proposal has been the use of opt-out clauses, by legislating either under the Agreement on Social Policy or within a legal instrument itself. An example for the latter option is the working time directive that allows member states to prescribe less stringent rules. Advancement is thus possible without imposing regulations on unwilling partners like the UK.

From the perspective of trade unions, the social, political and legal framework of a polity is of even greater importance than for other actors. They rely on it to overcome the structural inferiority of labour in its antagonistic relationship with employers, and therefore it is an essential source of their power. On a European level, a supportive structure for unions equivalent to those in the national arenas does not exist. Firstly, their members continue to be organized nationally and consequently demands arise from domestic circumstances so that the potential for transnational collective action, the ultimate weapon of unions, is low (Jacobi, 1990). Secondly, unions have no partner for the autonomous regulation of industrial relations, since European employers' associations have no mandate for collective bargaining (Lecher, 1991). Thirdly, there is no single authority through which labour friendly regulations can be established. Fourthly, wide variations exist in the structure of the member states, the national organization of labour and the ideology of unions. For instance, in Germany industrial relations are characterized by an extensive legal framework and trade unions that are in essence organized in one federation. In contrast, industrial relations are based on a voluntaristic approach in the UK, and in France the trade union movement is split into several, even competing federations (Barnouin, 1986; Visser and Ebbinghaus, 1992). Consequently, common transnational developments vary in their effect on national trade union organizations whose ability to cope with them also differs (Ferner and Hyman, 1992).

Why, under such circumstances, should national trade union federations focus their activities on the European level or cede competencies to a European umbrella organization? At least some of them are convinced that they can achieve more for their members in the national arena (Armingeon, 1991). Consequently, it can be argued that their involvement in EU policy-making is dependent neither on the substance of EU regulations nor on their potential influence on the supranational institutions. Instead, it is based on an organization's quite distinct needs and opportunities to maintain or improve regulatory conditions, its standing in the domestic environment and its position within the national movement. Thus, for consolidated union movements like the German Trade Union Federation (DGB), EU policy-making tends to be a side aspect of their domestic policies. For weaker movements, like the British Trades Union Congress (TUC), however, it is a replacement for the current partial exclusion from domestic policy-making (Minkin, 1991).

ETUC

The main trade union actor on the European level is the ETUC. It represents forty-six national federations and sixteen European industry committees, which are associations of national unions covering the same economic sectors. The role of the industry committees, however, is secondary to that of the federations within the ETUC, and also to that of the ETUC in EU policy-making. Together, affiliated federations represent about 47 million employees from twenty-two countries equivalent to roughly 86 per cent of the unionized workforce there (Visser and Ebbinghaus, 1992). Thus, the ETUC includes, with a few exceptions, all relevant labour organizations in Europe outside the former Eastern bloc. It is the main voice of trade unions on the European level and EU institutions recognize it as the representative of employees' interests in the EU (EU Commission, 1993).

Nevertheless, effective decision-making power still rests with the national federations, so that the ETUC's general task is to represent their common interests *vis-à-vis* the EU institutions (Rath, 1991; ETUC, 1991a). It is not a supranational organization with its own exclusive competencies to represent union members in certain areas. Since its foundation in 1973 the ETUC's functions, however, have developed beyond being merely a source of information and an instrument for cooperation among the affiliates. Today it increasingly forms a framework where policies are formulated that serve as guidelines for national unions and are represented collectively to EU decision-makers (Platzer, 1991).

Policy-making within the ETUC is split between a committee structure, through which the affiliates participate, and a secretariat. *De facto*, the latter is in charge of formulating, coordinating, and implementing policies. Under the overall responsibility of the general secretary, policy areas are allocated to seven departments that conduct policy-making more-or-less autonomously within the secretariat. Each department comprises a senior official, one policy and one administrative assistant. Altogether the ETUC employs forty-nine people, including support staff (ETUC, 1993). About the same number work for four bodies that are closely connected to the ETUC. They provide additional resources and are financed mainly by the Commission. The most important one is the European Trade Union Institute (ETUI), the ETUC's research arm (ETUC, 1991b). Although the ETUC is therefore one of the best resourced European interest groups, this does not overcome the principal impediment of the Secretariat: its resources are inadequate compared with the amount of legislation originating from the EU, the plethora of organizations representing business, and the number of government officials concerned with EU affairs (Platzer, 1991).

The ETUC's formal decision-making body between the four-yearly congresses is the executive committee whose main task is to direct and sanction activities. Basically, it is composed of senior officials from the affiliated organizations. From its midst a steering committee is elected that acts on its behalf between sessions. Its members are in effect the permanent representation of the affiliates, although it meets formally only eight times a year. The steering commitee, supervises the secretariat and conducts high-level lobbying. In the detailed work of the secretariat, the affiliates participate through eight standing committees and six working groups. Each meets twice yearly and comprises middle-ranking union officials (ETUC, 1991a, c). However, all these are unwieldy bodies through which policy coordination and formulation is difficult. Their membership is too big and diverse for focused discussion. Neither do they meet frequently enough to keep abreast of EU developments or to deal with all relevant issues for which the ETUC is responsible.

Ultimately, the committee structure does not provide an adequate mechanism for aggregating common interests and exercising control over ETUC activities. Policy-making, therefore, very much depends on informal channels, centring on the respective departmental head in the ETUC secretariat. Firstly, there are personal contacts, based especially on national affinity, that serve as a source of informal technical and political advice and which also give affiliates an interlocutor who has an intimate understanding for their concerns. Secondly, networks on particular issues emerge. These networks include representatives of affiliates whose expertise is useful for, or who cannot be ignored in, the formulation of an ETUC policy. Nevertheless, the linkage remains insufficient for close and permanent cooperation, since the European arena and the national arenas are not integrated either within the ETUC or within the EU. Hence, actors participate in policy-making with only a partial view of the overall picture; they are very much confined to their own sphere. As the authoritative voice of trade unions on the European level, a departmental head is relatively free in pursuing policies, based on his interpretation of positions put forward by the federations' representatives. Policy-making relies very much on his or her competency, experience and intuition. His discretion is, however, limited by the relevance of issues to affiliates and the degree of affiliates' intervention and agreement.

Although decisions can be made by a two-third majority of the executive committee or congress, affiliates and secretariat still 'endeavour to reach the widest possible measure of agreement' (ETUC, 1991a, Articles 10 and 16). This is prompted by the absence of any mechanism for enforcing ETUC decisions. Nevertheless, larger affiliates, particularly the DGB, can press for or attempt to block specific policies (Turner, 1993; Dolvik, 1993). ETUC officials also have to consider that many members are part of their respective national arrangements. ETUC policies that would contradict national ones are therefore in danger of being rejected or ignored by the respective affiliate in order to maintain domestic influence. Furthermore, their position in the national arena gives unions access to EU decision-makers without the need to dilute their positions within the ETUC. Consequently, the discretion of the secretariat ranges from relative independence on uncontroversial issues to policies, especially concerning non-decisions, that are virtually prescribed by member organizations. Policies are formulated and executed according to a more or less strict framework made up of the essential concerns of affiliates.

The outcome is often incoherent, reflecting the disparities within the trade union movement, but also being vague enough to allow everybody to agree and to interpret policies according to own needs. As a result, the ETUC as a whole is able to project a common approach to the outside world while everyone, secretariat and affiliates, is left with the opportunity to work through its own channels and thus to maximize its individual impact on the EU policy-making process. Each can argue that it is backed by the whole movement, and affiliates can highlight points, referring to their concerns in the ETUC position, but expand on them with special reference to national conditions. In the end, however, everyone has to rely on its own strength. The ETUC is not a means to overcome an affiliate's domestic weakness.

Influencing EU Institutions

Besides acting through the ETUC, national federations have two other options to participate in EU policy-making. Firstly, they may approach EU institutions directly. Influence may be exerted on the Commission, the Council or governments of other countries; they may also act through their representatives in the Economic and Social Committee (ESC) or by targeting members of the European Parliament (EP). Secondly, federations can utilize their normal domestic arrangements and resources. The focus in this section is on the ability of the ETUC and national federations to influence the different EU institutions (for this section, see ETUC, 1991b, pp. 36–44).

Beforehand, however, it is worth looking briefly at the so-called social dialogue. Under the auspices of the Commission, the social dialogue brings together the social partners: the ETUC and the two employers' associations UNICE and CEEP. Although some non-binding joint agreements have been reached, for instance on education and vocational training, its impact on policy-making has been small. The exception, albeit by chance, is the 'Agreement of 31 October 1991' on which the Maastricht Agreement on Social Policy was largely modelled (*European Industrial Relations Review*, no. 216, January 1992, p. 2). In the end, the social dialogue has some moderate influence on the EU agenda. It is, however, an instrument neither for policy-making nor for developing a common approach on specific policies among the social partners (their positions are too antagonistic).

The main target of ETUC interest representation is the Commission, due to its leading role during the preparation of legislative proposals. As already mentioned, the ETUC and employers' associations are consulted formally, though most issues raised have already been discussed bilaterally with the Commission beforehand. On an informal level, relations focus on those sections of the Commission bureaucracy dealing with social and labour affairs, namely DG V and the commissioner in charge of it. Good contacts also existed with President Delors, based on his championship of a social dimension and his ties to the French union movement (Turner, 1993; Platzer, 1991).

The ETUC's relationship to the Commission is underpinned by the need of the latter to gain information and support to counterbalance the expertise and power of the twelve governments (Barnouin, 1986). Since employers are often opposed to legislation in the social field, the ETUC is almost by default the only available partner in the early drafting stage. It is then that the ETUC secretariat has the greatest impact (Turner, 1993). Later, the Commission has to accommodate other interest groups too. Moreover, when the Council enters the process, the Commission's objective changes to finding a compromise among the member states: social interests then take second place (Hull, 1993). Besides the ETUC, national trade union federations and even single unions have opened offices in Brussels and have established their own contacts with EU institutions. Nevertheless, they are generally seen by the Commission as an additional source of support and information. Overall, ETUC officials remain the chief players *vis-à-vis* the Commission. They are the only ones who can wield the combined influence and authority of the ETUC member organizations.

With regard to the EP and the ESC, the influence of the ETUC and its affiliates is, in contrast, roughly balanced. In Parliament, MEPs are elected nationally and thus relationships to unions are dominated by personal entwinement and loyalties on the domestic level. One example is the quasi-institutionalized arrangement between the TUC and British Labour MEPs. Besides extensive informal contacts, ETUC officials meet monthly with the Trade Union Intergroup bringing together MEPs mainly from the Party of European Socialists and the European People's Party. Despite the EP's limited powers, it has been helpful in advancing trade union policies, particularly as there is at present a socialist majority and there are many supportive MEPs from other parties. Parliament is used mostly to introduce changes to a legislative proposal that have not been taken up by the Commission beforehand or to react to alterations by the Council. To do this effectively, the actions of the ETUC and the affiliates have to be coordinated: a common line has to be found and pressure has to be exerted on those MEPs over which each organization has influence. Because of the heterogeneity of the ETUC, it is a difficult task.

The role of the Economic and Social Committee (ESC) is even smaller than that of Parliament. It merely has to be consulted on some legislation, yet even then its work is widely ignored by other EU institutions (Nugent, 1991). Nevertheless, its opinions sometimes have an impact on policy developments, particularly on broad political issues, if they reflect a consensus among the ESC's three groups representing employers, workers and other interests. One example was the adoption of the Social Charter (Rhodes, 1991). The ESC workers' group is almost entirely composed of serving trade union officials from ETUC affiliates so that cooperation with the ETUC secretariat is very close – even to the extent that the policy-making processes are sometimes interlinked. The secretariat is involved in the selection of the rapporteurs from the workers' group and supports them in their work. Conversely, the rapporteurs are often entrusted with the formulation of ETUC policies in parallel with their ESC work, and often they are also in charge of the respective issue in their federation. In the end, the policies of the workers' group very much parallel those of the ETUC: they have the same constituency and thus arrive at a similar consensus.

The limited role of the ETUC in influencing EU legislation becomes especially evident when a proposal is tabled in the Council. During this phase, negotiations are conducted mostly at expert level in the Council's working party for social affairs and are tightly controlled by national ministries. The ETUC secretariat, therefore, relies largely on the influence of the national federations. Its own role is mainly to collect information throughout Europe about the governments' bargaining positions, and indeed, it is able to gather a fairly accurate picture. This information allows the identification of problems and governments that must and can be targeted to forward trade union interests. Influence is then exerted in close cooperation by the secretariat and the respective affiliates. The aim might be to organize support for trade union positions or a blocking majority, enhancing the power of the EP, whose amendments will then stand. They may also try to convince a government to withdraw a reservation on a specific provision. On a few issues, such as the Maastricht Treaty, ETUC representatives visited all heads of government individually, except the British, to put forward trade union positions. Yet, the ETUC's function is that of a moderator trying to organize a common approach, whereas influencing governments remains the domain of national federations.

Strategies and Influence

Due to the non-centralized nature of EU policy-making, interest groups are faced with the problems that not only do the actors in charge change during the legislative process, but so too does the arena where influence is best exerted. Moreover, the Council is a collective decision-maker that is insulated from direct outside interference. Policies promoted by the ETUC or national federations have therefore only a chance to be considered, if they win at least the support of one member state or the Commission.

In most countries, trade union federations, as the authoritative voice of organized labour, are important players in politics and have privileged access to national decision-makers. Ideally, a federation would not need to exert much pressure on its government to influence EU policy-making. Both, together with the employers, would be tied up in an extensive institutional and regulatory framework. Policies would be based on a generally accepted status quo over the contents of regulation as well as the balance of power among actors. The discretion of all participants to pursue different policies would therefore be severely restricted, if one does not intend to unravel the existing equilibrium. Civil servants would be able, and would in effect be compelled, to anticipate trade union positions, even when comments would not be forthcoming. Labour movements from such a background are also advantaged by the character of EU policy-making on social issues: it emphasizes the protection of established structures. Convergence will therefore tend to move towards their systems, since defending these is a far easier task than dismantling them.

For these most influential affiliates, the ETUC is only of secondary importance, thereby limiting its potential to influence EU policy-making. Not only do they provide relatively few resources but they also tend to block collective policies that are not in line with their national requirements. Consequently the ETUC is not able to fill the role of an interest group that can negotiate authoritatively for its membership and agree on specific and detailed policies in its name. This precondition for the establishment of a tripartite structure centring on the Commission and dominating EU policy-making on social issues is thus lacking.

Nevertheless, the ETUC is an important actor in the European arena. Its influence, however, is based not so much on physical resources and internal consistency of policies as on the image that it can project. It represents trade union positions vociferously and is judged to possess at least the latent potential to rally affiliates around a policy and, therefore, to be able to exert pressure through some governments on the EU decision-making process. It is worthwhile for the Commission to include the ETUC in its deliberations and to take account of its proposals for future developments. Thus, the ETUC is a helpful means for national federations to influence EU policy-making, both with regard to agenda-setting and policy formulation while the Commission is in charge.

Yet, for trade unions without adequate access to government, such as the TUC, the ETUC is an insufficient instrument for overcoming their lack of influence at home. It cannot represent and put its resources behind nationally focused interests. These affiliates therefore have an incentive to develop their own channels to EU institutions. Direct lobbying is, however, faced by either of two problems: Firstly, the positions of unions lobbying directly take second place to other trade union actors with a closer relationship with the target (e.g. Commission/ETUC versus Commission/ TUC). Secondly, unions lobbying directly, depend on intermediaries for the presentation of their positions to Council members, thus requiring the accommodation of other interests (e.g. targeting the EP). To exert influence, such a federation either has to be content with policies that do not challenge those of actors who have a more direct say or it has to adapt its policies to theirs.

For national federations, a hierarchy of strategies to influence EU policy-making may be proposed. In the first place, national federations trust that the established regulatory and institutional system will perforce bind government to act on their behalf. If this is not so, they will try to approach national policy-makers first. The second option is to use the ETUC, and if even this is insufficient, they will target EU institutions directly. Of course, this is a simplification and federations will tend to use all strategies simultaneously, though with different vigour, depending on their opportunities and needs.

In the end, trade unions have to trust in the resilience of the domestic structures from those countries where they are strong and influential. The EU is not a means to advance labour interests beyond the level that has already been reached there. Nevertheless, the European arena may be used to push for upward convergence. After Maastricht, this is a feasible approach. Whereas in the past trade unions have generally been seen as less successful than business in influencing EU policy-making, this seems now to have reversed. Employers can no longer rely on a policy that aims at blocking the enactment of legislation. To be influential, they have to put forward positions that address the contents of proposals, a policy that has been pursued by the ETUC over the years on many stalled issues. Its viewpoints have therefore often become integrated into compromises already achieved in the Council that now await enactment under the Agreement on Social Policy. To effect changes now will be a difficult task for business.

Note

1.   This case study is based on information obtained from interviews with European, German and British trade union officials as well as with officials of EU institutions and the German government. It is also based on experience gained through internships with Euro-FIET, TUC, ETUC and the German Labour Ministry over the period 1989-94.

References

Armingeon, K. (1991) 'Die doppelte Herausforderung der europäischen Gewerkschaften', *Gewerkschaftliche Monatshefte*, vol. 42, pp. 371–381.

Barnouin, B. (1986) *European Labour Movement and European Integration*. London: Pinter.

Dolvik, J. E. (1993) Towards a Europeanisation or Renationalisation of Nordic Trade Union Strategies?' Paper presented at the conference 'Perspektiven europäischen Arbeitsbeziehungen: Sind europäische Kollektivverhandlungen möglich?', Gustav Heinemann Akademie in Freudenberg, 26–28 May 1993.

ETUC (1991a) *Constitution of the European Trade Union Confederation as Approved by the 7th Statutory Congress*. Luxembourg, 13–17 May 1991.

ETUC (1991b) *For a More Efficient ETUC* (Stekelenburg Report).

ETUC (1991c) *VIIth Statutory Congress: Report on Activities 88/90*. Luxembourg, 13–17 May 1991.

ETUC (1993) *Organigramme de la Confédération Européenne des Syndicats*. 5 February 1993.

EU Commission (1993) *Communication Concerning the Application of the Agreement on Social Policy*. COM(93) 600 final, 14 December 1993.

Ferner, A. and Hyman, R. (1992) 'Introduction. Industrial relations in the new Europe: seventeen types of ambiguity', in Ferner, A. and Hyman, R. (eds) *Industrial Relations in the New Europe*. Oxford: Blackwell, pp. xvi–xxxix.

Hull, R. (1993) 'Lobbying Brussels: A View from Within', in Mazey, S. and Richardson, J. J. (eds) *Lobbying in the European Community*. Oxford: Oxford University Press, pp. 82–94.

Jacobi, O. (1990) 'Bausteine einer Europäisachen Zukunftsgesellschaft',*Die Neue Gesellschaft/Frankfurter Hefte*, March, pp. 218–224.

Jacobi, O. (1992) 'Industrielle Demokratie und intermediäre Organisationen in Europa', *WSI-Mitteilungen*, vol. 45, pp. 773–779.

Lange, P. (1992) 'The politics of the social dimension', in Sbragia, A. M. (ed.) *Euro-politics: Institutions and Policymaking in the 'New' European Community*. Washington DC: Brookings Institute, pp. 225–255.

Lecher, W. (1991) 'Konturen europäischer Tarifpolitik', WSI-Mitteilungen, vol. 44, pp. 194–201.

Minkin, L. (1991) *The Contentious Alliance: Trade Unions and the Labour Party*. Edinburgh: Edinburgh University Press.

Nugent, N. (1991) *The Government and Politics of the European Community* (2nd edn). London: Macmillan.

Platzer, H. (1991) *Gewerkschaftspolitik ohne Grenzen? Die transnationale Zusammenarbeit der Gewerkschaften im Europa der 90er Jahre?* Cologne: Dietz.

Rath, F. (1991) 'Strukturelle Koordination gewerkschaftlicher Europapolitik', in Däubler, W.

and Lecher, W. (eds) *Die Gewerkschaften in den 12 EG-Ländern: Europäische Integration und Gewerkschaftsbewegung*. Cologne: Bund-Verlag, pp. 233–283.

Rhodes, M. (1991) 'The social dimension of the single European market: national versus transnational regulation', *European Journal of Political Research*, vol. 19, pp. 245–280.

Sbragia, A. M. (1992) 'Thinking about the European future: the uses of comparison', in Sbragia, A. M. (ed.) *Euro-politics: Institutions and Policy-making in the 'New' European Community*. Washington DC: Brookings Institute, pp. 257–291.

Scharpf, F. W. (1990) 'Regionalisierung des europäischen Raums: Die Zukunft der Bundesländer im Spannungsfeld zwischen EG, Bund und Kommunen', in von Alemann, U., Heinze, R. G. and Hombach, B. (eds) *Die Kraft der Region: Nordrhein-Westfalen in Europa*. Bonn: Dietz.

Streeck, W. and Schmitter, P. C. (1992) 'From national corporatism to transnational pluralism: organized interests in the single European market', in Streek, W. (ed.) *Social Institutions and Economic Performance: Industrial Relations in Advanced Capitalist Economies*. London: Sage, pp. 197–232.

Taylor, P. (1993) *International Organization in the Modern World: The Regional and the Global Process*. London: Pinter.

Turner, L. (1993) 'Beyond national unionism? Cross-national labor collaboration in the European Community. Prepared for the conference 'Rethinking the Boundaries of Labor Politics: New Directions for Comparative Research and Theory', Minda de Gunzburg Center for European Studies, Harvard University, December 1993.

Visser, J. and Ebbinghaus, B. (1992) 'Making the most of diversity? European integration and transnational organization of labour', in Greenwood, J., Grote, J. and Ronit, K. (eds) *Organised Interests and the European Community*. London: Sage, pp. 206–237.

Weidenfeld, W. (1990) 'Die Bilanz der Europäischen Integration 1989/90: Abschied von der alten Ordnung', in Weidenfeld, W. and Wessels, W. (eds) *Jahrbuch der Europäischen Integration 1989/90*. Bonn: Europa Union Verlag, pp. 13–27.

Conclusions

Justin Greenwood

Drawing conclusions from a book of nineteen different cases and issues in a diverse range of domains may appear to be a difficult task, yet a number of themes persist throughout this collection. Strategic decision-making in business is not possible without reference to the external environment. The importance attached by business to the European level is evident, both in studying public policy outputs/outcomes and in the resources invested in political and collective action. In all of the cases examined, no significant business actor could remain as such without paying attention to events in Brussels, Luxembourg and Strasbourg.

Impact of Business Interests on European Public Policies

Any reader still in doubt about the impact of business interests on European public policies need only glance once again at no more than two chapters, starting perhaps with Maria Green Cowles' case of the European Round Table of Industrialists (ERT), a 'rich firm club'. This is a case where business interests have not only influenced public policies, but also set and driven the European agenda, most notably through proposing the single market project and, where national governments showed signs of reluctance, by ensuring their support, if necessary by the threat of investment withdrawal (Case 16). This is as clear a case of the neo-functionalist 'spillover' mechanism as one could wish to find. Not only have large businesses, through ERT, driven fundamental economic issues on the European agenda, but they have also intervened effectively in infrastructure support areas, such as education and training of the workforce. Rather than the ERT having to 'pressure' a Commissioner to come to the meeting table, Green Cowles finds evidence of the reverse process, i.e. of the Commission coming to ERT for policy formulation. ERT members are sought for strategy meetings or to present the

285

Commission's case at press conferences. This type of ingrained involvement by private interests in public policy-making should make us reject popular images of pressure politics conducted through media campaigns, or of hired hands showing up one day bearing gifts and persuasion, not to be seen again until the next crisis emerges, as a characterization of the operation of private interests in public affairs. Those whose interests are secured through their involvement in 'policy communities' rely instead on their ability to exchange key power-dependent resources as a means of shaping public policies.

Resource Exchange: The Key Unit of Analysis

Some of the large firm members of the European Round Table of Industrialists have more resources at their disposal than do member states. It should come as no surprise that they are significant political actors in the European Union. There is most certainly a pattern evident when seeking to make sense of European interest representation; those in possession of key resources to exchange with public interlocutors become insider groups, while those without them remain outsiders. No matter how sharp the haircuts or suits are of 'case presenters', no matter how wily the tactics employed, interests not in possession of key resources cannot obtain insider access to shape public policy-making and implementation. Furthermore, as Dan Morrison shows in Case 15, neither can the 'purchasing' of key former officials with established networks of interpersonal contacts be a substitute for resource indispensability. Of course, employing the right tactics can contribute to the interest obtaining a satisfactory outcome, but the core issue remains possession and exchange of key resources.

This established, the question is then, which resources are key resources? The answer can only be given in full by studying the particular relationship between the private and public interest. For instance, the mere production of statistics about the economic value of an 'industry' product will not tell us everything we need to know in order to judge whether an interest will obtain insider status. We would need to know, for instance, how well those potential 'bargaining chips' are organized for representational purposes; how well defined a sector is; how strategic its resources are to the European Union; what degree of Euro competencies exist in the domain; and to what extent an issue is politicized, affording easier access to groups who might otherwise be outsiders (see, for instance, Case 6). Thus, the 'world's largest industry', tourism (Case 9), scores badly on most of these criteria, and it is therefore no surprise to find that tourism interests are more of outsider than an insider. Similarly, Airbus Industrie, a genuine European business alliance, has only recently enjoyed insider status in the Commission as a result of external events which forced the development of Euro competencies (Case 4). This suggests the dynamic, rather than fixed and static, nature of insider status, a concept which is illustrated clearly by the case of cement (Case 6), where the Euro association has had to reorientate itself to cope with entry into the policy arena by non-industrial groups as a result of the degree of politicization of environmental issues. As reviewed in the introduction, the work of Maloney *et al.* (1995) reminds us that there are different types of insider status. Thus, Philips and Thomson (Case 3) have found their core insider status disrupted by both the presence of other types of interest and a combination of circumstances. For each case under consideration, it is necessary to study the actors involved and the resources that are exchanged, whether actual, potential or latent, and to assess the stability of these factors.

Methods of Studying European Business Alliances and Public Policy

One methodological difficulty encountered by researchers in seeking to identify the dynamic nature of insider status concerns the focus of study. Decisions are an insufficient basis because 'non-decisions' can be just as significant, if not more so: failure to regulate on safety standards of say, sea-going passenger ferries, is likely to have just as far-reaching consequences as if regulation had occurred. We need to be able to know why non-decisions arise, particularly where there are groups whose interests would be better served by a decision. Inductive conceptualization (i.e. generating ideas from case study evidence) from sets of cases based around events is thus insufficient. Without privileged access to the corridors of power it is not always easy to identify non-decisions, and indeed the nature of these is that a non-decision might never be discussed, i.e. it is latent (Lukes, 1977). As Lindblom (1977) suggests, the power of business need not always be exercised to be present, and indeed Clegg and Dunkerley (1980) go further and suggest that the power of capital is enshrined within and throughout the routines of capitalist societies. As I have suggested above, resources as raw as 'capital' may need further organization to be operationalized in public policy outputs and outcomes. However, once the resources which are exchanged are fully identified, whether overt, covert or latent, it is possible to construct models which help us understand the extent to which these are likely to occur, such as neo-pluralism and neo-corporatism.

Neo-pluralism and neo-corporatism are terms which can be applied to particular sets of circumstances encountered, rather than to deductive, starting-point theories. Notwithstanding, they do help us explain both the outputs and outcomes of public policies; for instance, if the resources exchanged are of a particular type and significance, then such a symbiotic, intertwined relationship might arise that fulfils the characteristics of a tightly knit 'policy community', or neo-corporatism, from which policy outputs and

outcomes arise. However, for each particular type of relationship we study we need to be able to identify the resources being exchanged, including the type of policy under consideration. This does not mean, however, that we cannot proceed beyond the level of generating empirical detail. Ideas emerge from case study research which can be formulated into more general hypotheses. By selecting crucial cases (Eckstein, 1979) for the type of issue under investigation (i.e. most or least likely scenarios for issues to occur), we can investigate hypotheses through the selection of other cases. For instance, in the case of pharmaceuticals, I hypothesized that the ability of a European federation of national federations to work successfully was in part dependent upon the commonality of national regulatory experiences which members faced (Case 2). A search would then be made for another case where similar circumstances prevailed. For both cases, of course, it would also be necessary to isolate the factors involved as regards the presence of other contributory issues.

The approach here is inductive, using case study evidence as the basis for conceptual development, rather than deductive, involving prior theoretical speculation which has not arisen from case evidence. This is not to confuse the inductive method with 'logical positivism', though, where a concept has to be measurable in order to be investigated. Case study evidence can contribute to constructivist-type methodologies, where issues present themselves from cases and seem plausible, but which nevertheless cannot be empirically measured. Case studies can stimulate the theoretical imagination, where issues arise and can be investigated through other cases, without having to 'measure them'. Thus, the idea that bureaucratic agency fragmentation invites competitive interest representation through nourishing different sorts of symbiotic relationship cannot be measured, but it can be investigated through different case study evidence collection methods.

'Policies Make Politics': The Example of the Product Cycle

The 'policies make politics' approach described in the introduction indicates that we could expect to find in sectoral domains the sorts of influence evident in the case of ERT with macro economic policy, provided that particular types of resource exchange were present. Businesses have different types of interests. The first categorization is that between employer and producer-type interests. A second might be to subdivide these into different types of contexts and concerns. For instance, different types of policies, and associability, arise at different stages in the product life cycle.[1] Products based on significant new technologies require support to develop, enable and legitimize the technologies used. Established products from mature industries coming under competition from producers in low-cost, newly emerging economies require quite different kinds of policies to sustain them. Regulatory and deregulatory types of policies may also be linked to different stages in the product life cycle; typically, new products demand regulation while old markets may be characterized by a process of deregulation and reregulation. Both types of product market may require promotion, but perhaps of a different kind. 'Policies make politics' therefore provides the intellectual foundation for meso-level studies, and the methodological basis for case study research. Different clusters of interests emerge around different types of policies, and we should expect differences to arise between domains.

Forms of Associability 1: Rich Firm Clubs and Direct Membership

The European Round Table of Industrialists (ERT) demonstrates the importance of 'rich firm club' -type networks, where the organizational format is flexible enough to permit different configurations of firms acting in particular domains. This contrasts rather with the case of the business 'peak' organization, representing highly federated structures covering both producer and employer interests, where platform-building is notoriously difficult (Case 18). However, as Lanzalaco shows, such a weakness adds up to a strength when it means that the association is unable to enter into dialogue as a 'social partner' with trade unions, because it is precisely that form of dialogue which many UNICE members have sought to prevent developing at the European level.

Laura Cram's case of information technology shows that the influence of business at a sectoral level can be just as significant as that exerted at a more macro level. Here, another 'rich firm club', the European IT Roundtable, has been responsible for the development of a range of Euro competencies, this time in the formation of a key research and development programme, ESPRIT, which continues to dominate the EU budget for research. Here, large firms have been significant political players, although the Commission preference for collective structures means that a range of collective strategies, from associational, club, alliances and large-firm action is evident. Although the federation ORGALIME, in existence since 1954, has not been without its problems, it does represent a structure for both large and smaller firms, and hence its attractiveness to the Commission, concerned to see that acorns have the chance to grow into mature oaks. This sort of representational ability may sustain federated structures, and indeed one disadvantage of 'rich firm clubs' is that, by excluding the smaller firms they invite competitive interest representation, particularly in cases where the Commission considers that smaller firms have a strategic role to play. This pattern is evident in the case of biotechnology (Case 5). Where there is agency fragmentation there is considerable scope for 'rival' associations to sustain themselves by forming symbiotic relationships with one part of the bureaucracy concerned; the Senior Advisory Group Biotechnology (SAGB) enjoys a close relationship with DG III (industrial affairs; single market) and DG VI (agriculture), while the 'rival' European Secretariat of National Biotechnology Associations (ESNBA) has developed close relations with DG XI (environmental affairs), whose profile is not as friendly to producer groups than are those of DGs III and VI.

Having to cope with agency fragmentation is an important management task facing almost all business interests in the European Union. McLaughlin's quotation of a Commission official describing the relationship with a unit in another directorate-general (DG) – 'quite simply, it's war' – is stark. Managing diversity represents both a threat and an opportunity. A threat in the sense that policy outputs carefully negotiated with one DG can be disrupted by the activities (intentional or not) of another unit, but an opportunity too in that hostility can be contained by finding a sponsor 'department'. The SAGB has successfully steered a course through this minefield by ensuring the creation of the Biotechnology Coordinating Committee consisting of the four directorate-generals concerned, and in doing so has partly marginalized the more hostile DG XI. Its success in this endeavour partly explains Jacques Delor's comments that this 'rich firm club' is the most effective of all Euro groups.

Direct firm membership formats are evident in around half the cases examined. They have mushroomed since the development of the single market project, not least in response to the difficulties experienced by highly federated formats in platform-building and the ability to be able to respond speedily. Here, direct firm membership formats enjoy an obvious advantage, because their relationship to their members is that much more direct. The enhanced competency of the EU meant that business interests needed to be able to respond quickly and with coherence to developments. Interest groups in some domains changed formats from federated structures to direct firm membership, as can be seen in the case of automobiles (Case 12). The flexibility of direct firm membership formats is evident in both the ERT and European IT Roundtable, where the expertise of different networks of large firms can be used to respond to different types of issue. In both of these cases, an exclusive community of firms that know and trust each other has been formed. In turn, these have formed 'policy communities' with the relevant parts of the Euro bureaucracies, built upon resource exchanges between key actors, whether they be institutions or interpersonal.

Cawson (Case 3), Jacek (Case 14), Cram (Case 1) and Vipond (Case 7) show how large firms have been able partly to depoliticize issues through turning them into technical concerns, and in doing so have made issue management easier. This process has also assisted the creation of European political alliances: Cawson describes the case of two entrenched rivals, Philips and Thomson, teaming up to ensure the choice of the same technology use in consumer markets for broadcasting. A number of economic alliances have arisen from requirements to pool technologies, and, as these cases show, so too have political alliances. Technical issues therefore facilitate, and demand, collective action strategies: an issue returned to later.

Jacek (Case 14) and Morrison (Case 15) show how exclusion has helped American and Japanese firms find their own effective channels of influence in Europe. Although American firms have a tradition of operating on their own as 'freebooters', exclusion by European firms has helped foster a common identity of national firms operating together in Europe. The EC Committee of the American Chamber of Commerce (ECACC) is regarded as one of the most effective of all groups. In the case of Japanese firms, exclusion from Euro groups may have provided them with an advantage in the sense that they have not been obliged to act collectively.

Forms of Associability 2: Federated Structures

It is interesting that all the direct firm formats are 'rich firm clubs'; small firms do not have the ability to form direct-line membership Euro associations on their own, and indeed they are dependent upon the resources of larger players for European-level representation. Historically, problems have arisen in associations where large and smaller firm interests are given equal say, and part of the secret to coherence seems to be to balance Euro federations in favour of large firms while at the same time leaving sufficient say for smaller interests to retain their membership. Such a balance is evident in the case of the European Federation of Pharmaceutical Industry Associations (Case 2). Here, the delegation of a significant degree of autonomy to the secretariat, or a core steering committee, enables the association to resemble direct firm membership formats in speed of decision-making, and such a mechanism is evident in the cases of water (Case 10; described by Maloney as a core insider group) and retailing (Case 8), in addition to pharmaceuticals. These factors are key to the success of a Euro group. All of these industries, with the addition of textiles (Case 11), display examples of effective federations of national federations. In the case of Eurocommerce, agreement has been possible among the national business interests where national governments have failed to agree. Some of the above Euro federations involve private interests in public policies through both formulation and implementation, which fulfil part of the criteria for the 'neo-corporatist' label. Successful 'mixed' formats also arise, where members are both associations and firms, as is evident in the case of cement (Case 6) and shipping (Case 13).

Successful federated formats appear to strike a balance between utilizing own and member resources. The advantage of this is that it keeps the membership fees down (Case 10), while at the same time keeping members involved. In Case 7, Vipond describes how the European Banking Federation uses the resources not just of its national members, but of their constituent firm members. This seems an excellent way to legitimize the activities of a

highly federated organization to otherwise remote members. In Euro-
Commerce too, the use of national interest group resources is one of the
factors contributing to an effective Euro group (Case 8).

In addition to the factors reviewed above, a number of further
hypotheses for effectiveness in European-level federations are explored in
Case 2. These include:

- The similarity of national regulatory styles encountered by the
  member organizations.
- The level of experiences, coupled with the multinational nature, of
  firms in the domain.
- The presence of prior experience in engaging transnational
  regulatory authority.
- The status of industrial activities undertaken and their attractiveness
  to the Commission.
- The degree of regulation demanded.
- The track record of the group.
- The sectoral definition of the interest represented.

Some of these factors, such as the degree of regulation demanded, are present
in the case of other effective European-level federations (in this instance
water). However, the examples of EuroCommerce and COMITEXTIL do not
provide 'crucial cases' for the comparative investigation of these hypotheses
with pharmaceuticals, and further work is therefore required to explore their
plausibility.

More entrenched difficulties are evident in the case of the European
Trade Union Confederation (ETUC) (Case 19). Lanzalaco (Case 18) draws our
attention to the fact that the logics underpinning collective action which is
based upon the representation of organizations is quite different from that
which underpins the representation of individuals. Trade Union membership
is ultimately based upon the latter. Indeed, the ETUC's membership base is
extremely complicated, with cleavages among members by affiliation to
political, sectoral and denominational organizations, and this complexity
clearly contributes to collective action problems. Also important is the absence
of Euro competencies in labour market relations, partly arising from the
desires of capital. For British labour interests, the European level represents
the 'main chance' to influence public policies, ostracized as they are from the
domestic scene. For German interests, however, there are few inducements
to leave the cosy domestic fireside and head for Brussels. Labour nationalism
is still strong, both at peak and sectoral levels (Cases 19 and 11). The ETUC's
secretariat, spanning a range of sectoral as well as more macro competencies,
is under-resourced. These factors make the ETUC's job extremely difficult: it
encounters obstacles which do not lie in the path of most business
confederations.

Rationality of Group Membership

Vipond (Case 7) argues that:

> alliances, be they with other firms or collective actions through industry
> associations, are explicable in terms of the attempt by firms to make strategic
> business choices, some of which will involve anticipating or even shaping
> changes to market conditions . . . The language of management theory,
> especially strategic management theory, provides a rational choice model at
> the level of the firm and allows an expansion of the notion of an alliance.

In direct firm membership formats it is much easier to identify who the
member is, and therefore to ascribe to the member some degree of direct
choice to join the Euro association. Firms certainly appear to include in their
membership calculations hard assessments of utility, including an assessment
of the track record of the Euro association in question. In this way, the 'logic
of influence' impinges upon the 'logic of membership'. A sort of rough-and-
ready cost/benefit analysis may also apply, and indeed Maloney suggests that
one of the reasons for the 'encompassingness' of the European water
associations, EUREAU, may be the cheapness of membership (Case 10).
However, some groups are so highly federated that the firm only appears
several generations along the organizational chart. This complexity makes it
extremely difficult to apply some of the traditional theories of collective action
to the European level, such as those based upon hard choices made by
constituent member firms as suggested by Mancur Olson. Thus a range of
selective incentives may not be necessary in Euro groups as a supplement to
the goal-oriented role to entice membership. Rather, as Jordan and
Wadsworth (Case 8) and McLaughlin (Case 12) argue, the anticipated costs
of 'non-membership' by national (and even European) organizations, whose
task it is to represent and defend the interests of their own members, may be
too great a threat to the credibility of a member or potential member of a
European-level collective format. For some Euro groups, the ultimate
sanction is member expulsion, and in the European Round Table of
Industrialists the ability to remove members helps to keep discipline tight
(Case 16).

Non-membership costs include, *inter alia*, the lack of ability to influence
the association, which may adopt positions damaging to a potential member;
the Commission preference for collective actors and the loss of opportunity
to share in the group's dialogue with European institutions (including advice
fora); the loss of contact with the Euro association's own networks; and the
loss of vital information and trade networking opportunities. Because the
Commission is badly overloaded, it depends upon the resources brought
by outside interests such as information, expertise and implementation

assistance. In short, overload, as Grote (Case 17) reminds us, leads to a search for alternative types of governance. Because this will almost always involve Euro groups, potential members cannot afford not to belong.

Given the technical nature of much of a Euro association's dialogue with European institutions, the cost of non-membership can be unacceptably high. A key issue in the livelihood of a firm may be passed up in interactions between the group and the Commission, or may emerge or fall as a result of the unpredictability of European policy processes (Case 12). Firms therefore need to be part of the permanent information networks established in Brussels which relate to their business concerns. Given that policy responses to issues arise from their definition, the loss of ability to influence the definition of particularly technical issues would be crippling. This idea arises in particular from the work of Majone (1989), who draws attention to the impact of socialization upon the policy process. Norms arise and are reinforced by mutual exchange and dialogue, which provides a guide to action; not being party to this process would result in a loss of ability to exert influence. The absence of membership from a Euro group would therefore not appear, in most cases, to be a realistic option. In addition, as is clear from many of the cases, associability may be driven from a sense of loyalty and solidarity, or even from a sense of tradition. In Case 13, Ronit shows how traditions of associability in shipping discourage large-firm representation. This tradition may have facilitated the smooth partial reorganization of interest representation from the global to the European level in shipping.

Many of the factors reviewed above seem to apply equally to both direct firm membership formats and federated structures. 'Rational choice', whilst easier to ascribe in the case of direct firm member associations than in federated structures, therefore seems to be an insufficient basis on its own to understand European-level business alliances. However, there are some key differences between federated and direct firm formats. For smaller firms, the option to join the latter may not exist. This means that direct firm membership formats risk being seen as, rich firm clubs. The Commission has always signalled its preference for encompassing Euro groups, a norm which has gained importance in recent months in the shape of the Commission's initiative for openness. Part of this initiative includes a concern for a 'level playing field' between business and non-business interests, and between different types of business interests, particularly large and small firms. Many Commission officials make a habit of seeking out small-firm representatives, knowing that they often hear the voices of large firm representatives. This means that large-firm representatives have to act collectively through federated formats which also represent the interests of smaller players. The strength of small firms therefore, paradoxically, may lie in their weakness; where they are dominated by large firms, and where they are excluded, there lie incentives for their organization at the European level (Case 17). The power of small firms to force large firms into alliances arises partly out of a recognition by the Commission of their lack of strength and ability to make themselves heard.

One example of the insufficient basis of large-firm organization is provided in Case 5, where Greenwood and Ronit show how the Senior Advisory Group Biotechnology, perhaps the most admired domain-level 'rich firm club', having withdrawn from federated structures, has found the need to recreate one as an additional representative structure. This demonstrates the need to belong to an identifiable community of interests, i.e. to act collectively. Some dynamics encouraging collective action may be the same for direct firm membership formats and federated structures, but the example given implies that there may be important differences too.

European Business Alliances to the Year 2000

This rather ambitious subtitle indicates the expectation that European business alliances will continue to be a dynamic, rather than static, phenomenon, looking towards the turn of the next century. Since the first three collections of studies on European interest representation were written in 1991–92 (Greenwood *et al.* 1992; van Schendelen, 1993; Mazey and Richardson, 1993), we have a much clearer picture. The first concerns the mushrooming of direct firm membership formats as an effective way for business to respond to the enhanced competencies of the 'new Europe', in part due to the difficulties encountered by some highly federated formats in achieving coherence, alacrity in decision-making or satisfactory outputs/ outcomes in representing their members' interests.

The second issue concerns the elasticity of direct firm membership formats, that is their ability to organize themselves in particular configurations depending upon the type of issue at stake. This is most evident from the cases of IT (Case 1) and ERT (Case 16). In the latter case, the organization is flexible enough to be able to complement the work of UNICE and to act effectively on a range of sectoral issues. As Green Cowles shows, elasticity need not mean a weakening of the ability to act collectively, in that ERT operates with a high level of discipline, able to remove members if necessary. Configurations of large firms are likely to continue to develop, and in particular in the direction of networks which use alliances among firms to address different issues.

The third point to emerge clearly since earlier studies is, however, that to write off federated formats as universally weak and fatally flawed in design now appears to have been a rather premature and unsustainable generalization. As a number of case studies in this collection have shown, these federated formats can be effective, and the possible conditions for effectiveness have been set out. Federated structures are likely to continue and to develop through internal strengthening of structures because of the

Commission's preference to deal with these types of format, knowing that they seek to represent the range of interests in a domain. This means that large firms will have to continue in membership of federations where smaller players are also represented.

A fourth issue concerns the impact of information upon European business alliances. As Vipond (Case 7) suggests, the need for firms to seek market information in the single market will drive them into alliances. This means that it is essential to act in encompassing, federated structures which provide access to all other types of firm, including smaller ones, as well as in exclusive networks. Put simply, the costs of non-membership are too high. Hypotheses which emerge from these cases concerning the dynamics of collective action at the European level are further summarized below.

A fifth issue concerns the extent to which federations and direct firm membership formats present in the same domain can work together. In information technology, relationships are harmonious (Case 1); in biotechnology there are disputes (Case 5), whereas in tourism (Case 9) there is poor coordination. A further research task which can be identified is to locate the conditions under which federations and direct firm formats in the same domain can work together.

A sixth issue concerns the increasing focus upon the European level of interest representation relative to the national route, evident in almost all the case studies. Both routes will remain an important part of the picture. However, a mark of the developing ability of Euro groups to operate effectively is provided by Jordan and Wadsworth in the case of Euro-Commerce, where the respective national groups were able to reach agreement on an issue where national governments were unable to do so. This suggests rather an optimistic outlook for neo-functionalist analysis, where the interest groups are pushing ahead of national governments. There are also occasions when the use of the national route can be counter-productive, and the more direct 'Brussels strategy' is preferable (Case 11). Sometimes, the development of Euro groups has been fostered by a combination of external events. Central to the formation of the European association in the case of aerospace has been the completion of the Uruguay Round of GATT negotiations, forcing the intervention of the European Union in an arena where competencies have previously been absent. This acquisition of competencies has been an important factor in the development of the 'Brussels strategy', and therefore European forms of collective action.

The crystallization of our understanding in the past two to three years as set out above emerges from monitoring events and the development of conceptual tools. There is some way to go in the latter task, both for understanding European-level collective action and meso-governance, where there are part theoretical voids. Nevertheless, a number of useful hypotheses have emerged from case study research, including ideas generated from empirical and constructivist type methods. These clearly have a contribution to make to filling a theoretical void. We now know that Olson's theory of collective action does not offer too much help at the European level, but we have suggested instead that the costs of non-membership, together with factors such as commitment, a sense of belonging, socialization effects, and the format of collective action may be key dynamics. Indeed, one research agenda suggested by this collection is the need to investigate systematically the differences in collective action dynamics which operate in the cases of direct firm and federated formats. Nevertheless, there are also considerable dynamics encouraging non-collective strategies based upon large-firm action; for instance, seventeen automotive firms have their own public affairs facilities in Brussels (Case 12), and many American (Case 14) and Japanese firms (Case 15) continue to act as 'free-booters', sometimes to the detriment of European collective strategies (Case 2). The regulatory experiences of multinational firms in national environments provide an indispensable resource to the Commission, and in some domains there are suggestions that large-firm contact with the Commission is increasing in importance (Case 12). Nevertheless, almost all large firms will be members of collective formats for the reasons outlined.

Since the production of the first three research collections on interest groups in the European Union, the Commission has begun to develop a policy towards greater openness. Part of this involves seeking and maintaining a broader range of institutionalized dialogue than has been evident to date. This is part of a wider set of concerns with information flows in the EU flagged by the 1992 Sutherland Report, where the Commission was accused of being rather *ad hoc* in the ways in which it consults and too oriented towards business interests (Sutherland, 1992). This is inevitable, given the greater resources of business interests and their greater ability to maintain permanent bases in Brussels. McLaughlin and Greenwood have argued that the ingrained patterns of business interest involvement in European-level public policy-making and implementation are unlikely to be upset by something as loose, infant-like and, as yet, sporadic as the openness initiative (McLaughlin and Greenwood, 1995). Yet, as Cram (1994) has convincingly argued, there is no such thing as cheap talk; ideas develop a life of their own, and there is now a range of groups with interests in the new openness policy, not least of which involves access to information. The openness initiative is unlikely to remain symbolic, and the need to involve a wider range of interests in public policy formulation and implementation may have at least two consequences of relevance here. One is that 'rich firm clubs' may have to broaden into more encompassing sectoral formats, and there are already signs that this is now happening (Case 5). This means that the mushrooming of direct firm membership formats will have either to re-seek federated-type structures, as discussed above, or to make themselves accessible to smaller firms. A second consequence is that business interests will have to open up new fronts of dialogue with non-business interests. In turn, this may encourage the

development of the latter and develop patterns of collective action which are
not identical to those evident today. Given the idea of resource possession
and exchange on which this collection is based, we should not expect patterns
of European interest representation and collective action to descend into
chaos, fragmentation and competition, but rather to continue to be based
upon ingrained patterns of business interest involvement in public policy
formulation and implementation.

Many of the sectoral studies in this collection observe a trend towards
market concentration, partly driven by the dynamics of the single market and
the need for competitiveness. Two important factors in this concern the need
for economies of scale and the need to gain better information about market
conditions. Although different logics underpin economic and political
alliances, these concepts are also partly related. The logic of the single market
is to create European rather than domestic players. These need to be attuned
to the European political level, and the years to come are likely to see
increased resources devoted to this tier. Market concentration may tend to
accelerate the development of 'rich firm clubs' where these are not already
evident.

For the Commission's part, it needs to be able to draw upon the
knowledge and expertise of firms with economic and political experiences
transcending national boundaries. Political factors may therefore contribute
to the development of economic alliances, which in turn promotes European-
level collective action. 'Spillover' development of collective action is therefore
likely. The result of this process would seem to be in the direction of denser
networks of business alliances, extending across sectors. In turn, this may
require some elasticity in business political networks, involving different
configurations of firms. These processes are evident in the cases of the
European Round Table of Industrialists (Case 16), and information technology (Case 1). Indeed, the creation of the 'Euro companies shell' by the
Commission, the European Economic Interest Grouping (EEIG), makes the
formation of alliances between firms, organizations or individuals easy – five
of the contributors to this text recently formed one for research purposes.
Whilst the primary purpose of the EEIG was to facilitate economic and
technical alliances, there are political benefits arising from closer collaboration. The EEIG is a clear example of what is being predicted in this chapter
as part of the future of European business alliances, i.e. network configurations of firms able to act in a particular context. Examples of European
Economic Interest Groupings can be found in Cases 4 (aerospace) and 14
(American organization of firms).

Many of the case studies in this volume arise from original research
conducted for the purpose of this text. They open up a rich seam of issues,
some new, and some, as a text of cases, by necessity mine familiar territory.
In concluding them it has not been my intention to review every insight
offered, but to focus instead on the core subject of European-level business

alliances. In this respect, reading the conclusions is no short-cut to digesting the messages of the individual cases themselves. For both meso-level governance and collective action at the European level there is a research agenda stretching through the years ahead, and one to which most of the authors in this collection would wish to contribute. Our primary ambition in this volume on European business alliances has been a pedagogical one but, in offering case study material, further goals have been to provide focused, accessible evidence, to stimulate the theoretical imagination, and to offer hypotheses for future research.

Note

1.   I am grateful to Philippe Schmitter for this point.

References

Clegg, S. and Dunkerley, D. (1980) *Organisation, Class and Control*. London: Routledge & Kegan Paul.

Cram, L. (1994) 'Rationalising EU intervention: rhetoric and soft law in European policy-making'. Paper presented to the 9th International Colloquium of the Council for European Studies, Chicago, 27–29 March 1994.

Eckstein, H. (1979) 'Case study and theory in political science', in Greenstein, F. and Polsby, N. W. (eds) *Strategies of Inquiry*, Reading, MA: Addison Wesley.

Greenwood, J., Grote, J. and Ronit, K. (1992) (eds) *Organised Interests and the European Community*. London: Sage.

Lindblom, C. E. (1977) *Politics and Markets: The World's Political–Economic Systems*. New York: Basic Books.

Lukes, S. (1977) *Power: A Radical View*. London: Macmillan.

Majone, G. (1989) *Evidence, Argument and Persuasion in the Policy Process*. Yale: Yale University Press.

Maloney, W., Jordan, A. G. and McLaughlin, A. M. (1995) 'Interest groups and public policy: the insider/outsider model revisited', *Journal of Public Policy*, vol. 14, pp. 17–38.

McLaughlin, A. and Greenwood, J. (1995) 'The management of interest representation in the European Union', *Journal of Common Market Studies*, forthcoming.

Mazey, S. and Richardson, J. J. (1993) (eds) *Lobbying in the European Community*. Oxford: Oxford University Press.

Sutherland, P. (1992) *The Internal Market after 1992: Meeting the Challenge*. (Sutherland Report) Report to the EU Commission by the High-level Group on the Operation of the Internal Market. Brussels: Commission of the European Communities.

van Schendelen, M. P. C. M. (1993) (ed) *National Public and Private EC Lobbying*, Aldershot: Dartmouth.